NO ONE MAN
SHOULD HAVE
ALL THAT POWER

NO ONE MAN SHOULD HAVE ALL THAT POWER

HOW RASPUTINS MANIPULATE THE WORLD

AMOS BARSHAD

ABRAMS PRESS, NEW YORK

Library of Congress Control Number: 2018936258

ISBN: 978-1-4197-3455-7
eISBN: 978-1-68335-525-0

Printed and bound in the United States
10 9 8 7 6 5 4 3 2 1

Abrams books are available at special discounts when purchased
in quantity for premiums and promotions as well as fundraising
or educational use. Special editions can also be created to
specification. For details, contact specialsales@abramsbooks.com
or the address below.

Abrams Press® is a registered trademark of Harry N. Abrams, Inc.

ABRAMS The Art of Books
195 Broadway, New York, NY 10007
abramsbooks.com

To Ima, Aba, Marush, Rodi, and Allison

Lord Henry: There is no such thing as a good influence, Mr. Gray. All influence is immoral—immoral from the scientific point of view. Because to influence a person is to give him one's own soul.

—Oscar Wilde, *The Picture of Dorian Gray*

CONTENTS

INTRODUCTION

AS FAR BACK AS I CAN REMEMBER, I've been obsessed with control. Not the beneficent kind—not the kind exhibited by the truly motivational, the organically wise, the honestly magnetic. That kind is easy enough to understand. And if anything, our histories and cultures give too much credence to that archetype. It was always dark control that grabbed me. Maybe I say that due to some predilection for the unseemly. But I don't think so. Ask yourself who's a more compelling figure—the head of state, or the senior advisor yanking their puppet strings?

That's the classic format of untoward control: the elected public official and their shadowy right-hand operator. That's why Grigori Rasputin is our gold standard. He is the most famous behind-the-scenes operator in history. And I've been obsessed with him for just about forever, too.

The tale of Rasputin will always be more myth than fact, which is what makes it so seductive. What we know for sure is this: Once, to the horror and amazement of a generation, a long-haired peasant magicked his way into the uppermost echelon of Russian high society.

When he died in St. Petersburg in 1916, he did so as the most notorious man in the Russian Empire. Cause of death: a revolver shot to the forehead. Or a revolver shot to the heart. Or potassium cyanide–laced fortified wine and petit-fours. Or drowning. Or all four. Or none.

Rasputin's relationship with Nicholas II and Alexandra, the last tsar and tsarina of Russia, was odd, intimate, heartfelt, and feared. The royal couple trusted him, in part, because of his mysterious ability to provide physical succor to their frail young son, Alexei, a hemophiliac. From there Rasputin became something between a court favorite, a personal priest, a guardian angel, and a best friend. "Remember how last year all were against us and our Friend gave you the help and strength," the tsarina once wrote to the tsar, with existential flair. "You took over all & saved Russia."

And that's what got Rasputin offed. The conspirators who carried out his infamously botched assassination believed they were rescuing the Russian Empire. Rasputin had become too powerful, and he had to die.

Rasputin healed the weak. And he fucked and drank with aplomb. To some, he was a "God-man." To others, a depraved deviant.

The writer Nadezhda Lokhvitskaya, who published under the name Teffi, would have brief but dramatic encounters with Rasputin in turn-of-the-century St. Petersburg. Years later, she recalled the mania that surrounded him. At dinner parties, Teffi noted, hosts pleaded with guests to please, please discuss anything but the Mad Monk. A common sign decorated homes: "In this house we do not talk about Rasputin." She also passed along the infamous story of the "black automobile," an unsolved case in which a car sped through St. Petersburg over the course of several nights, firing shots from inside and wounding bystanders.

"It's Rasputin's doing," people were saying. "Who else?"
"What's he got to do with it?"
"He profits from everything black, evil and incomprehensible. Everything that sows discord and panic. And there's nothing he can't explain to his own advantage when he needs to."

In death, he became legend. Mere hours after the fatal incident, the myth was blooming. According to police reports, when Rasputin's body was discovered in the Neva, locals ran to the river to scoop up water that had touched the corpse—they wanted to capture some essence of the great man.

After his death, all biographical details took on the air of *more*. One alleged night in Moscow's Yar restaurant, drunk as all hell and hitting on all of the dancers, he was said to have flashed what would come to be known around the world as a stunningly prodigious penis. In the years after his death, a group of female Russian expats in Paris allegedly possessed the penis, kept in a wooden casket, and prayed to it as a holy icon. It was described in one memoir as "a blackened overripe banana about a foot long, resting on velvet cloth." As I write this, the Museum of Russian Erotica claims to have the original artifact, pickled for preservation.

Is any of it real? Then, as now, it was hard to say.

His name reverberates. He sinned and repented. He said he was a man of faith and he meant it, every word of it, even while doing all of these disreputable things. He had, effectively, groupies. And he had long hair and eccentric clothing and a command of any room. He was some kind of strange, strange star.

"The whole world reads books which are written in blood, and yet remains indifferent. Humanity of today is blind to everything save the small concerns of the moment, petty personal interests and the thirst for immediate success." That was written by Prince Yusupof, the man who murdered Rasputin. "Is not this also a form of Rasputinism, which has gained possession of our epoch, and of the whole of mankind to-day?"

Yusupof was writing from Paris as a free man, a decade after the black deed was done, in an unseemly attempt to justify the cold-blooded assassination. But the murderous prince was right, in his way. We are obsessed with what is directly in front of us. Right now, right this minute, we ask: Who holds power, and how did they get it?

And while Yusupof may have meant something quite different by the term he was coining, the prince was right on this, too:

Rasputinism has taken over. More than a hundred years after his death, Rasputin has fully become a symbol—an archetype, recognized all over the world. Wherever there is a puppet master, an éminence grise, a Svengali, a manipulator, a secret controller—that is a Rasputin.

Traditionally Rasputins have been understood to be shadow leaders, the ones with true, evil power. But the odd truth is that the natural habitat of a Rasputin is not only the high-stakes salons, the war rooms, the places where geopolitical waves are made. Not at all. The truth is, wherever power dynamics exist—from Congress to Hollywood to the break room at the Tommy's Pretzel Hut—a Rasputin can rise. It happens all of the time.

When I sat down to write this book, I realized that even through my many years as a culture reporter for Grantland, The FADER, and *New York* magazine, I'd been exploring this kind of control. Look at the chart-topping pop star, and then look at the producer who's breathlessly envisioned their whole career. Look at the world-famous movie star, and then look at the director who's callously manipulated every beat of their performance. Look at the hip-hop genius, and then look at the anonymous MCs he blesses, and curses, with fame.

Rasputinesque—a term that, yes, I made up—is, frankly, one we do not use often enough.

How do we define a Rasputin? By design, there's something *ineffable* there. Unknowable.

That said, there *are* a few bedrock qualifications. Seven, in fact—the Seven Rasputin Rules. Here we go:

#1—They must exhibit control over others. Simple enough: As Rasputin was to the tsar and tsarina, the controller must be to their thrall. The latter must be beholden to the former—for some reason, bewitched.

#2—Their control must be controversial. Exactly why can vary; as we'll see, Rasputin's own control was deemed unseemly for a remarkably long and varied number of reasons. But let's not forget: It's not boring-old beneficent control we're after here.

#3—They must have enemies. A direct corollary to #2: If their manipulations haven't won them enemies, then their control is not quite untoward enough for the status of true Rasputin. As such, it's more of a symptom than a condition of the disease. But it's important: there must be those who are desperate to break the bond between the Rasputin and the Rasputin'd.

#4—They must attempt to execute a personal agenda. Theirs must be a grand goal, one they could never carry out themselves. As for *the* Rasputin's agenda? Some say he wanted to save the downtrodden; others say he wanted to sink the whole damn Russian Empire.

#5—They must operate from behind the scenes. The controller must always appear beholden to those they control. It's inevitable that the Rasputin will gain notoriety, but they must never exceed the fame of those they are Rasuptining. For all his myths and legends, Rasputin always remained *behind* the tsar and the tsarina. How could he not have? They were royalty.

#6—They control others who are few, but powerful. A crucial distinction. We're not talking pastors with loving congregations or demagogues with fawning masses or young tech billionaires accidentally manipulating electorates through social media platforms. That's a whole other book. The definitive trait of the Rasputin is control over one or a few influential, famous, or prominent figures.

#7—They must lack the abilities themselves. The Rasputin doesn't act—he makes a powerful few others act. And the actions of those others reverberate. The pop producer cannot sing or dance. The ghoulish presidential advisors are unelectable on their own. And Rasputin could never be tsar. That's the heartbreak: The dark control always stems from a place of deep and profound longing.

Not all *our* Rasputins will encompass all of the traits of *the* Rasputin. But they all will reflect some piece of him. Maybe it's the strange personal charisma. Maybe it's the hair. Maybe it's the godliness. Maybe it's those healing hands.

Taken in total, the figures in this book explicate the realities of untoward control. Who wields it? How? Ultimately we might just learn, for better or for worse, even if just theoretically—even if we'd never *dare* practice the dark arts—how *we* would become Rasputins ourselves. How does one person influence another? How does one person influence the culture at large? And is it OK to do so? Is it ever fully ethical?

In planning my descent into Rasputinism, I began with a roster of names whose control I'd long wanted to explore. They were film directors and pop producers and fiction editors. As I moved forward, more names presented themselves, more ways to chart this phenomenon. Some came from tips or offhand comments; some came via breaking international news. Soon, the deeds were getting more dastardly, the influence grander. I moved from pop culture to pro sports, from pro sports to crime, from crime to terrorism. Eventually, I got to those who were said to control world leaders.

SOME HAVE CALLED Aleksandr Dugin "Putin's brain"; others have called him "Putin's Rasputin." When I met the long-bearded, warmongering, fascistic philosopher in Moscow in the first flushes of Russian winter, that question of ethics is the one he wanted to answer first.

Influence, he said—in his strong, coarse, cinematic Russian accent—is "the chhhiiiighest of the perversions. If you influence others you *impose* on them your own will, your *own* world vision. It is something very far from innocence. It alienates the human freedom. To be regarded as an influential figure is not only a kind of praise and a responsibility—it's as well an accusation. If someone affirms that we are influential, it is the same as the affirmation that that we are *sinners*. We are *formatting* others. We are *masters* who regard others as *slaves*. We are committing *very* special, *very* vicious acts."

He paused to allow me to take in his proclamation. And then he went on.

"So can I accept, myself, this kind of accusation?" And then he made it very clear: "Yes! Yes!"

Yes, he told me. In so many words, Dugin was saying, yes, he *was* Rasputinesque. And he was very, very proud.

CHAPTER ONE
The Real Rasputin

AND HOW DID THE ORIGINAL RASPUTIN come to be? The details of young Grigori's nineteenth-century life in the tiny Siberian village of Pokrovskoye aren't particularly interesting. There was, it's fair to say, a lot of farming. Later on, his enemies would self-servingly recast him as a reckless youth, one displaying all the signs of his future degeneracy. In this way, fortunately for us, they injected his tale with much more juice. He was said not only to be a horse thief—in Siberia, the lowest of the low—but the *son* of a horse thief, too. Allegedly, the townspeople would often catch Grigori red-handed, and punish him with vigor.

"Another man would not have survived such thrashings," Prince Yusupof, his murderer, would write, "but it was as if a blacksmith's hammer were beating on an anvil. Rasputin bore everything, and only grew stronger from such treatment." A priest and Rasputin critic named Father Alexander Yurevsky was even more specific: He described an incident in which Rasputin was repeatedly picked up and slammed on the ground, at one point "nearly crush[ing] his genitals." Like the bite of a radioactive spider, the drop gave him great powers and great responsibility.

"He could now keep an erection for as long as he liked," Father Yurevsky frankly explained. "Once he realized this, Rasputin used it as his ticket to win over the bored, sexually starved society ladies. Rasputin told them that none of this gave him pleasure, for what he was really doing was driving the Devil from them." According to Yurevsky, as Rasputin thrust, he would exclaim, "You demon of the flesh, be gone!"

He married at eighteen and had seven children, four of whom died of childhood diseases. Then, in his late twenties, he had his religious awakening. In one version of the story, the Orthodox Saint Simeon of Verkhoturye came to him in a dream. In another, a vision of the Virgin Mary materialized in front of him, gesticulating to the horizon, in a field. Douglas Smith, author of the masterful 2016 biography *Rasputin: Faith, Power, and the Twilight of the Romanovs*, wrote, "perhaps it was a form of mid-life crisis": Rasputin knew that if he stayed put, all that lay ahead was hard farm work. The awakening would change his life and the fate of Russia. He began wandering the countryside in the then-common manner of the *stranniki*—the "holy pilgrims."

Russia at the time was rich with religious sects, many of them peculiar and secretive offshoots of Russian Orthodox Christianity. Well known were the troubling *skoptzy*, who practiced devoutness through self-castration. Most feared were the *khlysty*; they held mass rituals of ecstatic whirling that led to hallucinations and physical fits. They whirled around a vat of water, thereby granting it alleged intoxicative powers; they called it "spiritual beer." Rumors that Rasputin himself was a khlyst circulated for years.

In this atmosphere, Rasputin set off on penniless trips throughout the Russian Empire, learning and praying. He would come and go from his family and into strange worlds. Stories of his personal magnetism spread, and by 1905 he came to the attention of Militsa and Anastasia, a pair of strategically minded nobles known collectively as the Black Princesses. They, in turn, introduced him to very top of the royal family—Nicholas and Alexandra. Ironically, the Black Princesses did so hoping to use Rasputin as their own imperial-family inside man. They wanted to Rasputin Rasputin. But it was not to be.

The royal couple was predisposed to fall for him. St. Petersburg in the early 1900s was awash with belief in men and women with extraordinary abilities. "'Boulevard' mysticism" like "tarot, phrenology, mesmerism, astrology" were constantly discussed and practiced, the historian Maria Carlson has written. A given night out might include "public and private séances," "demonstrations of hypnotism," or "fortune-telling and dream interpretation." The occult was everywhere.

As a spiritualist court favorite, Rasputin had immediate predecessors. Before him came Vasia the Strannik and Matyrona the Barefooted and Mitya "The Nasal Voice" Kozelsky. The latter man, no one could actually understand. His incomprehensible speech would be "translated" by his personal vassal, Elpidifor, and then largely received as prophecy.

None of them lasted. But none of them could heal Alexei.

FOLLOWING THE DEATH of his father, Alexander III, in 1894, Tsar Nicholas II ascended to the throne. He was the scion of the Romanov family dynasty, which had lasted nearly three centuries. He was a few months shy of his twenty-sixth birthday.

Alexandra's first four children had all been girls. The Romanov dynasty needed a male heir. Alexei's birth had thus been joyously heralded. In turn, the discovery of his hemophilia early in life was a tragedy—even the most minor incidents could lead to fatal bleeding.

Naturally, unjustly, Alexandra bore the brunt of blame. It was her responsibility to produce a son. And the tsarina understood that Alexei's disease imperiled the dynasty. But more than anything, she loved her boy. Even without the imperial implications, it's not difficult to imagine a mother doing anything to make her sick child feel better.

Enter the fugitive farmer from Pokrovskoye.

Official Russia could not accept that a peasant—motivations unknown—could get so close to the seat of power. But they understood how it came to be. "The empress is ill, seriously ill," a

3

high-ranking Rasputin opponent once said. "She believes that Rasputin is the only person in the whole world who can help the heir and it is beyond human capacity to dissuade her about it."

A pattern would repeat itself over and over: An incident would trigger Alexei's hemophilic bleeding; Alexei would be bedridden, with the Tsarina hovering over him in despair; Rasputin would come and offer blessings—and they would work.

According to one of his more fanciful biographers, Rasputin was out partying with Romani the first time he was fetched. "A messenger told him to take his horse and go to a 'certain residence'"—it was the royal family's home. Eventually he relented, but not before "Rasputin drunkenly refused and shouted 'More dancing!'"

In her own memoirs, Rasputin's daughter Maria recalled tagging along during these healing visits. "Open your eyes, my son," she quoted her father saying to Alexei. "Open your eyes and look at me—your pain is going away. You will soon be well. You must thank God for healing you."

Grand Duchess Olga Alexandrovna, the tsar's sister, recounted her observations of the aftermath of one incident. "The little boy was not just alive—but well," she wrote. "He was sitting up in bed, the fever gone, the eyes clear and bright, not a sign of any swelling in his leg. The horror of the evening before became an incredibly distant nightmare. Later I learned . . . that Rasputin had not even touched the child but merely stood at the foot of the bed and prayed."

The pattern had its greatest realization in an incident in the wooded Polish town of Spala. While riding in a carriage over a rough path, eight-year-old Alexei started expressing his symptoms once again. Back at the Romanovs' villa, he was diagnosed with a rapidly forming hematoma. Day after day Alexei would lie there screaming in pain; he was so badly off that last rites were read. He is said to have turned to Alexandra in his sickbed and asked, "When I am dead it will not hurt anymore, will it, Mama?"

Rasputin was back home in Pokrovskoye with his family, Maria Rasputin recalled, when a message about Alexei's dire condition arrived from the tsarina. It was dinnertime. As Rasputin prayed, the family was "frozen like statues." Finally, "his face streaked with perspiration," Rasputin looked up, made the sign of the cross, and walked down to the village to send a telegram back: "Have no fear. God has seen your tears and heard your prayers. Do not grieve; your son will live."

For one day, Alexei's condition stayed exactly the same. Then, suddenly, he snapped back to life. A perfect, full recovery. It was remembered as "the Miracle at Spala."

But Alexei's health was only part of the story. Faith healing aside, there was an undeniable magnetism to Rasputin. In St. Petersburg, his uncouth ways would prove to have an effect far outside the royal family.

Tales of his abilities varied wildly. He cured a sick dog; he turned a clump of dirt into a rose; he granted a paralyzed woman the ability to walk by telling her to get up and do so. He developed something like a harem of true believers. They would collect and cherish sunflower husks he'd cracked or hair from his beard or trimmings from his fingernails. Locally, they spread the gospel of Rasputin—his very own evangelists.

What was it that they found so attractive? Most agreed the key to his appeal for St. Petersburg high society was his simplicity. From his table manners to his nearly illegible scribblings, he was through and through a true Russian peasant. When he preached the lessons of the Bible, he did so in his blunt, rough ways. And his speaking was all the more potent for it.

Then there were his eyes.

In his memoirs, Prince Yusupof would tell a highfalutin tale about being voluntarily hypnotized by Rasputin. It happened one afternoon during the sham friendship that preceded the assassination.

"My body seemed paralyzed. I tried to speak, but my tongue would not obey me, and I seemed to be falling asleep, as if under the influence of a strong narcotic. Yet Rasputin's eyes shone before me with a kind of phosphorescent light. From them came two rays which flowed into each other and merged into one glowing circle."

Eventually, the prince explains, he summoned the great internal power necessary to break free of the evil man's hypnosis.

Did Rasputin really shoot laser beams from his pupils? Probably not! But Yusupof was just one of many to obsess over Rasputin's eyes. They were "irresistible," according to a firsthand account. They "radiated a suggestion of some profound mystery," according to another. From a third witness: "I can't, I can't handle those eyes. They see everything." People said he could freely expand and contract his pupils; people said he could look right into your mind.

Yusupof would describe the eyes as "amazingly repulsive." They gave off "a feeling that a needle was piercing you through"; they "convey[ed] a feeling of some hidden, supernatural force."

It was a common theme, even for his detractors, to ascribe to Rasputin a singular presence. "He seldom washed and he smelt vilely; at the table he plunged his greedy hands into his favorite fish soup," wrote one critic. "His lechery had a barbaric quality that made him more like a beast than a human being."

It's meant to be dismissive, but it's illuminating. Because that particular underlying current would repeat itself over and over. He had an animal-like force. He had *pure* energy.

Writing in 1964, the British author Colin Wilson imagined a day where we'd understand Rasputin's magic as true. "His real significance may not be recognized for at least another century," Wilson wrote, "by which time, one hopes, telepathy, second sight, and pre-vision will be accepted as simply another form of psychology." (This is neither here nor there, but in an another aside from this passage, Wilson mentions having done, over the course of his life, a massive amount of mescaline.) Wilson also offered a more prosaic approximation of Grigori's control, and a very compelling one. Of those who fell under the sway of Rasputin, he said, "They believed again in man's power to control his own destiny. It was impossible to be a fatalist in the presence of this power."

Everybody wants to believe.

THE RUMOR ABOUNDED far and wide that Rasputin was sleeping with the tsarina. According to popular innuendo, this was all happening, implicitly, with the tsar's full awareness and even his support. The rumor even went international. During World War I, the Germans air-dropped copies of a cartoon over the front lines. It featured Kaiser Wilhelm II of Germany measuring a long artillery shell next to Tsar Nicholas doing the same with Rasputin's large, erect penis.

In reality, the relationship between Rasputin and the tsarina seems to have been of an altogether different sort. In his letters, Rasputin would refer to the tsar and the tsarina as Mama and Papa.

Alexandra was born into the royal family of the then-extant German Empire. She became the tsarina through marriage, and while her love for Nicholas was very real, she'd never adapted to her position in Russia. Rasputin, then, was uniquely positioned to offer her solace. "The pathologically shy woman felt herself to be a stranger in a hostile country," Wilson wrote. "Then Rasputin appeared, a personification of the Russian peasantry, and assured her that she was loved by all simple Russians."

Nicholas, for his part, was known as a weak-willed ruler. He loved his family. He believed wholeheartedly in the legitimacy of Russian imperial autocracy. But he had no known convictions. Some called him "a man without insides."

Yusupof quoted Rasputin describing a total control over the royal couple. "I don't beat about the bush with them," he claimed

Rasputin said. "If they don't do what I tell them I just bang on the table with my fist and get up and go, and then they chase after me and start begging 'don't go away Grigori Efimovich, we'll obey you in everything if you will only stay with us.'"

That's a weirdly comic rendering, in line with Yusupof's self-interested exaggerations. But by the time World War I broke out, Rasputin *was* offering unsolicited opinions on troop movements and strategy. He suggested that low-level criminal offenders be conscripted and sent to the front lines, a policy that was duly carried out. He was also made privy to the tsar's classified locations so that he could offer special blessings for his safety.

In their private conversations, Rasputin often tried to buck up the tsar—to remind him to wield his great power. Rasputin believed that the tsar's sovereignty was divine fiat. He wanted Nicholas to remember it, too.

Among his interventions: he weighed in on the hirings and firings of various influential governmental officials. Sometimes these were protective measures; Rasputin knew he had enemies everywhere. Other interventions were attempts to help those he considered legitimately downtrodden. He opposed hikes in train fares and pleaded with the tsar to handle food shortages: "Little Father, we must transport more corn and less soldiers and guns." Over and over, he advocated on behalf of minority groups, from the Tatars to the Jews to a renegade band of monks known as the Name-Glorifiers. If there was a throughline to Rasputin's ideology—if he had an easily definable agenda— it was this: a defense of the poor and oppressed.

Rasputin's status got him paid, but in a roundabout way. Followers would bring him gifts of velvet pants and embroidered shirts; influential friends would lend him money. At his Gorokhovaya Street apartment in St. Petersburg, there was a constant stream of the "politically ambitious," Maria wrote: "Mothers with sons seeking positions in the civil service, businessmen looking for government contracts, people seeking introductions to cabinet ministers, they all flocked to see my father."

With some of the stuffier officials, he'd offer preposterously strong raw country vodka. Then he'd watch them gag it down. He called it Rasputin's Revenge. For the most part he loved the nonstop circus. Accruing personal wealth was not his motivation, though. Whether with his home or his money or his booze, he was a gushingly generous fellow. And what he really, truly loved was to party.

His vice of choice was Madeira, the fortified wine from the Portuguese island of the same name. He was a happy drunk, pushed by wine into passionate soliloquies about his God or into wild fits of dance to Romani music. As his daughter Maria wrote of the Romani, using the then-popular term for these peoples, "These were people after his own heart. There was always a fiddler to play the wild, sometimes sad, sometimes gay music, and this, in itself, was intoxicating. And like himself the gypsies never tired of dancing and could go on until the small hours of the morning." Prince Yusupof's memoir is full of rebuffed entreaties from Rasputin that he and his future murderer go party with the Romani at Novaya Derevnya, their regular settlement in St. Petersburg.

The most famous night out of Rasputin's life happened at the Yar restaurant in 1915. They say he danced the *mattchiche* (also known as the Brazilian Tango) and made advances with the singers on the stage. It's a wild tale, so much so that some biographers doubt it ever really happened. (It was possibly invented or elaborated by his enemies as character assassination.) But a less-discussed incident, on the Tovarpar train later that same year, almost certainly did happen, and exhibits the same tendencies.

Rasputin—drunk beyond control, alternating between crying, singing, vomiting, and passing out—bothered a whole train car full of passengers. "Everyone says I only kiss women but this man here's taken my fancy," he told one fellow, "so I'd be happy to kiss him too." Then he sang a song: "Let me in to play for the night! / Your bare white breast I want to caress / Come accept all my charms!"

Writing in Paris in 1924, Teffi published a long account of her brief encounters with the man. At one point, she describes attending a bizarre dinner party at which Rasputin brought his own gang of village musicians and was quickly inspired into a madman burst of dance: "He thrust a knee forward, shook his beard about and circled round and round. His face looked tense and bewildered. His movements were frenzied; he was always ahead of the music, as if unable to stop . . . [he was] leaping about like a goat. Mouth hanging open, skin drawn tight over his cheekbones, locks of hair whipping across the sunken sockets of his eyes, he was dreadful to behold."

Rasputin was notorious for his lechery. He was utterly unfaithful to his dutiful wife. He was constantly touching and squeezing and fondling the women around him, always pleading for physical attention.

Even his daughter's account of her father's life as a "holy pilgrim" is full of sexual adventuring. The housewife who "withdrew her arms from the sleeves of her dress permitting it to fall to her waist and turning in order to display her full firm bust"; the young women in the river who, "after having frolicked with him for a suitable period so that he was no longer a stranger accepted his lovemaking one by one, on the grassy bank." Maria describes one religious ritual Rasputin joined that sounds like the world's earliest recorded body shot: "The sacramental wine was poured into [a women's] navel, from which the priest drank."

She even talks about the lore of her father's famous penis and the sexual/spiritual rituals that surrounded it. "Whichever of the female disciples was the first to perform fellatio upon him did so in a sense of a religious practice . . . endowing it with mystical qualities for it was an extraordinary member indeed, measuring a good thirteen inches when fully erect." In these tellings his lecherousness was redeemed, allegedly, by his faith. The idea was to sin so that you could repent—to touch God via extreme emotions.

Similarly, at the strange dinner party, Teffi recalls Rasputin pursuing her tirelessly, to her great offense. "Don't you know we all love sweet tears, a woman's sweet tears?" he told her at one point, attempting a strange pickup line. "Do you understand? I know everything."

She rebuffed him totally. She was immune to his bizarre charms. And yet, watching him dance, she almost slipped. "The spectacle was so weird, so wild, that it made you want to let out a howl and hurl yourself into the circle," she wrote, "to leap and whirl alongside him for as long as you had the strength."

IN THE SUMMER of 1914, while at home in Pokrovskoye, Rasputin was stabbed with a fifteen-inch dagger wielded by Khionya Guseva, a thirty-three-year-old woman who'd lost her nose as a teenager to an undiagnosed disease (alleged but never conclusively proven to be syphilis), an experience that damaged her emotionally. She was also a loyal follower of one of Rasputin's fiercest enemies, the monk Iliodor. According to an outlandish account of the incident, at the moment of impact Guseva screeched, "I have killed the Antichrist!" Rasputin stumbled away, then noticed her still chasing him, the assault knife in hand. He managed to bonk her on the head with a large stick, ensuring her arrest.

He survived the attack. But as has been well-documented, a close brush with assassination can have a serious deleterious effect. In the fall of 1994, two years before he was killed, the rapper Tupac Shakur was shot in the lobby of New York City's Quad Studios. Afterward, a certain fatalistic doom famously settled over 'Pac. On one of his biggest posthumous hits, "Thugz Mansion," Tupac imagined finding solace only in an alternate version of the afterlife. "Will I survive all the fights and the darkness?" he rapped. "Trouble sparks, they tell me home is where the heart is, dear departed." A similar doom, it seemed, consumed Rasputin after Guseva's attack.

Rasputin would predict his death to friends and associates. "I pushed death away once more," he said. "But she'll come again for me . . . like a hungry virgin she'll find me."

"Yes, they want to kill me," he told others. "Well, so what! The fools don't understand who I am. A sorcerer? Maybe I am. They burn sorcerers, so let them burn me. But there's one thing they don't understand: if they kill me, it will be the end of Russia."

He coped, in his way—namely, with more drinking, more Romani jams. Rasputin knew what kind of mess he was in. It was all around him.

By the end of his life, Rasputin would have enemies everywhere, from the St. Petersburg police to the elected officials in Russia's governing body, the Duma. At the height of his infamy, he was constantly tailed. Agents saw him carousing at the *banyas*, picking up prostitutes, and heading to and from the imperial family's palaces. He had a personal security detail as well as packs of agents duly following any given number of visitors from the floods of them he'd entertain. Roughly five thousand policemen were tasked with the monitoring and safety of Rasputin and his cohorts. His police code name was "The Dark One."

The most virulent anti-Rasputin forces saw him as an active German spy. To this day, rumors persist of the British secret service's role in his assassination. The German affiliation, if unproven, makes sense: If he had convinced Russia to abandon the war, then the Germans would have had one less front to fight on.

For Douglas Smith, the Rasputin biographer, the summer of his assassination attempt was the man's greatest moment.

"Summer of 1914," Smith tells me, setting the scene. "Europe is rushing headlong into war. Rasputin's in Siberia and he's attacked, nearly murdered, by a crazy woman with no nose. And he writes from his hospital bed this amazing letter in which he begs the tsar not to go to war. To not listen to the calls for blood, to ignore the warmongers. He says he sees nothing but unending misery, seas of darkness, chaos, this kind of thing."

As Smith recounts in his 2016 biography, Rasputin "requested pen and paper and wrote what must be considered the most prophetic letter ever written to a Russian monarch by one of his subjects—'I know they all want war from you evidently not realizing that this means ruin.'"

"We know Nicholas got the letter," Smith adds. "Unfortunately, he didn't follow the advice."

World War I was triggered by the assassination of Austrian archduke Franz Ferdinand in Serbia in 1914 by an agent of the Black Hand, a Serbian nationalist group. In response, Austria-Hungary and its allies—which included Germany—waged war on Serbia. In turn, Russia, Serbia's ally, engaged in war with the so-called Central Powers.

In Smith's reading of history, if Tsar Nicholas II never mobilizes the Russian troops in response to the German aggression, the Austria-Hungary–Serbia confrontation remains a local Balkan conflict, and the then-unfathomable widespread destruction engendered by World War I is, quite possibly, avoided. Furthermore, without war, the Russian Empire likely doesn't collapse, the Bolshevik revolution never happens, and neither does eighty years of Soviet subjugation of the Russian people.

"Papa threw himself into the quest for a quick peace with all the fervor he knew," Maria Rasputin recalled of her father's attempts to stop the war. "Our flat became the nucleus of his activities and I had a feeling of exhilaration knowing that I was in the midst of history being made, rubbing elbows with the participants and feeling caught up in the onrush to wherever it took me."

Modern historians like Smith believe it's highly unlikely Rasputin was anti-war for reasons of international subterfuge. The man does seem to have had a genuine predilection for peace. But what really matters for our purposes is not necessarily *why* Rasputin was advocating for peace. What matters is this: By the end, this is the power people believed Rasputin possessed—the power to stop wars.

"A court favorite—it's a shadowy figure," Smith tells me. "And there's a shadowy unknowability. People are never really clear on the extent of power that these figures have and how they've gained it. It comes with a whiff of illegitimacy. They wield great power without rightfully being given that right."

From that unknowability comes great fear. And fear, in the end, is what got Rasputin killed.

In November of 1916, Vladimir Purishkevich, a member of the Duma, addressed the assembly. War was raging. With verve and punch, Purishkevich detailed the source of the existential threat looming over the empire. He pointed not toward the bloody front lines of the Imperial Russian Army, but toward one man. Not long after his speech, Purishkevich would join Prince Yusupof in the conspiracy to kill Rasputin.

"Over the years of the war I have assumed that our domestic quarrels should be forgotten," he said. "Now I have violated that prohibition in order to place at the feet of the throne the thoughts of the Russian masses and the bitter taste of resentment from the Russian front."

The cause of the anguish? The weakness of the tsar's ministers, "who have been turned into marionettes, marionettes whose threads have been taken firmly in hand by Rasputin—the evil genius of Russia."

CHAPTER TWO
The Pop Rasputins

THINKING ABOUT GRIGORI EFIMOVICH RASPUTIN did something to me: It started to make me see Rasputins everywhere. Here was Person X—and there was Person Y, enjoying a strangely intimate control over Person X. I'd bring it up constantly in conversations, and, soon enough, friends and family started suggesting them to me, too. *Check out* [name redacted]'s *therapist! Check out* [name redacted]'s *assistant! Check out* [name redacted]'s *personal manicurist!* The "frequency illusion," also known as the Baader–Meinhof phenomenon, is the strange sensation we get once someone mentions something very, very specific—a new car model, an obscure World War II battle, a gang of German student-terrorists—and we start to see it and hear about it everywhere. That was happening to me: Rasputins were taking over my brain. And I loved it.

Again and again, in those early Rasputin-mad days, I came back to one field: music. Joyful, pure music. It's uncomfortable, but it's true: Few disciplines have been as rife with Rasputins as the music industry. For our descent into the darkness of Rasputinism, it's a perfect place to start.

The formula is maddeningly easy to grasp, because this is how our music, at least our pop music, naturally functions. The star at the front of the stage gets the mass adulation and the magazine covers; the operator behind the curtain maintains the control. This is how we—the engaged fans, informed about the full machinations of the song machine—generally believe the *best* pop music is made.

Rasputins have been persuasive in pop not just because they promise money and fame, but also because they promise grandness.

That's the currency of pop. An aspiring pop star doesn't just want fleeting red-carpet glitz: they want the stature, the legacy, the *iconicity* that pop can grant.

An actor can dazzle millions with a vulnerable debut performance. A novelist can hit the bestseller list with a thinly veiled autobiographical debut. But the pop star never just arrives fully formed. Even when the pop star's rallying cry is individualism above all else, we know there has been a process.

Which means the string-puller—the one who orchestrates the process—is elemental. Rasputins regularly occur in other artistic fields. But in pop, they're so baked into the system that they have their own industry-specific term.

HE WAS "A tall, bony individual," George du Maurier wrote in his late-nineteenth-century novel *Trilby*, "well-featured but sinister." He had "bold, brilliant black eyes," a "thin, sallow face," and a "beard of burnt-up black which grew almost from his under eyelids." And "he went by the name of Svengali."

That is the first-ever appearance of a character that has been both obscured and made notorious by the passing of time. It was with pure villainy and literal hypnotism that Svengali transformed our titular heroine—the joyous Parisian commoner Trilby, with whom everyone fell in love—into a dead-eyed international singing sensation. Throughout the glorious opera houses of Europe, and all while under his masterful trance, she became a prima donna star known as "La Svengali."

Trilby was a populist smash in its time, birthing multiple theatrical and cinematic adaptations. And somewhere along the way, as its lore grew, the prototype gave way to an archetype. Most of us don't know du Maurier's tall, bony individual. But we know the Svengali: the dark figure that, with undue control, manipulates another into greatness.

Du Maurier's book was published in 1895, a decade before Rasputin made his entrance onto the St. Petersburg scene. Over a century and change, the two archetypes—both sinister, both bearded—have conflated.

IN THE SIXTIES, Phil Spector's obsessively deliberate "Wall of Sound"—layers and layers of guitars and strings and glockenspiels— elevated girl-group pop into high art. But he created that sound, so heart-quaking and eternal, with creeping dictatorism. Five years after Spector produced "Be My Baby" for the Ronettes, he married their lead singer, Ronnie, then virtually imprisoned her in their home. "I was brainwashed, he wouldn't let me out of his sight," Ronnie has said. "All he wanted me to do was stay at home and sing 'Born to Be Together' to him every night." He told her mother there was a gold glass-topped coffin in the basement, and that the only way Ronnie would ever leave him would be in that coffin.

Ike Turner is the man who may have invented rock and roll. His "machine-gun bursts of tortured, quivering chordal slams," wrote the *Los Angeles Times*'s Robert Palmer in 1993, "were like nothing heard before" and "have rarely been equaled" since. But while Ike was possibly a genius, he was no pop star.

He found his greatest muse in Anna Mae Bullock from Nutbush, Tennessee—the woman who would meet the world as Tina Turner. Ike's vision, as summed up by Steely Dan's Donald Fagen: "The band plays tight; Tina goes berserk."

Years later, rendered ignominious by Tina's accounting of his brazen philandering and physical abuse, Ike would still take outsized pride at his role in crafting his ex-wife's famed showmanship. "The lights came down on *her*, there was no spotlight on me," Ike told *SPIN* in 1985. "She'd stroke that mike and shit like that—I was the one who told her to do that . . . And Tina being the sex symbol, that's what happened. People think that came from the visual part of an Ike and Tina show, but man, that's not it. I styled her that way—I made it happen. I gave the drummer the signal, and it sounded like a gunshot."

In the mid-seventies, Malcolm McLaren created the Sex Pistols, who almost immediately bucked against his control. The band broke up after one album—long enough to become icons and create the bedrock for hallowed London punk. It was McLaren's single greatest act of Rasputinism. But McLaren didn't really care about punk music per se; it was the manipulation he liked. Later, he'd go on to manufacture cheeky hits for Bow Wow Wow ("I Want Candy") and alongside the proto-hip-hop act the World's Famous Supreme Team ("Buffalo Gals"). He was an "arch-manipulator of people," he'd brag. "I was always trying to find an identity and the one way you found an identity was to create some sort of surrogate family and the way you did that was to create a gang."

Paying respect to McLaren after his death, Bow Wow Wow's bassist Leigh Gorman released a loving statement that captured the man's blatant strategies and his many contradictions. "He didn't play an instrument but he could play a musician for certain." His "manipulations" were "terror-inducing." And, in the end, he "got you to play better than you'd ever dreamed of."

Right around the same time McLaren was plotting his schemes in London, Frank Farian was in West Germany doing the same. Farian was an actual musician, but his genre of choice was disco, and he had an inkling that it'd go over better if it wasn't being sung by a white European. So he concocted a quartet of black musicians called Boney M to front as the band making the music. The ruse would be successful for years, even when it became widely known that Boney M didn't actually get to sing their songs. One of their greatest hits? "Rasputin," a very loose retelling of the epic story of our guy Grigori. Over a quasi-Slavic disco beat, Boney M sang, "Ra Ra Rasputin / Lover of the Russian queen . . . Ra Ra Rasputin /

Russia's greatest love machine." Years later, Farian would dream up another classic, tragic lip-sync act: Milli Vanilli.

Rick Rubin is now the most famous music producer alive. In the early eighties, he was instrumental in transforming the Beastie Boys from hardcore kids to a hip-hop phenomenon. He himself was just an NYU underclassman, working out of his dorms. He gifted the Beasties the big drums of their early sound; he bought them matching Puma tracksuits. But they would grow to resent his outsized role and his egging-on of boozy frat-boy antics. To recuse themselves of Rubin's control, they would quit Def Jam in its prime and run off to California.

In the nineties, Lou Pearlman funded the Backstreet Boys and *NSYNC with money generated from a pyramid scheme built on blimp rentals—then later stole millions from the boys to desperately prop up said pyramid scheme. Justin Timberlake has said working with him was like "being financially raped." When the warrant for Pearlman's arrest for fraud was issued, he fled to Bali, where he was eventually found registered at a hotel under the name "A. Incognito Johnson." For the last years of his life, until his death in 2016, he was held in federal prison in Texarkana, Texas, and Miami, where he swore he could whip up a new hit boy band if just given regular access to a phone line.

All of these singular talents, from Tina Turner to the Backstreet Boys, deserved, and may well have enjoyed, long careers even if they'd never met their Ikes or their Pearlmans. But the Ikes and the Pearlmans would never admit that; they had a vested interest in presenting themselves as the secret geniuses and, therefore, in a way, the true talent.

In Jewish folklore, there is a character called the golem. It's a monster made from clay and brought to life by a rabbi wishing to protect his fellow Jews from pogroms and anti-Semitism. In some popular accounts the rabbi loses control of his golem, and the monster eventually runs murderously wild. The golem is an obscure, mystical, mythical figure. But it's surprisingly relevant. Because the life of the golem's builder echoes the pop Rasputin's life. They breathe life into their creation; eventually, their creation nearly destroys them.

SOME OF THESE people are, possibly, true sociopaths. Decades after his abuse of Ronnie, Phil would be convicted of killing Lana Clarkson in his California home by shooting her through the mouth with a Colt Cobra .38 revolver. This tragedy was made worse by its foreshadowing. For decades before, tales of an arms-crazed Spector pulling guns in studio sessions—with John Lennon, with Leonard Cohen, with the Ramones—were passed along and gawked at.

Most of the time, though, these types of Rasputins seem driven by something less than out-and-out mania. They believe their control is warranted by their singular talent and their uncompromised vision. And in that, they find some kind of complicated redemption.

Is abuse justified if it produces great art? Most of us wouldn't have a hard time answering this question. The respective greatness is irrelevant. Human abuse cannot be justified by artistic product.

The Rasputins would disagree. And in that, they are cheered by the public response. As long as the true extent of the control is kept secret, the art can stand on its own. The fans love it, and the Rasputin is proven right. But once the control is revealed, the fans—confused, dejected, bitter, and combative—turn on the Rasputin, who is left shouting, from deep within bowels of theoretical gated mansions, "But you loved me before you knew!"

FEW RECENT RASPUTIN stories in the music industry have been as blatant—and as ugly and as public—as the story of Kesha Sebert and Dr. Luke.

In the winter of 2016, a legal battle between the music producer Luke and his former protégée Kesha, once known professionally as Ke$ha, dominated music-industry news. Kesha alleged that over the decade of their collaboration—which had produced chart-topping hits like "Tik Tok" and "Die Young"—the producer abused her both verbally and sexually. In a civil lawsuit filed in hopes of voiding her contractual obligations, Kesha made a string of nightmarish allegations, including that she was once given what Dr. Luke called "sober pills" and woke up the next day naked in his bed without memory of the night before.

Dr. Luke denied all charges, releasing a statement saying Kesha was "like my little sister." He would also suggest the charges stemmed from a misguided attempt at a more favorable contract renegotiation.

If this story weren't so horrible, it would sound clichéd. Kesha was eighteen when Luke signed her, an aspiring starlet from Nashville with a country music background and a lovely natural singing voice. She had dropped out of high school and moved to L.A. But when she broke through a few years later, it was as an unbathed, whiskey-loving, quasi-rapping delinquent.

Dr. Luke, born Lukasz Gottwald in Providence, Rhode Island, in 1973, was a protégé once, too. His mentor was Max Martin, the Swedish songwriter who has dominated the pop landscape for decades. From the outset of his career, Martin was eager for total control: Robyn, the dance-music experimentalist, was in the Martin camp as a teenager, but bristled under his command and often shook off his directives. "I really wanted to stand on my own two feet," she would later say. In the late nineties, Jive Records introduced Martin to their new artist: the then-unknown, sixteen-year-old Britney Spears. And he found his blank canvas.

Years later, Luke would, too. He'd crafted smash hits before, for the pop stars Kelly Clarkson and Katy Perry. But Kesha was the first act that Luke had discovered and developed himself; to Luke, perhaps, this suggested a natural ownership over Kesha's career.

Kesha's lawsuit described a working relationship in which she had no say over her creative choices or her public persona. Kesha says Dr. Luke made his control explicitly clear; during one spat, according to an affidavit, he icily told her that he could "manipulate my voice . . . in his computer . . . to say whatever he wanted." When taking aim at Dr. Luke's Sony-backed Kemosabe Records, the lawsuit paints the label as less of an unwitting participant and more of a pimp. It claimed the label "provided Dr. Luke with unfettered and unsupervised access to vulnerable female artists beginning their careers . . . who would be totally dependent upon Dr. Luke for success."

Kesha's case brought a wave of discourse about the ugly things that happen in the back corridors of power. It also brought attention to this storied tradition of behind-the-scenes pop music abuse—and reminded us quite how rife it is.

Dr. Luke fulfills almost all of our Rasputinesque requirements. Despite the flashy stage name, he was happy to exist in the shadows. And as his controversial control was revealed, the enemies came. An online swell of support for Kesha broke forth, demonizing Luke in the process. In the wake of the scandal, Sony broke ties with Luke in the spring of 2017, firing him as CEO of his Kemosabe imprint.

Some might find that harrowing—was the public acting as judge and executioner? Looked at it another way, Sony wasn't so much giving in to a virtual mob as being practical. At the point of his firing, it had been years since Luke was regularly snapping out number one hits like widgets from a pop machine.

Luke never intended to fulfill the tenets of a Rasputin, not all the way. Yes, he wanted to exhibit control (Rasputin Rule #1). Yes, he wanted to operate from behind the scenes (#5). Yes, he wanted to execute his personal agenda (#4). But he never *intended* to have enemies (#3). He never *intended* for his control to become controversial (#2). He just wanted his artist to fall in line forever.

There's one more important foundational Rasputinesque element Luke couldn't avoid—Rasputin Rule #7: "They must lack the abilities themselves." Dr. Luke can't sing, can't perform, can't fill the spotlight. To have hits, he had to manipulate others.

On YouTube you can find footage of Kesha onstage, back in her Nashville days, unfurling the natural strength and range of her singing voice. When Luke began working with her, he chucked all that aside. Luke's vision for her was ceaselessly one-note. With one line on her first breakthrough "Tik Tok," she'd define herself for years: "Before I leave, brush my teeth with a bottle of Jack." In subsequent interviews, Kesha would even claim that gargling with whiskey is a thing she really, really, really did.

Was Luke truly, sincerely passionate about creating a party-monster golem? I would guess not. I would guess he was simply pushing forth what he was wagering would work. He was right, of course. Kesha's first album, *Animal*, sold nearly 1.5 million copies. "Tik Tok" went to number one on the *Billboard* charts and stayed there for nine weeks.

Did Luke find any kind of personal joy in that? Did he find his creative impulses fulfilled? I would guess not. I would guess that his agenda went only so far as finding what it was that worked. In interview after interview, he spoke of his obsessiveness over making songs that were huge. That was the dream: to be huge.

Legally, Kesha would be stymied, and forced to continue recording for Sony. Personally, she would triumph. In mid-2017 she'd release *Rainbow*, her first album in five years. Officially a Kemosabe release, it's the first album of her career to feature no co-writing or production from Luke.

On its lead single, "Praying," she addresses the man without naming names. "Well, you almost had me *fooled*," she sings, pounding the words. "Told me that I was *nothing* without you / Oh, but after *everything* you've done / I can thank you for how *strong* I have *become*." The piano line circles. The drums kick in. Kesha unleashes the full might of her capable lungs: "I hope you're somewhere / *praaaaying*."

It's a punchy ode to resilience, to strength through pain. And it is very, very on the nose. But that's OK. The Rasputin is an outcast. The former puppet is playing sold-out shows and crooning on the Grammys. Can we blame Kesha for talking her shit as bluntly as possible? "Praying" is massive. It's perfect. I love it.

The lesson of Kesha's story seems resoundingly clear: Avoid men who tell you you need them. And yet, it's not hard to imagine her arc playing out again and again. A high school dropout moving to California and throwing her lot in with a producer she perhaps should not trust? There will always be raw talent. And there will always be "bony individuals" believing they should, by any means necessary, shape raw talent into supernovas.

Take Ike Turner. To the end, he was unrepentant. He believed he was the only one who understood how hard it was to create a force as commanding as the young Tina Turner—the only one who could have pulled it off. And years later, some music historians would grapple with a problematic, widely shared thought: that the brilliant, violent Ike had died not being paid his proper due. Wrote the *LA Times*, "perhaps [Ike] played the behind-the-scenes Svengali too seamlessly for his own good."

Let's go back to du Maurier. By the end of his book, everybody dies. Svengali has a sudden heart attack mid-performance; finally free of his hypnosis, Trilby passes away soon after of a vaguely defined illness. We, the readers, are meant to be happy that Trilby moves on with some measure of peace. But there's a lamentation, too. Despite his lecherous treachery, despite his cowardice and greed, we're left feeling regret that the music that was Rasputin'd into existence is no more. "[H]er voice was so immense in its softness, richness, freshness, that it seemed to be pouring itself out from all round," du Maurier writes. "If she had spread a pair of large white wings and gracefully fluttered up to the roof and perched upon the chandelier, she could not have produced a greater sensation. The like of that voice has never been heard, nor ever will be again."

CHAPTER THREE
The Anti-Rasputin

IKE TURNER, MALCOLM MCLAREN, SVENGALI: They were powerful. But they are the past. To understand the present I go to West Hollywood, to the inner sanctum of a lovely ivy-covered townhouse with a big black door and a small black plaque reading, in gold lettering, "Believe." These are the offices of SB Projects. This is where Scooter Braun, the man who gave the world the pop star Justin Bieber, does his work.

Still shy of forty, Braun is the most famous manager in the industry. And he's well-protected. To get to this precipice, I went through two rounds of off-the-record vetting with Braun, first on the phone, then in person (I got the feeling Braun wanted to look me in the eyes). Months passed. I pushed and pressed and pleaded and, finally, was granted an invite. He was, without a doubt, the hardest person you'll meet in this book for me to get to.

My first wait on the morning of our scheduled appointment is at the front reception desk, looking out at the office's lovely pin-striped wallpaper and framed portraits of clients past and present (Kanye looking pensive; Justin in a tree). Then I'm ushered, through a courtyard strung with Christmas lights and dotted with potted Valencia orange trees, to a second, higher-priority reception desk.

Finally, I'm taken into Braun's sprawling personal office.

I sink into the couch and, waiting for his arrival, look around the room. Behind a wide wooden desk a frame holds four words: "Imagine," "Create," "Execute," "Deliver." Another frame holds the phrase "We used the stars to guide us home." On the wall in front of me is a huge spread of small black-and-white photos. There are portraits of Scooter locked in an embrace with his wife and of Scooter locked in an embrace with Whoopi Goldberg.

He comes in on the phone, mouthing his apologies. He's in a hoodie, a dad hat, and sweats. On his feet are a pair of the very rare semi-frozen-yellow Yeezys. He appears to be dictating for a client a response to some negative press coverage. "So what you wanna do is . . ." I hear, before he steps back outside the office. Then, muffled, from the other room: "Don't be upset about that 'cause you'll look like a crazy person." A big laugh. "I mean, that's up to you!"

His call over, he reenters and sits. Already, I feel a sense of accomplishment. My interview with Scooter Braun is finally happening.

I ask, "How do you get really famous people to listen to you?"

"Ummmmmmmmmm." Long pause. "I think respect. When I'm trying to get clients to say 'yes,' I ask them why they're saying 'no.' I listen to them. Then I pick one thing within their argument that I can acknowledge. And I let them know that I can see why they feel that way. Now they're softening so that they can hear me. And then I slowly change their perspective. In a *respectful* manner."

I imagine Braun's track record of success helps. So was it harder earlier on, when he was a nobody? "I worked with acts that no one wanted!" he shrugs. "It wasn't like they could say, 'Oh, I know what the hell I'm talking about!' They were just as much in the trenches as I was." Scooter, with careful calculation, had young Internet kids looking up at him with eyes wide open. Once they were famous, they were still kids. As far as power dynamics go, it's a pretty stable one.

Braun grew up in leafy Cos Cob, Connecticut, then enrolled at Emory University in Atlanta, where he went about purposefully reinventing himself. His given name, Scott, was certainly a strong one. But he decided to brand himself professionally with a goofy nickname he'd carried on and off through his youth. Now, he was Scooter again. He started throwing huge parties that broke out of the college circuit and roped in the city's hip-hop scene.

Jermaine Dupri, the Atlanta impresario behind the beloved hip-hop and R&B label So So Def, hired him as director of marketing. Braun dropped out of school. He was a twenty-year-old executive; everything was beautiful. Then, a few years in, Jermaine Dupri's mother, a dominant figure within the label, fired Braun for perceived insubordination. He was a twenty-three-year-old flameout.

He looked around, identified what he believed were openings in the industry, and made a plan. He wanted three things: a white rapper; an eighteen-year-old Britney-meets-P!nk hybrid; and a solo pop teen.

The first became Asher Roth, a kid from Pennsylvania who'd have a radio hit with a cloyingly effective number called "I Love College" (sample lyric: "Man I love drinking / Man I love college.") It was Braun's first modest success. The second, he never found. "It just wasn't out there," he says.

The third was Justin Bieber, the global superstar whose success became the bedrock for everything Braun would come to build. It all feels inevitable now, when Bieber's presence permeates mass culture. But Braun was the one who found Bieber on YouTube, bankrolled his inchoate career, and whipped him into stardom.

Braun had grown up on classic hip-hop; he'd come through an Atlanta rap scene enjoying a true golden era. His business plan, though, was utterly agnostic. It couldn't be about what he liked. It had to be about what would work.

"Usher"—the R&B star—"asked me to come to NHL All-Star weekend in Atlanta," Braun recalls. "He was performing. And the Jonas Brothers went on right before him. And the place went nuts for these little kids. And I was like, 'What the hell is going on?' I wasn't a huge fan of their music. But I was like, 'OK, someone in this space—with really great records? That's missing.'"

Braun has been this strategic about wielding influence since he was a kid. He used to devour books by Phil Jackson, the legendary NBA coach. He fixated on the manner in which Jackson would finagle, coddle, and push his superstar, Michael Jordan. Then, at nineteen years old, while reading *The Operator*, Thomas King's classic biography of entertainment magnate David Geffen, he had a revelation.

"There's a point where David's trying to sign John Lennon's solo career," Braun recalls. "And I'm sitting in my bed in my freshman dorm room saying, 'Go to Yoko Ono, go to Yoko Ono. Why is no one respecting her. Go to Yoko Ono!' And I turn the page and it's like—'Geffen was the only one who went to Yoko Ono.'"

Braun beams. "It clicked. Like, 'My brain works this way—I can do this.' That book changed my life."

Geffen had once commented that the particulars of the music industry made it the best arena for a young man to rise fast. Braun took that to heart. "For a young entrepreneur, it was the place I could create my own destiny," he says. "The stock market has regulations. There's players' unions in every athletic league. There's unions with movies and TV. Music has no regulations! It's the Wild Wild West!"

He tells me a story about the old days, in Atlanta. "There was this guy Blue who was managing Outkast," he says. "One year him and Puffy"—aka Sean Combs, rap's timeless Renaissance man— "did this huge party at the Velvet Room. It was crazy and amazing and everyone was going nuts. The following year Outkast breaks up. Puffy comes back to Atlanta and does a party and I'm like—*Blue's name is not on that party invitation.*"

Both Blue and Puffy were associated with specific acts: Outkast for the former, Biggie Smalls for the latter. But Blue had latched himself just to that one act, and he had gone into relative obscurity.

After working with Biggie, Puffy went on to create a brand built on success in, like, all-encompassing totality. That was the lesson: It was OK to be closely associated with a massive star. But the name Scooter would have to mean success, too.

Braun's current client roster includes acts that, like Bieber, he found and built into fame. It also has included previously established names, most notably Kanye West, who were drawn to Braun's carefully manufactured aura of success. (In 2018, Kanye officially parted ways with Braun, although the two remain friendly.) That aura has even meant Braun's been able to transition to other industries.

He rattles it off. "I'm in Uber, I'm in Dropbox, I'm in Coupang . . ."

"Pardon? Coupang?"

"Oh, it's a great company out of Korea. You don't know it?" He goes on: "I'm in film, I'm in TV, I'm in tech, I'm in real estate, I'm in art, I'm in cannabis . . ."

"Cannabis? What do you have in cannabis?"

He smirks. "We'll see."

At the time we speak, Braun is on the cover of the latest issue of *Variety*. They have dubbed him "The Rainmaker." "The people who probably hate my press more than anyone are my own artists," he tells me. "Some of them are proud of me. Others are like, 'What are you doing?' But we built this brand so it stands on its own."

I had wondered one thing: Why, really, was he talking to me? Sitting down with a trade publication like *Variety* had strategic purpose, I could see that. It upped, or at the very least maintained, this image, this brand of never-ending success. He'd made Bieber. Now, he was messaging to the world, he could make anything else he wanted.

But what was the strategic purpose here? Where did my book fit into the master plan?

He smiles. "Everyone on my team told me not to do this interview," he said. "'You can do your own book, *da da da da*.' But I'm curious. You come in, with your limited knowledge of me, and you write about me—it's gonna be a fun exercise, to see how someone who comes into my life for such a short period of time dissects me."

And besides, it was risk free. The way I'd seen it, I'd broken through the vetting. I was going to get Scooter Braun to tell me his secrets. But he reminded me that I'd called in a favor to get here.

It was true. The convoluted backstory: My girlfriend's sister's best friend happens to be Scooter's younger sister. That had gotten our initial correspondence going. And it was also, as Braun saw it, indebting me to behave, or face his sister being mad at her best friend, and her best friend being mad at her sister, and her sister—my girlfriend—being mad at me. As he saw it, I'd already compromised myself. He had the upper hand.

"You know, when you and I first met, I wanted to know—who is this guy? What's the deal with the girlfriend? Now I know who you are, so I can feel more safe. Because I know what life is throwing at me. Life is throwing at me someone who, if he goes rogue on me and tries to fuck me over for no fucking reason, his life is going to get fucked up!" I nod. We both laugh.

I'D STARTED THE conversation by asking Braun how he influenced famous people. Now I was on to my second big question: How does Braun influence the culture at large?

I know the answer, broadly: through the hits he connives into existence. That's what makes a character like Braun so interesting. He doesn't sing, he doesn't write, he doesn't play an instrument. But he is as much the author of the pop music we listen to incessantly as are the artists on his roster. Hundreds of millions of people, literally *hundreds* of *millions* of people, cry and kiss and fight through heartbreak with these songs. He is, as much as anyone, controlling the last vestiges of the monoculture.

With huge hits, there's always an air of inevitability after the fact. This chorus is so catchy, it must have been predestined by the gods. But take something like Carly Rae Jepsen's "Call Me Maybe." One of the all-time great earworms. A massive global smash. When Braun came across it, it was idling at a piddling Number 36. On the *Canadian* charts.

As Braun tells it, Bieber had just returned from his home nation with the song stuck in his head and was absentmindedly singing it. "I was like, 'What was that?'" Braun recalls. "He's like, 'Oh, it's a fun little song.' And I was like, '*This is more than a fun little song*. This is big.'"

Quickly, Braun secured worldwide rights to Jepsen's music. Then he concocted a bit of viral promo: a video of Bieber and his famous friends dancing along to the song on goofy laptop cam footage. "Oh, you mean the 'organic' video," Braun laughs, putting up air quotes, when I bring it up. It would indeed rev up "Call Me Maybe," which now has over a billion YouTube views. (The ancillary video itself would crack seventy-five million views.)

That's a drop in the bucket compared to "Gangnam Style," the 2012 phenomenon from South Korean artist Psy. With over three billion views, it's one of the top ten most played YouTube videos of all time.

"Scott Manson, my COO, sent it to me when it had sixty thousand views," Braun says. "He was like, 'Haha, isn't this funny.' And I was like, '*Find him*. Sign him.' And he's like, 'You're joking, right? You wanna do it in English?' And I said, 'No, I wanna keep it in Korean.' And he's like, 'You gotta be fucking kidding me.' And I was like, 'Dude, I can make this the number one song in the world.'"

In pursuing Psy, Braun flashed back to the old novelty dance songs he'd lived through as kid: "Cotton Eye Joe," "Macarena." He also thought back to Snow's "Informer," an infamous nineties arti- fact in which a white Canadian (real name: Darrin O'Brien) does an imitation of a Jamaican patois accent. "To this day, we have no idea what he was saying. But we all tried to memorize the words. And I was like, 'The kids are gonna do that with Korean.'"

As throughout our conversation, Braun seems to be offering what is primarily an agnostic analysis. I don't actually know how Braun genuinely felt about "Gangnam Style." I just know he didn't have to care for "Gangnam Style" one way or the other to believe that it would work.

At the time we speak, the song "Despacito," from the Puerto Rican artist Luis Fonsi, had just recently concluded a long run of chart domination. Braun recognized its potential early. "We have a bunch of management companies that we've owned that we've never talked about publicly," he says. "In country, in hip-hop, in Latin. My guys in the Latin market, they were like, 'This is a big number, it's *going*.'"

He maneuvered to get Bieber on the remix. Unsurprisingly, Braun says, Fonsi's reps readily agreed—but they wanted him in English. They were planning to cross the song over by dropping the Spanish. Braun demurred. "I'm like, 'Guys, I took a number one in Korean.' Like, Spanish is as spoken as any language in this country. This is gonna work."

Braun speaks of a "formula" for analyzing chart success. "Just understanding how many streams, how much radio play is needed—how to spike all the right things at the right time. Study- ing the charts and putting the plan together to get us there."

Braun estimated that, with his formula, he could get "Despa- cito" to number one on the Billboard Hot 100 for a week. It made it for a week. And then it made it for fifteen weeks straight after that.

All summer, America couldn't get out of its head. With more than 5 billion views, it's now the most played YouTube video of all time.

This is a very particular kind of influence: the influence to dictate what it is a whole country hears.

As a thought exercise I ask Braun: Imagine I was an artist on your client roster. How would you sell my book?

He grins. "This has nothing to do with the interview, right?" And then he shifts into business mode. "I've made a couple of best-sellers. My brother's book"—Adam Braun's memoir of charitable work, *The Promise of a Pencil*—"was a *New York Times* bestseller. Originally they weren't going to print enough copies to get him on the list. I came in and managed him in that process."

He instructs me to keep it simple: "Figure out a really easy way for people to understand what it's about. Just like with artists, people wanna compartmentalize. Artists always say, 'Don't compare me to this or that'—stop fighting that! If you can compare it to something else, people will understand, and you'll be able to sell your book."

Then Braun hands over a bit of proprietary strategy that he'd used effectively before. It's crafty, simple, a bit deceptive. It is really quite good. But he tells me to keep it off the record, for myself.

"Do you feel like you could create a hit song in, say, the next two weeks?" I ask.

"Yes."

"Is that something you continuously need to plan for? To train yourself to be able to do?"

"No."

It's the only time in our conversation he's monosyllabic.

BIEBER WAS A twelve-year-old nobody singing R&B covers in Stratford, Ontario, when Braun found him on YouTube. In an early article on Bieber's ascent, Bieber's mother said that after Braun got in touch, she asked the Lord a question: "God, you don't want this Jewish kid to be Justin's man, do you?" Soon enough, clearly, she realized this *was* the way Jesus had intended it to be.

Those were sweet, innocent, naive times. Early drama came from haircuts. Bieber had emerged with a trademark floppy bowl cut. And when he wanted a trim, Braun says, "I fought it! We were doing so well and the haircut was such a big thing for us, and he was so sick of it. And I'm sitting there like, no! If it ain't broke don't try to fix it!'"

Right around the time he turned eighteen, Bieber began an extended public meltdown. There were all manners of incidents: arrests for drag racing in Miami, a lost pet monkey in Germany, citations for noise violations from parties in Calabasas, bucket-peeing in NYC. It looked, from the outside, like perhaps the young man was breaking free from a once tightly-held yoke.

It's times like these that give the music industry a certain tinge of inevitable disfavor. The years after his discovery were a maelstrom. Bieber became the most famous pop star in the world. That was the point, for sure. But even if you meticulously game-plan for the most insane success, no one knows what that feels like from the inside. No one knows what that's going to do to a kid.

Technically, Braun checks the Rasputin boxes. He is a behind-the-scenes operator, executing a personal agenda through the vessel of another. He doesn't sing or dance. (Although when I bring that up, he argues the latter point by showing me an Instagram video of him very cleanly executing some tricky backup dancer stage moves.) He even has the required enemies.

"My competitors, most of them are my *boys*," he tells me. "But there are some people who would love to see me fail. Who would love to see me fall on my face." But does he exhibit controversial control? Perhaps, once, he did. Then Bieber grew up. And he let him go, to make monkey- and pee-related mistakes.

It's inevitable that fans will imagine Braun as the puppeteer. In the summer of 2018, both Bieber and Ariana Grande, another client of Braun's, announced their engagements (to Hailey Baldwin and Pete Davidson, respectively). The ensuing media attention was huge. For Grande, the attention conveniently came just as she was set to release her fourth album, *Sweetener*. In response, one cheeky fan tweeted, "the devil works hard but Scooter Braun works harder."

This understanding of Bieber, or of Grande, or of any pop star—as a commodity yanked by stronger forces—does not grant them much agency. And Braun's own understanding of Bieber, unexpectedly, is that he is a young man who makes his own decisions. It has been a tricky thing to navigate, he says. But for more than a decade, through rocky times, Scooter and Justin are still together and still tight and still here.

"The line between influence and manipulation can be thin," I say. "Have you ever . . ."

"Manipulated? Yeah. A hundred percent," Braun shoots back. "Justin, when he got healthy"—after the meltdown period—"he was like, 'Man, there were times that you were manipulating me that made me really upset. But now I realize that you were only doing it to help me. You were never trying to manipulate me to hurt me— you were trying to manipulate me to stop me from hurting myself."

"How so?"

"That's personal details between me and him. But I basically was maneuvering behind the scenes to push him into situations where he was safe. And, um—that's a tricky business when you're playing that game. And it's not something you wanna necessarily do, but there are times when you have no choice. When you feel like you have to make those moves."

"That's the only time?"

"On a day-to-day basis, no, I don't manipulate. I try to be so transparent it's overwhelming. Manipulation, I think, should only be used when it's a life-or-death situation. If you're manipulating and you know in your *heart* you're doing something malicious— then you're just an awful person. If you're in a situation where you're manipulating something and you truly, one hundred percent believe it's for their betterment—that it's for the benefit of others—then that's a justification I've found in the past."

He now seems to be suggesting that he has the power to manipulate at will, but that he only uses it for good. I try to understand exactly what he means—I try to understand what the rules are here. "For their benefit—could that mean, you know, manipulating them into doing something that'll net them a hit song?"

He stops me. "This is probably not gonna go in your book but—at this point in your life, you don't have complete financial freedom. You have rent, or a mortgage. You gotta pay bills?"

I concur. I am far, far from financial freedom.

"A lot of your questions, I feel like, are coming from the perspective of *your* life. So I'm trying to see from your eyes. But the things you think I'm hopeful for, I don't think like that. I still wake up every morning like I'm going broke. But I know, financially, I'm OK. I wanted to make ten million. That was my number. I passed that when I was twenty-seven. To manipulate to get more success—I don't think like that."

And here, Braun, always voluble, picks it up a notch.

"My grandma, who I loved more than anything in the world, was working in a sweatshop for eighteen years after surviving the Holocaust. I know I come from that. So I look at my life—getting on private jets, hanging out with celebrities, living in a big house—and I just think to myself, there's no way I get to keep any of this."

I think of the photo of Braun and Whoopi. His life does seem sweet. But before I linger there, I hear: "I don't know when I learned about the Holocaust—I've always just known! It's from my grandma, telling me stories about, you have everything, and then one day an army showed up and took it away.

"They actually study survivors' [families], and we're like a different breed because we truly believe that it can disappear"— he snaps his fingers—"tomorrow. I took fourteen hundred dollars and turned it into a company worth hundreds of millions! I don't think my life is deserved! It sounds naive. It sounds like bullshit, I assume. But I can do things from a really honest place. I can now just care for people.

"One of my friends pointed this out to me, and I loved it. There are Fortune 500 CEOs who have killed themselves, and we're like, 'That's tragic,' but we're not shocked. But if we said, 'Oh, this person who worked in a soup kitchen killed themselves,' we'd be like, 'What! That makes no sense!' Because people who give to others never kill themselves. You don't see Mother Teresa being like, 'I just wanna die!'" He laughs, in incredulity of the image. "It just doesn't happen!"

Braun is in a very good place, he tells me. A place of peace. He doesn't want to manipulate anybody. He wants to do good. He wants to change the world. He just wants to help.

As we say our good-byes, I see that a group of cheery men and women are waiting for Braun in his elegant, gorgeously lit office foyer. I recognize a few of the faces. One's a powerful veteran music exec; the other's a well-known, flashy, industry jack-of-all-trades. The younger faces, I don't know. Maybe they're songwriters or producers. Maybe they're would-be new pop stars. I hear something about "Got the full swag today" and "Don't sit on that, that's an antique." I hear a lot of laughing. I leave them to it, to plot the hits that—soon, very soon—we all, surely, will be using to soundtrack our kisses and our tears and our heartbreak. It's out of our control.

CHAPTER FOUR
The Literary Rasputin

POP MUSIC IS OUR LINGUA FRANCA. But the short story? In the grand imagination of American culture, the short story is the underloved kid brother. If you produce pretty much any other cultural product, you're most likely higher on the cultural totem pole than the short story writer. (OK, yes—technically poetry enjoys less popularity than the short story. But poetry has an inherent artsiness, and inherent artsiness goes a long way.)

All of which is to say, it's hard—goddamn near impossible— to get famous as a short story writer. You have to be really, really good. And to get famous as a short story *editor?* You must be doing something crazy. Gordon Lish, of New York, New York, was definitely doing something crazy.

Lish's first flush of fame came in the 1970s, after he hustled his way into the job of fiction editor at *Esquire* and used the position to launch a string of previously unknown writers. At that point, Lish had run a few small, influential literary magazines where he'd published the likes of Amiri Baraka, Grace Paley, and Leonard Gardner. But the combination of the cachet of *Esquire*, then at its peak relevancy, and the bold new stuff Lish was finding branded him a young master of the form. He'd later brag that he had a gift for reading a page of a good manuscript and immediately getting a feel for its value. With characteristic grandiosity, he'd describe it as an actual physical sensation. People in the industry would call him, with his explicit encouragement, "Captain Fiction."

And there was no one writer that Lish was more closely associated with at *Esquire*—and, subsequently, for the rest of his life—than

Raymond Carver. Carver died of lung cancer at the age of fifty in 1988. At the time of his death, his legacy was established: then, as now, he was considered one of American fiction's all-time greats.

Carver grew up in Yakima, Washington. His mother was a waitress; his father worked in a sawmill. Early in life, Carver bounced between menial jobs at gas stations and hospitals while managing short stints studying creative writing at Humboldt State University and California State University, Chico. He was, like his dad, an alcoholic. Describing the severity of his problem, he once told an interviewer, "Let's just say, on occasion, the police were involved, and emergency rooms and courtrooms." His famous stories were clipped and enigmatic and punchy and populated by humdrum infidelity and bare violence and the kind of hard-drinking blue collar folks he'd grown up with. After his death, the *Times* of London dubbed him "the Chekhov of middle America."

Lish and Carver first met in the late sixties in Palo Alto, California. They were both on the masthead of the lit mag *December*. One night, Lish, drunk on Wild Turkey, came over to the Carvers' home raving about one of Carver's stories—and explaining precisely how he'd have changed the ending if he'd written it. Maryann Burk, Carver's first wife, told Lish, "Well, that's just the point, Gordon. You didn't write it."

A year and change after the incident, Lish was across the country in Manhattan, at *Esquire* magazine on Madison Avenue, and thinking of his friend. In 1971, Lish published Carver in *Esquire* for the first time. The story was "Neighbors," a beguilingly strange piece about a couple whose next-door cat-feeding duties become wracked with envy and invasiveness. It was the future titan's first big look. Soon after, Lish would call Carver "*our* Raymond Carver—ours because he was uncovered in 'slush' here, and because our publication of his 'Neighbors' was his first outing in a national magazine, and because I say he's ours. . . ."

In the ten years to come, Lish would move to a senior editor job at the publisher Alfred A. Knopf. He would edit the seminal Carver collections *Will You Please Be Quiet, Please?* and *What We Talk About When We Talk About Love.* And the two men's lives would become complicatedly intertwined. As the novelist Brian Evenson explained it in his novella-length 2018 appraisal, *Raymond Carver's What We Talk About When We Talk About Love*, "Lish arranged an agent for Carver . . . read Carver's stories on the radio to publicize him . . . engaged a typist for Carver's revisions. Lish would seem to have been a promoter, editor, and publicity agent rolled into one."

Evenson holds a peculiar spot in the saga of Carver and Lish; he himself was edited by Lish. Furthermore, Evenson was the one who tipped off the world at large to the extreme, canon-altering degrees of Lish's editing—of Lish's intense creative Rasputinism.

Many years after the controversy broke, Lish would explain to *The Paris Review* that he only got the job at *Esquire* in the first place because he'd promised he'd be publishing some wild shit. "I was faced with the problem of satisfying [*Esquire's*] notion that I was going to turn up something hitherto unseen," he said. "The New Fiction. I saw in Carver's pieces something I could fuck around with. There was a prospect there, certainly. The germ of the thing, in Ray's stuff, was revealed in the catalogue of his experience. It had that promise in it, something I could fool with and make something new-seeming."

EVENSON WAS AN undergraduate student at Brigham Young University in Salt Lake City in the late eighties when he first heard of the magnetic pull of Gordon Lish. At the time, Lish was running *The Quarterly*, another one of his tastemaking lit mags, and was soliciting submissions from young writers. Evenson remembers his pals at BYU submitting manuscripts and getting them back severely chopped up or marked full of changes. For hungry, unpublished, vulnerable young writers, these were horror stories:

Writers would reject the changes and, in turn, have their stories rejected outright; writers would accept the changes and be rewarded with a fresh batch of dramatic edits; writers would accept *multiple* rounds of changes and still not see their stories win approval for *The Quarterly*. Cowed by the tales, Evenson—as ambitious as any of his peers—never submitted to Lish.

Just a few years later, Lish came into his life nonetheless. After his undergrad years, Evenson moved to the University of Washington for a graduate degree. There, between pursuing his PhD in English literature and critical theory and his coffee shop day jobs, he worked on a novella called *Siege*. It was, as Evenson would later describe it, about "an odd group of misfits living in a desert fortress, one of whom goes crazy and seals the fortress down, shooting anybody who tries to leave" while "others slowly starve to death, go crazy themselves, wander around in underground caves, and so on." Not thinking anything much would come of it, Evenson submitted it to publishers' slush piles. Then one evening, he got a call. Someone had actually read the manuscript. Gordon Lish had read the manuscript.

"I talked to Lish for perhaps ten minutes," Evenson would write in his appraisal of *What We Talk About*. "*Siege*, he said, was not a novel, not something he could publish as a book, but there was still something there, something original. I had potential, he said, and he could bring that potential out, could make me one of the best writers of my generation, just as he had done for"—oh, yeah— "Raymond Carver. But I should move to New York. I should abandon everything and come to New York to take his writing class."

Carver was one of Evenson's all-time favorites and the spiel was naturally persuasive. He didn't drop everything and go. But, despite his past suspicions, he did begin working with Lish. First he attended a few Lish seminars in San Francisco and Portland, in which Lish would workshop stories with small groups of young writers. On the East Coast, Lish was famous for these seminars. They'd last hours and hours; they'd become heated and contentious. As some kind of oppressive outward display of willpower, Lish would never excuse himself to go to the bathroom: "Urinating is probably the first index of a less-than-literary heart," he'd explain. Years later, his son Atticus, himself a novelist, would blame this practice for his father's "boggy bladder." (It has undergone multiple surgeries.)

"I never saw him yell," Evenson recalled to me of the seminars. "I saw him be very cutting to people sometimes. I saw it as almost performative. But if it was happening to you, it was not pleasant. If he didn't like something, he would make it very clear he didn't like it. He would not mince words at all." Evenson took copious notes during the Lish seminars, and he shared them with me. They are a bizarre, fascinating document. Some contemporaneous, out-of-context Lish thoughts, all furiously scribbled down by the eager young Evenson:

- "Nature and reality are no friends to us, they kill us in the end"
- "One cannot write until one has given oneself permission to be God"
- "Writing as a means of sustaining oneself from horror"
- "You must establish presence, even if it means cutting your fingers off and writing with the stumps"
- "You must speak in tongues"

Lish was also already flexing. This was the early nineties, a few years before the Carver scandal broke. But Evenson notes Lish already bragging that it was he who "designed" Carver—who "gave him his affectlessness."

Lish became Evenson's regular editor. And Evenson eventually established himself as a genre-informed, critically acclaimed novelist. Then, at some point in the mid-nineties, Evenson heard something interesting: Lish had sold his papers to Indiana

University–Bloomington's Lilly Library. To this day, Evenson can't recall if it was a fellow writer or an academic or Lish himself who tipped him off to the fact. But immediately, Evenson was piqued. He'd seen Lish's editing firsthand. He wanted to see what it looked like when applied to his heroes as well: folks like Don DeLillo, Amy Hempel, and Carver, still his favorite.

Chasing that scholarly curiosity, Evenson found himself at the Lilly Library digging through papers. He'd known that Lish could be extreme with his cutting, of course. And it'd been years now that he'd heard, in roundabout ways, that Carver himself had suffered the same fate. But, as he writes in his *What We Talk About* analysis, "Even in that context, the revisions were more extensive than I had imagined. Looking at them felt, in some respects, like a violation. I felt like I was seeing something that, ethically speaking, I wasn't sure I should see. Something I wasn't sure I wanted to see."

The cuts were massive, and they were ceaseless. Thirty, fifty, seventy percent of stories were eliminated. Nuance and mitigating thoughts and emotional undertows had been stripped away from characters. Blunt and brand-new closing sentences had been slapped down by Lish. Carver was world-famous for his minimalism. And suddenly, it was revealed to Evenson, that minimalism may have been forced upon him by Lish.

Then things got stranger.

Fairly quickly, Evenson decided to write an academic article about what he'd found. He knew that in order to reproduce selections from Carver's stories, he'd need clearance from Carver's estate, then as now handled by Carver's second wife, the poet Tess Gallagher. He intended to wait until he had a proper draft of the piece before reaching out for approval. But before he could, Evenson recalls, "I get a letter from Gallagher's lawyer, essentially a kind of warning not to pursue the papers."

Gallagher had gotten wind of Evenson's piece and moved to shut it down. Evenson wrote back politely pleading his case and explaining his benign motivations. He even said he'd be happy to share a draft before publication. He heard back, again via mail: "It was a strongly worded letter from the lawyer saying, basically, that they would sue."

Evenson was cowed. "It was frightening," he recalls. "I'd never been threatened with a lawsuit before. And I was pretty young, and I had a young family, and I had just started a new job in the university, and I didn't really have any money. Several people encouraged me. 'Oh, they don't have a case, you should just go ahead with it.' But it was really discouraging. Eventually I thought, this is not what I was headed to do. This is becoming this work of exhaustion."

"From very early, I thought, nothing good was was going to come from *not* talking about this stuff," Evenson continues. "My notion was, 'I'm going to write a scholarly article on this and publish it in a little scholarly journal and that'll get the conversation going.' That seemed like the most productive route. I think that her preventing people from talking about this in the way she did—it ended up being quite harmful for Carver's reputation. I really wish the information had come out first in a scholarly way. It's not that I don't like D. T. Max's article. I just think it allowed for there to be this kind of scandal."

The article Evenson is referring to is "The Carver Chronicles," an August 1998 cover story for the *New York Times Magazine* written by the journalist D. T. Max. The piece is a riveting, surprisingly dramatic chunk of literary hullabaloo. It's the first time the behind-the-scenes Lish–Carver drama was publicized.

Of flipping through the Lish archives himself, Max wrote, "It looked as if a temperamental 7-year-old had somehow got hold of the stories . . . Lish's black felt-tip markings sometimes obliterate the original text . . . When Lish got hold of Carver, [characters] stopped crying . . ."

In some stories, Lish "cut away whole sections to leave a sentence from inside the story as the end: 'There were dogs and there were dogs. Some dogs you just couldn't do anything with' . . . 'Carol, story ends here,' he would note for the benefit of his typist."

Once Max got wind of the rumors of Lish's edits, he contacted Evenson, who gladly shared the research he'd done before abandoning his article under Gallagher's pressure. Evenson was relieved; he never wanted to be the sole caretaker of the explosive information. The fact that Gallagher had already threatened Evenson with a lawsuit didn't hinder Max: the *Times* was a major publication with an in-house counsel.

Recalling his reporting for the piece, Max told me, "I felt like Lish was waiting to talk about it." Lish was then in his sixties and already semi-retired and quasi-hermetic in his Upper East Side apartment—the same one where he lives now, in deeper seclusion. When I reached out myself, I heard back from a representative that "Mr. Lish is, owing to a bad patch health-wise, unavailable."

When Max came calling on Lish, Carver had been dead for a decade. "Lish used to give these very celebrated seminars, and those had ended at some point," Max says. "It was the case of a guy who had a reason to tell his story, maybe, because he was no longer publicly what he had been. I remember him in his apartment with his flowing white hair. I imagine him with a black cape on. I don't think he really did have cape on. But I can imagine it. He was, you know, famous as a magician of sorts." The story that Lish told, that *he* had been the one to find the genius in Carver's raw material—"it wasn't that hard to believe."

In the years after Lish first published him in *Esquire*, Carver's life went through a series of dramatic turns. His writing made him famous. He left Maryann Burk, his first wife, with whom he'd had a tumultuous relationship, and began living with Gallagher. In 1977, he was nominated for a National Book Award, for *Will You Please*. And he stopped drinking.

In July of 1980, he wrote Lish a letter full of foreshadowing. Carver had submitted the manuscript of *What We Talk About When We Talk About Love,* and Lish had returned it with his regular heavy hand. Once, speaking of Lish's editing on "Neighbors," Carver had written of the final product, "My only fear is that it is too thin, too elliptical and subtle, too inhuman." It sounds there, almost, as if Carver himself was not a fan of the famous Carver style. In the past, he wasn't in a position to argue. His alcoholism weakened his resolve. And Lish dangled fame in front of him, and Carver didn't want to fuck that up.

Now, in his July letter, he laid it all out and pleaded with Lish to, for once, leave his raw material alone. "I feel it, that if the book were to be published as it is in its present edited form, I may never write another story." He goes on, "I'm not unmindful of the fact of my immense debt to you, a debt I can simply never, never repay." Crediting his feelings in part to his recent and still-fragile sobriety, he says, "my very sanity is on the line here. I don't want to sound melodramatic here, but I've come back from the grave here to start writing stories once more."

A few days later, in another letter, Carver caved. He accepted the edits. Carol Sklenicka, Carver's biographer, has relayed a few theories as to why. One is that Lish simply, flatly rejected Carver's pleas. Another is that Lish won him over with his regular shtick. (As the Boston *Globe* once put it, Lish had "the oratorical skills of a roadshow preacher.") Yet one more is that Lish won the battle with a hint of blackmail: In this scenario, Lish told Carver that if he backed out now, Lish would reveal just how much deep editing had gone on for years and years.

So Lish would win the battle for the soul of *What We Talk About.* (Today, it's arguably Carver's best-known work.) But by 1983's *Cathedral,* Carver was in the driver's seat. Lish was once again his editor, but Carver preempted any attempt at Lish's usual editing grandiosity. The stories are fuller, richer, warmer. Characters once again get to feel.

There are many theories, as well, over what finally led Carver to steal back his agency. That his sobriety wised him up to what was happening here. That his success emboldened him to reclaim his life's work. But this is a study of Rasputins. And so for our interests, the most interesting theory is that Carver effectively gave the space that Lish had occupied in his brain over to Gallagher. That he'd swapped one Rasputin for another.

Lish himself has suggested as much. "For all those years, Carver could not have been more enthusiastic, nor more complicit—or complacent," he's said. "That mood reversed rather sharply when he appeared at the YMHA"—a venue in New York, for a reading; this would have been the early eighties—"and I met Carver and Tess Gallagher for drinks across the street. Things between us were quite obviously going south. I took it that from that point forward she was increasingly participating in what work Ray turned out."

In his *Times Magazine* piece, D. T. Max points to a 1992 PBS documentary called *To Write and Keep Kind* in which Gallagher boasts of her contributions to Carver's later work. Gallagher states that the idea for the title story from *Cathedral*, one of Carver's most beloved pieces, had come from an anecdote that she had told Carver about a blind friend of hers, and that "Carver 'scooped' her" on the story; as Max writes, "She spoke of the story as a joint effort."

Of the ending, Gallagher says on-camera, "Ray had written many, many drafts and didn't know how to get out of this story . . . I was empathizing with his waiter character and I said, that waiter is going to be looking down and you know what he's going to see? He's going to see that cork that popped out of the champagne. I think the ending is involved with his response to that cork, and that he's going to bend down to get that and we're going to know something from that gesture, that action."

Evenson holds no ill will toward Gallagher, his one-time foe. When I bring up the Gallagher Theory—aka The Replacement Rasputin Theory—he considers it with a chuckle. "I think she probably did have a big influence on him, but I also don't know to what degree that translates into her actual revising things on the page. I think having someone in his life who was there to stand up to him, and to his fiction, was huge. We don't have any kind of manuscript evidence to confirm that. Maybe that's something that will eventually be published or be given to an archive. I honestly think it's very possible."

And Gallagher did have another, much more massive and documentable influence on Carver. "She was so adamant about trying to control that information"—the truth about Lish—"that it ended up being harmful," Evenson says. "Because if there's nothing to cover up—you don't cover it up!"

Gallagher hasn't spoken much publicly about Lish. But she did once say in the press, "What would you do if your book was a success but you didn't want to explain to the public that it had been crammed down your throat? He had to carry on. There was no way for him to repudiate the [edits]. To do so would have meant that it would all have to come out in public with Gordon, and he was not about to do that. Ray was not a fighter. He would avoid conflict, because conflict would drive him to drink."

At the top of this chapter, I called short stories "underloved." But not out of malice. I love short stories. I love Carver. I only did it to make one small point: that even in the relatively low-stakes world of short fiction—less money, less prestige, less attention—the Rasputins can rise. It's a peculiar thing, too. What seems like a small act—cutting some sentences, changing some words—is, in fact, a grand invasion. Carver's stories *were* his worldview. Lish stole that away. Lish entered his brain. Which of our other Rasputins can lay claim to such a feat?

The way that the saga of Lish and Carver was made public, over the protestations of Gallagher, gives it an air of delicious melodrama. But as any attentive English major could tell you, the tale of the overzealous editor is a staple of literary history. With a few influential personal letters, F. Scott Fitzgerald chopped down his pal Ernest Hemingway's *The Sun Also Rises*. Maxwell Perkins cut tens of thousands of words out of Thomas Wolfe's classics. Ezra Pound fashioned a strange mess of a T. S. Eliot poem called "He Do the Police in Different Voices" into "The Waste Land."

One of my personal favorite complicated editor–writer pairings is the knottier example of Franz Kafka and Max Brod. The two met as university students in turn-of-the-century Prague. Kafka was a sickly and eternally insecure introvert; Brod was the pronounced alpha of the pair and, despite his small hunchback, apparently quite the ladies' man.

Both were writers. But Kafka was the genius and Brod, with no outward hint of jealousy, knew it. After Kafka's premature death of tuberculosis in 1924 at the age of forty, in a sanatorium, Brod dedicated his life to spreading the gospel of Kafka. Kafka burned an assumed 90 percent of what he wrote in his life and had barely published any of the rest. After his death, among Kafka's leftover belongings on the desk in his parents' home, Brod found a handwritten note. "Dearest Max, My last request: Everything I leave behind me . . . in the way of notebooks, manuscripts, letters—my own and other people's—sketches, and so on, is to be burned unread and to the last page." Brod, of course, did no such thing. And it is from his curation and editing that we have the final, public versions of the masterpieces *The Trial* and *The Castle*. So we don't actually know— no one does—what Kafka's writing was before Brod.

Brod is a relatively obscure figure. Kafka is canonized internationally. But as the novelist Elif Batuman once suggested, "Maybe there is no Kafka beyond Brod."

WE ARE LEFT with two recurring questions: Where does the person end and the Rasputin begin? And if the end product is worth our time, does it matter? More specifically to our interests here, what was Lish's goal? Did he want to be a Rasputin? Or did he just end up that way? He gave us Carver's classics. Should we hate him or love him for it?

Not long after Evenson had his first conversation with Lish, the one in which Lish promised to make him famous, he found out something interesting. It turned out, a fellow writer told Evenson, that Lish was prone to making these kind of calls. It was, in fact, something of a Gordon Lish stump speech. *Come to New York, and I'll grant you success.*

"It was amazing to hear," Evenson says of that first phone call. "And it was very convincing. You're hearing that speech and you're hearing 'I can be famous.' But the thing that you should be hearing is, '*I* can *make* you famous.'"

Knowing the speech had been trotted out before didn't bother Evenson in the long run, because he believed in Lish's bona fides. "He was very good at taking a writer and making them better. I'm very grateful for what he taught me. He saved me years of effort. Working with Lish is this intensive experience that felt abusive sometimes but ultimately was really, really helpful."

"What did he actually show you?" I ask. "Can you articulate it?"

"I can try to," he says. "I think he was very good at bringing attention to the language of the sentence—very good at really making you think about every word being important. He taught me how to be economical about what I was doing, but he also taught me how to *not* be economical—he just made you think about the degree that you did or did not need certain things."

I suggest that Lish's style was intentional—that Lish was purposefully frightening his young charges, who believed Lish held the secret to their success, into going along with his program.

"I don't think it was *quite* like that," Evenson says. "He was busy. He was trying to do a lot all at once. He *did* respect it when you would stand up to him—as long as you had reasons. It was as simple as, you know, 'I'm trying to talk to you. Don't waste my time.' And in fact, a lot of my interactions with him were very kind. I was going through my letters and realized just how much time he spent with me that had nothing to do with writing. He would send notes to my daughters. He would talk about philosophy."

In Evenson's point of view, Lish does not get enough credit for the hundreds and hundreds of hours he spent nurturing young writers. But he understands why that is. Because there was always that flip side. "If he didn't feel that a person was acknowledging him in a way that was proper, he would cut them. In some cases he would never speak to that person again. He was brutal about that."

Evenson argues that Lish earned the right. "He saw his job as someone who would be a provocation for people. And he was very provocative! I see that as performative. But ultimately, he wanted the writers he was working with to produce great work."

In later years, Lish would happily defend his work, and not only on the merits of its popularity. "I've been decried for a heinous act," he said after the facts had all come out and shook up the lit world. "Was it that? Me, I think I made something enduring. For its being durable, and, in many instances, beautiful."

So if Lish could make Carver's work beautiful, why couldn't he do the same with his own? He once promised, "I will never write, because I respect writers too much, and I know I don't have the talent." But starting in 1983 (right around the time, in fact, his intimacy with Carver frayed), Lish began publishing his own fiction. His bibliography, including novels, memoirs, and short story collections, now runs to nearly twenty books.

But none of Lish's original work touched the culture the way Carver's did. (In 2018, all of Lish's books combined sold . . .

seventy-one copies.) And in a later interview with *The Paris Review*'s Christian Lorentzen, Lish would admit as much. He just couldn't do it himself. He just didn't have the chops. He had to go through Carver. To make something beautiful, he had to be Carver's Rasputin.

"Was it ever your ambition to approach the sublime?" Lorentzen asks.

"Oh, sure," Lish says. "But never came close . . . I'm a poseur, a potzer . . . Shit, are you kidding? The sublime . . . not with respect to my own writing. Only, if ever, through my acts of revising the materials of others."

Lish then circles back to defending his work. "Had I not revised Carver, would he be paid the attention given him? Baloney! . . . I can't believe that what I had in my hands from Ray would have made its way into the hearts of those who have apparently been so undone by the work . . . But readers were seduced, and, I'm sorry, but it was my intervention that seduced them. In it, in doing this, I fashioned a golem that would be cheered to see me destroyed."

Looking back at the sordid story now, Evenson is waiting patiently for yet another twist in the story. "The unfortunate thing was that the response to it was more of a response to Lish's personality than to what was actually going on with the edits. I think it'll take twenty to thirty years and Lish's death before we start to get an objective sense as to whether Lish's edits were a good thing or a bad thing. The shame is, when you sit down to read Carver, you always feel like you're being asked to pick sides."

In his appraisal of *What We Talk About*, Evenson adds a few more salient points. Of Lish's editing, which so assiduously did away with Carver's sentimentality in favor of more boozy, hard-bitten tales, he says, "In that aspect of his editing, Lish strikes me as being somewhat like that old friend who wants you to still be the brash, reckless person you were when you were younger." And of the whole "epic" thing, he writes, "It's probably not coincidental that, after having thought seriously about Lish's severe editing of Carver, I went on to write a novel, *Last Days*, about an amputation cult."

In my conversation with D. T. Max, the journalist reflected on what he saw as the increasingly tragic, increasingly sympathetic figure of Lish.

"Your book is about manipulation?" he asked. I agreed that it was.

"And each edit is its own drama for all of us, right?" I agreed that that was true enough—for writers, comically touchy writers, each and every edit can feel like an attempt at manipulation.

Of Lish and Carver, Max said, "There's no doubt that there was a taking—almost a kind of a predatory way of swooping down on a talented but weak individual. Lish had great gifts, but maybe he didn't have the personality to be a great fiction writer. I think his contempt for the public, at the end, it just prohibited him."

Max gives me a good example. "Imagine a story in which a kid has a pet bunny that dies."

OK. Got it.

"The only way Lish would be interested in that story?"

Yeah?

"If it was the kid that killed the bunny."

But Max ultimately is more sympathetic to Lish now than ever. Lish, he argues, did what he had to do.

"He's an unattractive figure, but he's a self-acknowledged unattractive figure. He made himself into . . ." Max struggles to recall a name. "Who's Batman's nemesis?" He gets it. "The Penguin! He made himself into the Penguin. And he had enemies. I mean, not people that would cut his throat. But he was a star and he was beset by enemies. You can be a star and be hated."

CHAPTER FIVE
The Cinematic Rasputin

IN THE NINETIES, when I was first falling in love with movies, I was enamored with a Sicilian American artist from Buffalo named Vincent Gallo. At the time, Gallo was a ubiquitous, restless creative force: He was a director and he was an actor and he was an artist and he was a musician who put insane albums out on very cool record labels and he talked a lot of shit and he was great at it all. (Well, OK, mostly he was great at the directing and the shit-talking.) He was dark and handsome and profoundly off-kilter. He was deeply strange, and proud of it. He had long hair and a thick beard and he probably really wouldn't have much minded a comparison to Rasputin. I remember reading about how he declared he'd only agree to magazine interviews if they gave him the cover. I remember thinking that was so, so cool.

He made his directorial debut in 1998 with the semi-autobiographical *Buffalo '66*, in which he costarred with Christina Ricci as a freshly freed ex-con who kidnaps a young woman and forces her to pretend to be his wife. It's supposed to be a comedy. It's a gem of a movie. In 2015, recalling her experiences on *'66* in a *Huffington Post* interview, Christina Ricci said, "I spent most of that movie trapped in a car with a raving lunatic."

Ricci was seventeen at the time of filming and had largely worked as a child actress on big-budget movies, which meant strict rules and close supervision. On *'66*, Gallo dictated that Ricci's mother wouldn't be allowed on set. He also later bragged that he totally manipulated Ricci's performance into existence. "She's basically a puppet," Gallo said. "I told her what to do, and she did it."

Just like pop music and literature, cinema has always carried a promise of dark control. The domineering director has always been with us. Alfred Hitchcock once notoriously said, "Actors are cattle." In our list of Rasputin Rules, it's #4 that is most pressing here: "They must attempt to execute a personal agenda." The Rasputinesque director is an auteur. Their agenda is their true, pure artistic vision. And they are desperate to make it happen.

By the mid-2000s, Gallo had faded away. His shtick had curdled and become ugly and obscene. In 2018, after a long stretch of silence, Gallo reappeared with a bizarre first-person piece for the British magazine *Another Man*. He used it as an excuse to adjudicate petty, obscure old beefs. He claimed he'd made multiple movies that he'd chosen not to release. He explained that that was a good thing because "the possibilities of what a film could be, could never be realized with the public so in mind." It all felt like the ramblings of a long-forgotten man, one wrecked by his doubts and failings. (For the record, though, he did get the cover.)

In the years after Gallo disappeared, new problematic auteurs appeared in his place. In 2013, the French director Abdellatif Kechiche released *Blue Is the Warmest Color*, a three-hour romance starring the actresses Léa Seydoux and Adèle Exarchopoulos as young lovers caught in a tortured affair. The process of shooting it so traumatized them that they both vowed never to work with Kechiche again. Said Exarchopoulos, "Abdell doesn't want to see you act—he wants to take your soul."

The movie debuted at the Cannes Film Festival and won the Palme d'Or, Cannes's highest honor. The jury, led by Steven Spielberg, made a point of awarding the prize not only to the director, as is traditional, but to Seydoux and Exarchopoulos as well. In photos from Cannes, the director stands beaming and flanked by his two actresses, each laying a kiss on one cheek. In their well-tailored formal dress, the three of them look the very picture of gleeful prestige-film success.

Once Seydoux and Exarchopoulos began doing interviews in America to promote the movie, the scandal broke. In one dramatic early interview with *The Daily Beast*, the actresses seemed to unload all of their dark on-set memories.

Sex scenes, the actresses explained, were shot without choreography, emotional breaks, or verbal support. In fact, Kechiche did nothing that a director might generally do to desexualize a situation and make actors more comfortable. The movie's central, six-minute sex sequence was shot, laboriously, over the course of ten days. Every tiny moment got rehashed. Kechiche would shoot take after take after take.

In the movie, the characters first meet as they're crossing a street. They lock eyes. It's love at first sight. It's half a minute of screen time. They shot it all day long—over a hundred takes. By the end of the day, Seydoux had been spun into a dizzy state. In one late take, involuntarily, she let out a laugh. The director snapped. Seydoux recalls, "[Kechiche] became so crazy that he picked up the little monitor he was viewing it through and threw it into the street, screaming, 'I can't work under these conditions!'"

Anything disingenuous on set would be cause for similar panic. "I didn't use any tricks to make myself cry," Exarchopoulos would later tell *The Independent*. "Abdell would kill me. He hates fabrication. He wants to be close to the truth every time." They smoked real joints, drank real beer. Most dramatic of all was a scene featuring domestic violence. Exarchopoulos remembers Seydoux striking her over and over, and Kechiche screaming, "'Hit her! Hit her again!'" and crew members echoing his shout as well. "And she didn't want to hit me," Exarchopoulos said, "so she'd say sorry with her eyes and then hit me really hard."

Kechiche shot the scene with three cameras running constantly over the duration of one hour-long take. Again, no breaks. At one point Exarchopoulos cut herself putting her hand through a glass door. She was bleeding and crying, and her nose was running with the tears. Seydoux tried to comfort her, and Kechiche cut her off. "He screamed, 'No! Kiss her! Lick her snot!'" Exarchopoulos would recall. The shoot was planned for two months. It was extended, a bit at a time, until it stretched to nearly half a year. "We couldn't see the ending," Seydoux said. "It was horrible." Also: "In America, we'd all be in jail."

The inevitable end point of any conversation about unhealthy creative partnerships: Was it worth it? Does the art justify the means? In interviews with French media, Seydoux said: "I don't think artistic success justifies everything." Exarchopoulos, the much younger actress, was more equivocal. "Every genius has his own complexity," she said. "[Kechiche] is a genius, but he's tortured. We wanted to give everything we have, but sometimes there was a kind of manipulation." Ultimately, she saw it as an emotional spectacle, riveting and powerful. "I was so exhausted that I think the emotions came out more freely," she said of the end of the shoot. "You can see that we were really suffering."

Directors who shoot take after take after take often talk about beating the acting out of their actors. They want to push the actors past any of their tricks or mannerisms, past their shells. They want to get to a place of true, natural feeling. Kechiche seemed intent on the same thing—only more and more and more of it. He didn't just want his actors breaking down their shells. He wanted them, themselves, broken down. He wanted them too tired to think, too tired to push back. To convince someone to hit someone against their own will—that's a remarkable, ugly thing.

How was Kechiche able to accomplish this? Seydoux has suggested that his control was in line with a French tradition of filmmaking in which a director is preemptively granted serious authority. Exarchopoulos has suggested it was her age and her inexperience that got her to go along. She wanted to give her all to the production. She didn't know where to draw the line—she didn't even know she could *draw* one. For their own reasons, both actresses ceded control early in the process. With each take, with each tacked-on day of shooting, they got further away from the point at which they'd given up that control.

Neither Kechiche or Gallo invented their respective philosophies. Film history has long entertained, as the film critic Richard Brody has written, a certain idea "that extends from the content of the movies themselves to the particulars of their release, and even includes their marketing and distribution—the very idea that there is an optimal film, one that bears the total imprint of the total intentions of the absolutely domineering and visionary director, and that there's a platonic form of those intentions that the finished film (and even its presentation) are meant to realize."

And that idea, says Brody, comes as much as anything from "the ongoing cult of [Stanley] Kubrick—a cult that worked its power . . . on all of modern cinema."

When I look at all of the Rasputinism behind all of the movies that I love, I think about Gallo and Kechiche and Hitchcock—and even Michael Bay and James Cameron. But I keep on coming back to Stanley.

"NICOLE AND I talk about it so much at night. When we're 70 years old, sitting on the front porch, we'll be able to look back and say, 'Wow! We made this movie with Stanley Kubrick!' We know it may take a long time to finish, but we don't care. We really don't."

This was Tom Cruise speaking to *Entertainment Weekly* in 1996. The move in question was *Eyes Wide Shut*. His costar was his then-wife, Nicole Kidman. Cruise didn't yet know the crucible to come.

At more than four hundred days spread across two years, *Eyes Wide Shut* clocks in as the longest continuous shoot in movie history. That's remarkable given that nearly all of the film's action—including an infamous Illuminati sex-party centerpiece—consists of people walking or sitting or talking. A few days after the movie was screened for the first time, Kubrick passed away. He was seventy years old. In the last film he would direct, Kubrick gave full flight to his artistic, manipulative impulses.

In the name of creative exploration, *Eyes Wide Shut*'s scenes would be shot again and again and again. The unrelenting production bludgeoned the life force out of Cruise and, in the process, neutralized the actor's insatiable zest. Despite the conditions, Cruise pursued his performance with the same drive that has made him such an indomitable movie star. But this time would be different.

Kubrick would consciously play on Cruise and Kidman's real-life relationship, and not just for its commercial appeal. Before shooting, in secret conversations that eerily mimicked alleged Scientology auditing practices, Kubrick coaxed Cruise and Kidman to reveal their darkest thoughts about their relationship. But there was no room to analyze or respond to the disclosures; they were there only to cultivate fodder for the movie. "You didn't have anyone to say, 'And how do you feel about that?'" Kidman would explain. "It was honest, and brutally honest at times."

By the time *Eyes Wide Shut* went into production, Kubrick had been toying with a version of the project for more than three decades. He'd originally envisioned it as a follow-up to *Lolita*, his 1962 cultural brush fire, until his wife, Christiane, gently ushered him away. "Don't . . . oh, please don't . . . not now," she told him. "We're so young. Let's not go through this right now."

Born and raised in the Bronx, the teenage Kubrick was a wunderkind. By the age of seventeen he was shooting photographs of Frank Sinatra and prizefights for the powerhouse *Look* magazine. He'd quickly segue into documentary shorts and film noir features.

With 1956's *The Killing*, a meticulously plotted heist film, he'd prove himself a proper Hollywood director. In photos from the set, he's still decades away from the image with which we popularly associate him. Which is to say: a bit plump, a bit sullen, a lot bearded. Instead, clean shaven in a neat suit, with a glint of a smile in his eyes, he's the definition of boyish. Kubrick followed *The Killing* with *Paths of Glory*, a taut exploration of morality within the trenches of World War I starring Kirk Douglas. It elevated him again, this time from elite practitioner to true artist.

Next, he reunited with Douglas on *Spartacus*. Anthony Mann, the original director of *Spartacus*, was fired two weeks in. Douglas—who was not only the star of the movie, but also one of its producers—successfully lobbied for Kubrick to take over. But their second partnership would be an unhappy one full of creative clashes. Hoping to work through their issues, they actually went through a version of couples' therapy. It was during these sessions that Kubrick first came across the book that would form the basis for *Eyes Wide Shut*.

Forced to concede to his star's instincts on *Spartacus*, Kubrick stewed. For one, he never wanted to shoot the now famous "I am Spartacus" scene. This was the project that convinced Kubrick that in order to make the movies he wanted to make, he'd need absolute, total control. He was thirty years old.

The decades to come would bring a string of generation-defining, controversy-stoking classics: *A Clockwork Orange*, *2001: A Space Odyssey*, *The Shining*, *Full Metal Jacket*. He did it his way—he had complete control.

By the mid-nineties, his reputation as unassailable as ever, Kubrick would finally return to *Eyes Wide Shut*. He hired the writer Frederic Raphael to whip up a script. The source material was *Traumnovelle*, or *Dream Story*, by the relatively obscure, medically trained Austrian writer Arthur Schnitzler. (A strange side note: On the occasion of Schnitzler's sixtieth birthday, Sigmund Freud, a professional acquaintance, wrote him a letter confessing, "I have avoided you out of a fear of finding my own *doppelgänger.*") Not that Raphael knew that: For no reason the writer could discern, Kubrick gave Raphael Xeroxed pages of the text from which he'd physically cut out Schnitzler's name.

Raphael would go on to write a memoir of the process, *Eyes Wide Open.* In it he breached Kubrick's well-documented obsession with privacy to share a trove of unflattering details. He portrayed the filmmaker as indecisive, illogical, awkward, and petty. Still, intentionally or otherwise, Kubrick comes off as the decidedly more charming half of the partnership.

"The Holocaust—what do you think?" Raphael quotes Kubrick asking at one point. "As a subject for a movie."

"It's been done a few times, hasn't it?" Raphael says.

"I didn't know that," Kubrick responds.

Raphael's memoir is a fascinating account of a man locked in a battle he can't quite understand. A great admirer of Kubrick's films, Raphael—a novelist and Oscar-winning screenwriter himself—is intent on entering this collaboration as an equal partner. But everything about the fleeting, intermittent interactions he has with the mysterious man seems to throw him off.

Raphael first meets Kubrick at Childwickbury Manor, Kubrick's sprawling home in the English countryside. "He spoke as if unused to speech," Raphael writes. "He appeared both vain and self-effacing . . . he was wearing a blue overall with black buttons. He might have been a minor employee of the French railways."

Later, as he awaits further instructions, Raphael theorizes that the home invitation itself was an attack. "In the Mediterranean, the man who displaces himself to visit another is conceding his superiority by the very fact of traveling to see him." He feels every move by Kubrick has some hidden purpose: "I suspect that his concealment of the source of the text had been little more than a game which he was playing with himself and against me: the warm-up."

At one point in conversation, Raphael makes a slip-up by referring to "Central Park East," in Manhattan, a street that doesn't actually exist. "Kubrick grinned and said 'Central Park East is Fifth Avenue.' He collected my pawn with relish." Raphael was mortified.

Because we never hear Kubrick's internal monologue in Raphael's memoir, we never know if the screenwriter really is locking intellectual horns, or is just imagining as much. This is the victory that Kubrick has secured before even opening his mouth; the collected genius of his work has so intimated Raphael that the screenwriter preemptively knocked sideways.

Ultimately, Raphael realizes that his quest to be an equal partner in the collaboration was always doomed. Kubrick "never wanted a *collaborator*, but rather a skilled mechanic that would can crank out the dross he will later turn to gold." He concludes, "Directors are a cannibal breed. Their nature is to seek out those whose destruction will give them the greatest charge."

In the book, we hear Kubrick say almost nothing, but we feel his power through Raphael's fried logic. "What I dread and cannot help probing is the possibility that the Kubrick myth will perish under close inspection," he thinks at one point. "I need him to be great, and yet I probe for his flaws." And by the end of their time together, Raphael all but throws in the towel. He never did gain some higher understanding of Kubrick's internal gifts, but, he says, "I still have to believe in Kubrick's genius. Imagine if all these too obsequious months have *not* been in the service of a transcendent talent!"

The end result of Raphael and Kubrick's tense collaboration was a finished script that would update the novella from early-twentieth-century Vienna to modern-day Manhattan but, otherwise, remain surprisingly faithful. An attractive married couple—Cruise is Bill Harford, a doctor; Kidman is Alice Harford, a mother to their young daughter—attend a fancy party during which both are separately, unsuccessfully seduced. In the fuzzy exchange that follows, Alice offers a confession: Last summer, while on a family vacation, she saw a handsome naval officer she was so intensely drawn to that she would have, she believes, thrown her life away to be with him.

She never took step one to consummate the fantasy, she explains. But the revelation is enough to unmoor Dr. Harford, who almost immediately begins a long night of profound sexual weirdness. Much of it is scored to the odd plink-plink-plink of the composer Györgi Ligeti's "Musica Ricercata II," a piece of music written in Soviet-occupied 1950s Hungary and imagined, according to Ligeti, as "a knife in Stalin's heart."

First Harford receives a confession of love from the bereaved daughter of a dead patient. Then, a pleasant, chaste encounter with a quiet, dangerous sex worker. And finally, one inimitable sex party. There, masked men in robes watch other masked men have sex with naked, masked women as atonal chanting—actually choral recordings of Romanian priests, run backward—rings out. It's an honest-to-God orgy.

That Eyes Wide Shut has its detractors is not only understandable, it's inevitable. All these years later, the question persists: What is this thing?

Practically, it's an attempt to explicate internal drama. If sexual jealousy so often feels epic, it's just as often rooted in empty paranoia. Eyes Wide Shut walks a line—for all its sights and sounds, it presents no actual unfaithful copulation from either husband or wife.

It's also a manifestation of the strange, dark fears within. Schnitzler describes them in the novella as "those hidden, scarcely suspected desires that are capable of producing dark and dangerous whirlpools in even the most clear-headed, purest soul." It's surreal, but only to a point. It's an attempt to play out what might happen if one were to let those fears take over.

The answer: Why, you'd end up with your life threatened by a powerful masked sex cult, of course.

The leader of the cult is a man in a red cloak and a gold mask that is never removed. His presence is hypnotizing; his voice is powerful and strange. I can't tell you how many hours my high school buddies and I spent quoting his booming declarations: "*Would you kindly remove your mask . . . now, get undressed. . . .*" And so when I met the man who played the red-cloaked figure in a cluttered Manhattan film-production office, I happily told him as much. And to my delight, he responded by cackling lightly and quoting himself: "*May I have the password, please . . .*"

His name is Leon Vitali, and he's not an actor. Well, not anymore. Now in his seventies, he's spent most of his life in service to Kubrick. It's a long, fascinating story. While Kubrick was alive, Vitali was his endlessly versatile, endlessly pliable right-hand man. He did everything from casting to dialogue coaching to archive maintenance to VHS-cover editing; he was slavishly, proudly devoted to Kubrick. And the the craziest part: Kubrick first met Vitali during an audition. The latter was a working actor in the UK; Kubrick cast him in a sizable role in his 1975 movie *Barry Lyndon*. After *Lyndon*, Vitali won praise and attention. He most likely could have chosen to ride that clamor into a long film and theater career. Instead, he gave it all up to execute every last particle of Kubrick's vision.

You would think Kubrick's 1999 death might have freed Vitali from the hold. Instead, Vitali has committed his life since to caring for the manifold restorations and technological transfers of Kubrick's films. He's now devoted to making sure they last forever.

When we meet, he's in a black leather jacket and a black beanie, a pair of black sunglasses folded in front of him on top of that morning's *New York Times*. In person, his voice is less imposing, more alluring. The years have given it a soothing, even-more theatrical richness.

Vitali first fell in love with Kubrick after seeing *A Clockwork Orange*. Just getting cast in *Barry Lyndon*, he told me, felt like an unbelievable coup. Then, after a few days on set, Vitali recalls, Kubrick pulled him aside to tell him that he liked what he was seeing and that he wanted to write him more scenes.

"He asked me, 'What do you think?'" Vitali says. "And I thought, 'That's a stupid fucking question. I can't think!'" Vitali laughs. "I've smoked some dope in my life, but I've never been as high as when he told me he wanted more scenes from me."

As an actor, Vitali was struck by Kubrick's ability to focus. "It didn't matter how many people were there [on set]," he says. "There was nobody else—just you and him. And he never said, 'I want you to sit down' or 'Put your arms in your face.' It was, 'Do it the way you think you're gonna do it.' And 'Don't hold anything back—don't save it.'"

Later, when working with Kubrick's actors as a dialogue coach, Vitali would train them, first, to know every last line past the beyond of memory—to get to a point where "it becomes an absolute sort of reflex." And "that's why he's renowned for thirty, forty takes sometimes. He was going to keep you doing it until you gave him what you wanted without him having to say 'I want you to be *this*' . . . '*this* degree of frustrated or angry' or whatever it is. Stanley was always after that inner thing."

So his control wasn't about dictating every last motion and line. It wasn't about on-set domination, either. On the set of *The Shining*, Vitali says, "If the crew didn't want to work Saturdays, they'd have to vote so on Fridays. And Jack [Nicholson] used to say to them, 'You get champagne on set if you vote no.'" Impersonating Kubrick's response, Vitali jokingly mutters, "I hate Jack, I hate him!" But Kubrick did let the voting (and the bins of champagne) roll on. And more often than not, Kubrick's crews would go along with what appeared to be his madman desires. "Sometimes they'd say, 'Oh, I don't understand this at all,'" Vitali recalls. "But amazingly, and beautifully, they resolved themselves to go along with it. Even if they thought it was silly! Which was touching. It really was."

Vitali remembers Kubrick only becoming upset when people made "careless mistakes. If he thought that you were trying—if the mistake was an honest one—there was never a problem. But there were times when he got, I always said, *incandescent*. You could see this glow getting bigger and bigger and bigger. And you'd go, 'He's gonna hit the fan!' But it was all very transparent for me. And he'd admit when he wasn't in complete control."

That reminds Vitali of 1953's *Fear and Desire*. Made when Kubrick was twenty-five years old, it is officially the master's directorial debut. But Stanley loathed the end product, and the film faded into obscurity.

"I found a copy of it," Vitali tells me. "He thought they'd all been destroyed. I told him, 'It's in the projection booth.' And he said, 'Leon—promise me you'll never look at that film.' And I said, 'Oh, no, I won't.' And he said, "No—*promise* me you'll never look at that film.' And I never have."

"What happened to the copy?" I ask.

"I think it's burned," Vitali says.

Stories like that remind us of Vitali's devotion to Kubrick—and of Kubrick's ability to get people to do precisely what he wanted. But, Vitali insists, Kubrick didn't just "have control. He fought for it every time. Every movie was a battle."

I ask Vitali if he feels it's fair to say Kubrick manipulated people. Vitali tells me that, yes, in a way, he accepts the wording.

"But it's a part of everyone's life, isn't it?" he asks. "You manipulate your mum and your mum manipulates your dad and vice versa. We always used to say, you get three people in an office and you've got a pyramid of power!" He cackles. "That's all there is to it. It's very human. And I mean, it got to a point where—"

Suddenly, in the corner behind us, a precarious pile of rolled-up posters goes tumbling to the ground. We both look over, smiling. Vitali, the old actor, takes the bait.

"Oh, hello Stanley!" He cackles again. "He still has his ways!"

EYES WIDE SHUT is a startling piece of evidence of Cruise's courage in giving himself to Kubrick. Unlike Raphael, he never felt the need to hang even. Happily, wisely, he bent the knee. As Vitali puts it, "It was fantastic. It was bliss. Not a peep of worry or complaint. By the time of the Master Ball"—the showpiece sex party—"the calls were getting later and later. We were working until two or three in the morning. Tom went with it. No complaints. He really, really went with the way Stanley wanted him to work. Unquestioning, absolutely."

In her book Tom Cruise: Anatomy of an Actor, film critic Amy Nicholson recounts the breadth of Cruise's devotion—"[a] perfectionist himself"—to "his master," Kubrick. The sprawling shoot, with no solid end date. The repetition—at one point, Cruise did ninety-five takes just walking through a door. The ulcer Cruise developed on set and kept hidden. The blatant emotional manipulation.

"To exaggerate the distrust between their fictional husband and wife, Kubrick would direct each actor separately and forbid them to share notes," Nicholson explains. For the footage of Alice's fantasy with the naval officer—which periodically plays in Bill's mind throughout—"Kubrick demanded that Kidman shoot six days of naked sex scenes with a male model. Not only did he ask the pair to pose in over fifty erotic positions, he banned Cruise from the set and forbade Kidman to assuage her husband's tension by telling him what happened during the shoot."

It wasn't only the names at the top of the call sheet that suffered at the hands of Kubrick's calculated coldness.

Rade Serbedzija—the great Hollywood character actor, and a star in his native Croatia—appears in the movie's most explicitly comical scene, in which Dr. Harford convinces Serbedzija's disheveled character, Mr. Milich, to open up his costume shop in the middle of the night. For a character often criticized as a cipher, this is Harford at his most active—he *needs* to get to that sex party.

It's a small hurricane of a performance from Serbedzija. He swerves from peevishly lamenting his hair loss to suddenly imprisoning the Japanese men with whom his pubescent daughter, played by Leelee Sobieski, has been cavorting in the middle of the night—all while calmly executing his business transaction with Dr. Harford. Appropriately, it has a bitter coda: Mr. Milich willingly conspires in the pimping of his daughter.

"It was kind of torture, what [Kubrick] did to me," Serbedzija tells me over the phone from Brijuni Islands, a beautiful archipelago in the Adriatic Sea. "He wasn't satisfied with anything I brought. He said, 'It's very bad.'" Serbedzija laughs heartily as he explains how Kubrick, essentially, fucked with him. Over and over, Kubrick cut Serbedzija off, bluntly explaining how execrable he was just a few sentences into each take.

"I said, 'Well, tell me what I have to do.' He said, 'I don't know, you are the actor.' 'OK, what do we do now?' He said, 'Let's try it again.' And then I started again. And again he said—'It's awful.'

"And then I thought, 'My God. Which game is this guy playing with me?'"

Eventually Kubrick, sensing the actor was on to his tactics, ordered a break in shooting and called Serbedzija and Cruise into his office.

"He was very angry with me. And he put on my tape from the audition. And he was laughing. You know? Watching this tape, he was laughing. Tom was watching [for the] first time and he was laughing, too. And Stanley said, 'This guy is excellent! He's fantastic.' And he turned to me and he said, 'Can you try same as this guy?' And I said, 'My God. What's going on?'"

Mulling it over for the night, Serbedzija had his breakthrough. "I was thinking, He must know I'm a pretty good actor. Maybe he wanted to say to me, 'I don't want to see your acting.' He wanted me to be really mad. To be really crazy. And I started to play games with [the] whole world."

For his male star, Kubrick's trick was to strip it all away—the charm, the charisma, the Cruise-ness of it all. Early in the movie, in a wonderful weed-stoked marital spat, Kidman menacingly drawls an accusation at her handsome doctor husband: "You are very, very *sure* of yourself, aren't you?"

As the movie goes on, Cruise begins giving us a strange, frozen version of his famous grin. It's a death mask. By the end—after the events of the evening have unfolded—Cruise is a whimpering husk.

Cruise gave everything to Kubrick. He let him into his marriage. He lent him his movie-star charm and he let him smash it into a million pieces. Cruise believed in Kubrick so completely that for two years he was brave enough to do more takes than he could remember—to produce all that raw copy and to leave it all in Kubrick's hands.

As the director and actor Todd Field, who played the piano player Nick Nightingale, said of Cruise on set: "You've never seen [an actor] more completely subservient and prostrate themselves at the feet of a director."

The idea of the director as manipulator threads through Hollywood all the way back to the icon Hitchcock himself. You force your will onto your cattle.

But that's just a pure, blunt power game. It's the manipulative likes of Kechiche and Kubrick that are truly diabolical—true Rasputins. They have their agendas, and they manipulate to get their way. But Kechiche did it with young actors; like Scooter Braun before him, he had the upper hand by virtue of his relative age. Kubrick's feat is more impressive: He pulled his Rasputinism off with the biggest star in Hollywood.

And while Léa Seydoux and Adèle Exarchopoulos gave themselves up in the name of a greater cause, they then vowed to never do it again. For Cruise, was it also too much? Being Rasputin'd?

It was certainly rough. Before the shoot concluded, Cruise and Kidman sued the tabloid *Star* for reporting that on-set "sex therapists" had been hired. The film's eventual reception could be best described as befuddlement. And within two years of the movie's release, Cruise and Kidman were separated.

Did *Eyes Wide Shut* mess him up? Cruise has never said as much, never even suggested as much. Well into his fifties, he remains a huge box-office draw. But his choices would never be as bold again. He has never again touched anything as psychologically exposed or potentially damaging. And he never again approached a film with sexual themes.

"Some people told me, 'Well, Tom Cruise is good but, maybe somebody else [could] play this part,'" Serbedzija told me. "I really feel it's not true. He's so fantastic in this film because he's actually [doing] less acting. He was being this simple man. It was beautiful."

Of his own experience being Rasputin'd by Kubrick, Serbedzija told me, "Some madness I tried to bring, and everybody was afraid of me on set. Everybody except him. He was watching me, laughing from his eyes. So there is something that is more than acting. Some real madness, you know?"

Serbedzija stops. "That's it. He was really a magician."

CHAPTER SIX
The Pro Ball Rasputin

CONTROLLING A MOVIE STAR isn't too shabby. But then there *is* one role in American society that outranks the Hollywood A-lister. Only the quarterback potently and fully evokes the idealized Great American Male in the twenty-first century, with all of his exalted values: individualism, unflappability, pluck; an unimpeachable, inoffensive handsomeness; and, of course, the pure physical talent of those truly touched by God.

Tom Brady, of the New England Patriots, is the greatest quarterback of all time. That gives him a rarified kind of cachet. A cachet so rarified it might just convince you that you can cheat death.

Because Brady didn't just become the best. He managed, as he rolled into his late thirties and early forties, to stay the best. There is no precedent for this. Not just in football, which is so punishing it famously, regularly kills careers when they're young. Nowhere else in sports is there precedent for this. No one this old stays this good. It's inexplicable.

Well—inexplicable to anyone but Brady. To Brady, there's a very good explanation for it all. And it is: the singular methodology of his body coach and best friend in the world, Alex Guerrero.

THE DAY I meet Guerrero is blustery and cold. A proper, hard Massachusetts fall afternoon. It's the middle of the NFL season, and Guerrero is busy. That season, he was on the road with Brady for every Patriots game. That way he could most efficiently tend to Tom's needs and aches, along with the twenty other Pats roster members he was regularly healing. (All of which is just a part of his overall clientele, which includes athletes across the major sports.) This afternoon, I'm told, he would have some rare time to talk.

I'm directed to the TB12 Sports Therapy Center in Foxborough, directly across the street from the Patriots' Gillette Stadium and just a few storefronts over from a Toby Keith's I Love This Bar & Grill. Under the vaulted ceiling of the lobby, silver canisters of proprietary TB12 protein powder are elegantly stacked, proprietary TB12 knee braces are proudly displayed, and proprietary TB12 snacks (Sorry: "superfood energy squares") are waiting to be purchased. TB12 soccer scarves hang off a back wall, festooned with the TB12 catchphrase: "Sustaining Peak Performance." From a supersized cover of *The TB12 Method*, Brady's bestselling self-help coffee-table opus, the QB smiles out at us knowingly.

A tall glass wall separates the lobby from the actual training facility. It's blue and opaque. I wait in a cozy leather chair and listen to the sound of a medicine ball being slammed somewhere in the beyond and watch silhouettes move toward greatness.

Alex Guerrero has been working with Tom Brady since 2004. They opened this place together in 2013 as an "education platform." Now they're business partners. And this is the flagship of their potential empire. In *The TB12 Method*, Brady extols Guerrero's underlying ideology, which is all about "pliability"—basically, soft, flexible muscles. Make yourself as soft and flexible as possible, the ideology dictates, and you will rarely get hurt. As Brady says in the book, when he's hit, he's able to deflect damage because "my brain is thinking only *lengthen* and *soften* and *disperse*."

At the time I come to Foxborough, Guerrero and Brady are planning to open TB12 centers all over the country. Before that will come a certification program: They want folks all over the world to be able to teach the methodology themselves. And already here for the public is the TB12 app, available at time of launch for a simple subscription price of $199.99 a year. It is now a content-based business, they say, with one goal: Get the message to the masses.

As Brady writes in *The TB12 Method*, "we can decelerate the aging process as most people experience it today." The medical community may not totally agree. But the quarterback seems to be suggesting he's figured out how to push back death.

Close Brady watchers have known about the intimacy of his relationship with Guerrero for years. Guerrero helped shape basic tenets by which Brady religiously lives. (Bed by nine. No meal portions larger than the palm of a hand.) The two spend a whole lot of time together; Guerrero is the godfather to Brady's younger son. Guerrero used to be known as Brady's idiosyncratic trainer. Now, he's rightfully recognized as the fervent ideologue behind it all—the man behind one of history's greatest athletes.

As Guerrero has gotten more and more attention, so has his sordid past. Thanks to exhaustive reporting from *Boston* magazine's Chris Sweeney, we know that Guerrero has twice been shut down by the Federal Trade Commission for marketing sham nutritional products; has twice been sued for fraud for having bilked investors out of hundreds of thousands of dollars; and once allegedly swindled a former client, the boxer Genaro "Chicanito" Hernández, out of his life savings.

"He says he's a sports medicine doctor that works with cancer patients, and I don't know, he did me a tremendous disservice, and I believe he's still doing it to other people," Hernández said in an interview before his death from cancer in 2011. "This guy is out there taking advantage of innocent people, and he being part of my family and [to] do something like this and leave me broke is just shameless."

Guerrero was first busted by the FTC in 2005, when he'd been pushing a vitamin supplement via a late-night infomercial. The supplement was called Supreme Greens. And it was being marketed as a cure for cancer.

As *Boston* magazine reported, in the infomercial Guerrero looked into the camera, identified himself as a doctor, and told his audience that his father-in-law "had lost his right arm, scapula, clavicle, and three ribs before dying of skin cancer," and that Guerrero "vowed that nobody in my family would ever suffer from that disease again." The FTC found out the sham product had pulled in over $16 million. They forced Guerrero to pay back his share of the earnings (presumably concerned he wouldn't be able to make the payments, the FTC also gave Guerrero the option to turn over the title to his 2004 Cadillac Escalade). The FTC further ruled that if Guerrero had misrepresented his "financial condition," then an "avalanche clause" would kick in, meaning Guerrero and the company behind Supreme Greens would immediately owe $1.47 million.

They also barred him for life from ever referring to himself a "medical doctor, Doctor of Oriental Medicine, or Ph.D." In fact, it turned out, he had no official medical degree at all.

AFTER TEN OR so minutes, Guerrero appears and takes me beyond the tall blue wall. He's in blue running pants and a heather gray TB12 shirt that curves over a slight paunch. His hair is cropped short and neat with bits of gray speckled in the sides. There are light wrinkles around his kindly eyes, as well as a few light liver spots. He greets me with a slight, sly smile, which he holds often. He has the slight air of a marionette come to life. We sit in a massive glass-walled conference room, side by side, and he tells me how he built his empire.

Guerrero grew up in Southern California to Argentine expat parents. As a kid he played baseball and tennis and Pop Warner football, but he wasn't a natural athlete. "I didn't gain much size," he points out, with a bit of winning self-deprecation. He also wasn't always such a fanatic about the far reaches of human ability. "I would say probably when I was in school getting my master's degree in traditional Chinese medicine—*that's* when I really began to understand what a marvelous thing the body was." (According to *Boston* magazine, Guerrero's master's is from Samra University, "a school in California that no longer exists.")

While in school he was certified in massage therapy; he supported himself in part by churning out massages, $60 a pop. By his mid-twenties, he was working in physical therapy. "When I first started, my vision wasn't what it is today," he says. "I started originally in track and field, and it was all injury rehab. Then I was able to get them better and faster. They would go and get personal record times, and I realized, 'Oh my gosh, that is a really cool thing!'"

By the 1990s, Guerrero was working with pros. One of his most loyal clients was Willie McGinest, a former Patriots linebacker. In the mid-2000s, McGinest led Guerrero to Brady. And early in their professional dalliances, Guerrero proved his mettle.

It was the offseason, 2007. Brady had already won three Super Bowls with the Patriots by then, but the team's last season had ended in a disappointing AFC Championship loss. He was a few months shy of thirty, an age by which lots of players have washed out of the NFL altogether, and he was suffering serious groin pain. There would have been reason to believe that this was the beginning of an inevitable decline.

According to reporting from the *New York Times*, Brady was scheduled for surgery to cut a tendon that was pulling his adductor muscle. The Patriots told him the operation was necessary. Guerrero talked him out of it. Instead, he showed Brady a series of workouts to create the aforementioned, all-important pliability. Brady says his pain dissipated in days. By most accounts, he's been a true believer ever since.

At the heart of Guerrero's work with Brady has been what would commonly be understood as, well, massages. No half-hour sessions for the QB, though. These are deep, intensive affairs.

Guerrero is methodical, constant, and tireless in his approach. Brian Hoyer, Tom Brady's former backup, has recalled seeing Guerrero spend an entire day by the QB's side, through meetings and practice, steadily working one of Brady's injured fingers.

Brady and Guerrero believe the term "massage" vastly undersells the impact Guerrero is having. As Brady once told the *Times*, "It's like giving a chef flour and eggs and saying, 'OK, we'll make biscuits.' Well, sure, everyone is going to make them different." But Alex's biscuits, Brady explained, would be "perfect." They say Guerrero is "re-educating" muscles. They call it "body work."

I ask Guerrero if he teaches his proprietary "body work" techniques to his employees. Can he pass along the secret of his magical hands?

"That's a great question," Guerrero says. "Tom asks me that all the time. I can teach the theory, but I just don't know *how*"—he crumples his fingers in the air, demonstrating the elemental source of his power—"to teach *this*."

GUERRERO'S RELATIONSHIP WITH Brady is the source of much speculation. (The *Times* called him Brady's "spiritual guide.") I ask Guerrero to define it.

"Tom and I, we're, you know . . ." he trails off, smiling, then swoops back in. "He's my best friend! And we've been together for a long time. We never really disagree. We've never really had issues. We certainly hear all the stuff and read it, too, and we snicker and laugh at it. We always laugh and joke, 'Nobody knows us better than us.'"

As we spoke, the Patriots were halfway through their 2017 season. Once again, they were one of the powerhouses of the NFL. Once again, Brady was one of the league's best, most consistent players. "When we look at the program, we evaluate two or three years ahead of time," Guerrero says. "The Tom Brady that everybody sees today—we planned for that a couple of years ago. He's getting better with age. They call him, who's that"—Guerrero pauses, fumbling for the name—"Benjamin Button!

"You see these other quarterbacks going out," Guerrero says, ticking off the injuries that had piled up that past NFL season. "Aaron Rodgers, breaking a collarbone. Carson Palmer, breaking his forearm. Matthew Stafford, hamstring. Marcus Mariota, hamstring. Sam Bradford, with his knee. And then here's Tom Brady, who is forty and sustaining a lot of impact and he's playing every game."

There is a certain unblinking certainty to the way Guerrero speaks. He does not like to attribute any part of Brady's fortunate good health to pure luck. Effectively, Guerrero is suggesting that he can predict the future.

"I know how Tom feels every day," Guerrero assures me. "He says, 'I don't have any soreness. I'm ready to play again. Those are things that we thought would happen, and now we're seeing the reality of them happening. Do I think Tom can play to a high level at forty-five? Absolutely."

"OK. How about fifty?"

Guerrero laughs. "I mean, why not? I've never put limits on myself, and I've never put limits on any of my clients. I'm a big believer that everything is learned behavior. You tell an athlete, 'You're gonna be done when you're thirty,' well, the brain begins to believe that, and all your neuro-programming is based on, 'OK, I'm thirty, I'm old.' But I don't think the brain understands the concept of time. It doesn't understand *age*. Right? How would your brain know you're whatever *age* you are? I always tell Tom, we're not gonna tell our body what we wanna do. We're gonna tell our body what we want *it* to do."

Excitedly, Guerrero tells me about some of the clients he works with at the TB12 facility. A seventy-year-old woman who runs marathons. A seventy-year-old guy who plays in soccer leagues with folks half his age. An eighty-seven- and an eighty-five-year-old, a pair of best friends, who went out last summer and cycled the Tour de France route together! "We laugh. Age is a number to us. Everything is learned behavior. Wire your brain to understand that. To me, that's sustaining peak performance. That's *living*."

It is here where I cannot deny that I am being yanked forward by this line of thought. I've never been a good athlete. But I've loved playing basketball my whole life. I've also known that one day I would have to stop.

Or—if I follow Guerrero's logic—could I rewire my brain with the TB12 method? Could I be pulling up for threes when I'm ninety? Could I sustain peak performance? Could I, too, in my way, live forever?

AT ONE POINT in our chat, Guerrero tells me about the first time he helped an athlete recover from an ACL injury. The standard at the time, Guerrero says, was nine to twelve months of rehab. Guerrero says he got his client back in six. "They thought I was out of my mind. Everybody said, 'Oh, Alex, you're gonna hurt this athlete.' At first I was an absolute loon. Now guess what everybody's rehab time on ACLs is? Six months."

Guerrero is acutely aware of skepticism toward the TB12 model. First, it's the grandness of the promise that raises hackles. Then, it's the vagueness of its underpinnings. ("There's biomechanics and Feldenkrais massage technique and reiki and craniosacral therapy," Guerrero tells me at one point. "I couldn't say there's any *one* thing that really inspired me.")

As much than anything, though, it's the money that seems to bother people. Because nearly all of the stated innovative TB12 methods come paired with high-priced TB12 products. The box of superfood snacks is $50. The protein's $54 a can. A medicine ball goes for $90. A weight vest is $140. A vibrating sphere will run you $150.

"The whole damn thing feels like a con," the ESPN personality Bomani Jones once railed on his radio show. "Imagine somebody walk up in your crib talking about 'That's my homeboy, he say he got the cure for cancer [and] I'm out here exercising my brain to where I know that when I get hit I tell my muscles what to do, and you, for the very very low price of $250, can get started.'"

"You know, Tom and I always say, 'If you're explaining, you're losing,'" Guerrero tells me, by way of explanation. "So we don't! I wait for people to come around. Most of the people that have said a lot of funny things about us are now coming in and are clients! And now they're like, 'Oh my gosh, I just didn't understand.' You know, in the book Tom says, 'I drink a lot of water, therefore I don't get sunburned.'"

Guerrero's not bringing it up to deny it—the "avoiding sunburn by drinking water" technique really is in the book. There were many other quirky details. ("Try not to drink too much water during a meal, as it can interfere with digestion," Brady counsels. "Wait an hour or so after you're done eating before you drink water." The book also heavily recommends staying away from "nightshades"—that includes potatoes, tomatoes, tomatillos, strawberries, eggplants, and okra—altogether.) But the water-sunburn quote became one of the most widely shared passages from *The TB12 Method*.

"And then people use that to say the TB12 method isn't based in science," adds Guerrero. "Well, it's all science!"

If Guerrero were just another trainer with quirky ideas on wellness, there wouldn't be anything particularly notable about him. But with Brady's influence at his disposal, he's now uniquely positioned to spread those ideas far and wide, and to make a lot of money doing it. And this from a man once busted for pushing phony cancer cures.

I bring up the criticism and the serious charges illuminated in *Boston* magazine's reporting on Supreme Greens. "How do you respond to those allegations?" The calmness in his voice never wavers. The smile, in the trained manner of late-era Tom Cruise, never cracks.

"I don't. I don't respond to it," he tells me. "They never talk to me. The research into the things they write about it is erroneous. They never source anybody! It's always, 'Sources say. Sources are talking.' Say whatever you want. I don't have to agree with what you say.'"

Boston's reporting was not based on anonymous sources, but on FTC filings. Furthermore, they reached out to Guerrero himself, and had conversations with his lawyer.

In a statement, *Boston* would later tell me, "To the extent Mr. Guerrero may be referring to *Boston* magazine's coverage, he is incorrect. The magazine has contacted him and his representatives multiple times for comment before publishing, and he has never responded to our inquiries. Nor have we become aware of any inaccuracy in our reporting about him. All of our pieces are thoroughly fact-checked before publication, and we are confident that our coverage of Mr. Guerrero has been both accurate and fair."

I ask Guerrero, "Do you feel like you've made mistakes?"

"There's a lot of things that I would do differently. But the mistakes that people talk about me making are not the mistakes that I've made. One day I'll tell my story. When I feel compelled to, I'll tell my side."

"You don't want to tell me?" I asked. "Now?"

"Nah. I don't feel like I need to give up my power. And if I come out and express my story then they're just gonna ask more questions. And then I'm just giving up my power."

The day after *Boston* magazine first reported on Guerrero and Supreme Greens, Brady went on the Boston sports radio station WEEI. In a wide-ranging interview, the QB vociferously defended his friend.

He soft-pedaled at first. "Everything in life is more than meets the eye," Brady told WEEI, addressing the Supreme Greens scandal specifically. "A lot of people were involved in that business. Alex has said that he wishes he had done things differently."

But when it came to Guerrero's actual ideology, he went full bore: "When you say, 'Wow, this sounds like quackery,' there's a lot of things that I see on a daily basis in Western medicine that I think, 'Wow, why would they ever do that? That is crazy. That doesn't work' . . . you guys may think I'm full of crap, but I'm the proof, what you see on the field." He added, "I'm the best advertisement I could ever have."

It went without saying that he was the best advertisement Guerrero could ever have, too. It was a remarkable bit of radio. A live performance of rare, unceasing loyalty.

A few months after my sit-down with Guerrero, news would break out of Foxborough: The Brady-Guerrero axis was threatening the Patriots dynasty. First, the *Boston Globe* reported that Patriots coach Bill Belichick had revoked Guerrero's access to the Patriots plane and to the sidelines during games. According to the *Globe*, tension between Guerrero and the Patriots' medical staff had existed for some time. As Guerrero had pulled more and more of the Patriots roster into the idiosyncratic TB12 Method, that tension had ratcheted up. But when he fielded internal complaints about Guerrero, Belichick would say, in so many words, *Tom wants him. What am I supposed to do?*

After the *Globe*'s report, ESPN followed up with an even lengthier piece by Seth Wickersham digging into the drama. Wickersham heard from a friend of Brady's that "Tom changed . . . that's where a lot of these problems started." He heard from team staffers that the strictness of the TB12 Method was beginning to feel "like a cult." The underlying schism was this: Belichick and the team on the one side; Brady, Guerrero, and the TB12 method on the other. As the ESPN article put it, Patriots players had to ask themselves, "Do we risk alienating the NFL's most powerful coach or risk alienating the NFL's most powerful quarterback?"

Parallels to Guerrero are hard to come by. A few years back there was the case of José "Pepe" Imaz, a former Spanish tennis pro turned coach/personal motivational speaker for the Serbian great Novak Djokovic. Imaz started touring with Djokovic on the ATP Tour in 2016, right around when Djokovic's dominance in the game began slipping. Some observers suggested it was Imaz's style—a famously hippie-dippie love-all approach—that was causing the once ultra-aggressive Djokovic to soften.

In one promotional video, Djokovic explains Imaz's approach: "We are all looking for love, happiness, and harmony. We need to be able to look inwards and to establish this connection with a divine light." As *The Guardian* wrote of post-Pepe Djokovic, "if he wins, [he] cups his hands from his heart towards the crowd, seeking a public embrace he plainly hopes is mutual. To some, it is an unalloyed gesture of love by a caring and sensitive man; to others, it is an embarrassing affectation." In 2018, Djokovic rehired his old coach, Marián Vajda, and let go of Imaz. Said Vajda at the time, without naming names, "You must focus on where to hit the ball, not think about Buddha."

There's also Carlon Colker, a preposterously jacked medical professional who's worked with everyone from Shaq to Justin Bieber. Like Guerrero, Colker has unorthodox methods—he's super into squatting—and a history of legal problems. One lawsuit accused Colker of altering clinical studies to produce more favorable results for his employer, Xenadrine-EFX, which manufactured the widely banned substance ephedra. He was also once involved in a far dumber scandal: When the actor Jeremy Piven quit a 2008 Broadway play because of what he claimed were doctor's orders after sushi-induced mercury-poisoning, it was Colker who was then

NO ONE MAN SHOULD HAVE ALL THAT POWER

acting as his personal physician. In his latest reinvention, Colker is the personal trainer to the New York Knicks' Latvian wonderboy Kristaps Porziņģis. By all accounts, the young star is in thrall to the good doctor.

For the most part, when imagining a powerful behind-the-scenes operator in sports, you wouldn't think of the likes of Pepe or Colker or Guerrero. In fact, your mind would generally wander to a head coach like Belichick. He's part of a lineage of domineering coaches who have sustained success for so long that their presence goes far beyond the actual mandate of their jobs. They are believed to be able to magick victory out of thin air.

But even a coach like Belichick is ultimately beholden to the limits of the game. His sales pitch is powerful, to be sure. He promises championships, and the sports immortality that comes with them. Guerrero, though, doesn't have to dabble in the minutiae of X's and O's, of wins and losses. He hints at immortality, writ large.

After the ESPN report, Guerrero was moved to release a rare public statement. It was a blank piece of fluff. "I get that many of my beliefs are not mainstream, and I know they may differ from others," he wrote. "I wish nothing but the best for everyone, and for each of us to be able to live our lives to our utmost potential." Guerrero surely knew it didn't much matter what he said. As long as he still had his most important client in his corner, he was gold.

And on cue, Brady was back on WEEI to offer his backing. When asked about the *Globe* and ESPN's reports, the QB said, "I don't have any comment on that, other than to say Alex has been a huge part of what I do, and I'm so fortunate to have him not only as a friend, but with everything we've been able to do together . . . It takes a lot of people for an NFL player to achieve. Your career and teammates and coaches and family and support and friends, and Alex has been a huge, huge reason why I'm still playing."

Back in the TB12 Center, I ask Guerrero how he managed to get such strong of support out of Brady. "I've never once asked him to do anything like that for me," Guerrero says. "He sees how unjust it is. He knows my story. He made the decision for himself. Tom knows the truth. Right? The truth is what it is. Tom knows the truth."

In August of 2015, a chunk of Brady's emails were released as part of discovery in an unrelated lawsuit between the NFL and the NFL Players Association. Digging through the emails, Deadspin reporter Timothy Burke found a long correspondence between the quarterback and Francesco Aquilini, the co-owner of the Vancouver Canucks. Aquilini had requested that Brady come speak to the Canucks. Brady agreed, with one stipulation.

"I have been very fortunate to learn the right information from the best person in the world whom I work with," he emailed. "His name is Alex. He is my body coach and the person who I am blessed to have learned from. I would like to bring him also so he can answer some technical questions if the guys have any. He hasn't been wrong 1 time in the 11 years we have worked together."

How did Brady come to have this kind of belief in Guerrero? How did Guerrero come to have this kind of pull over Brady?

The most optimistic answer is that, despite a lack of stated remorse, Guerrero has reformed himself since his Supreme Green days. That he is not just cynically pushing new sham products, and this time with the might of Brady behind him. That Guerrero really is an innovator, and that Brady is right to believe in him in total.

The more pessimistic answer is this is all happening because of some form of superstition. That Brady saw himself playing with excellence later and later into his career, and that he needed a reason to believe it wasn't just happening because he was genetically blessed. That it wasn't just happening because he'd flukily dodged that one crushing blindside hit that can end careers. That it wasn't just happening because he was plain old lucky. It was because he had Guerrero. In this reading of the situation, Brady is holding on to Guerrero like Dumbo and that feather.

The answer, as usual, is more complicated than either extreme. Selling sham cancer cures is just about as despicable a thing a person can do. Telling people they'll avoid sunburns if they drink enough water does sound like pure quackery.

And by the way: Even though the book is based entirely on his systems, Guerrero isn't listed as a co-author on *The TB12 Method*. It's quite possible Guerrero purposefully left his name off the book, just in case some of the more unfounded tenets of *The TB12 Method* would once again get him in trouble with the federal government. The FTC wouldn't comment on a theoretical violation of Guerrero's 2005 order. But that order does state that he's banned for life from "misrepresenting that any dietary supplement can prevent, treat, or cure any disease" or "from making false or unsubstantiated health benefit, performance, efficacy, or safety claims."

Guerrero has managed to make Brady, with his bare hands, feel good. Once, long ago, in St. Petersburg, Rasputin healed young Alexei, too. We know the placebo effect is real; we know amelioration can come just from a doctor's visit. We don't quite know how Rasputin healed the little heir to the Russian throne. It didn't really matter, though. His touch was medicinal. And that granted him an incredible influence. The magic of the healing hands seems unbelievable, as in "impossible to believe." They seemed unbelievable in Rasputin's time, too. But those who felt them swore by their power.

And it's not just Brady who swears by Guerrero's touch. There are all the other NFL guys, from McGinest to Brady's current and former teammates Julian Edelman, Rob Gronkowski, and Danny Amendola. (That they have not managed to uniformly avoid injury, à la Brady, has apparently not made them any less faithful.) Two separate reporters have written pieces about coming to Guerrero with serious physical ailments and then watching in awe as he made those ailments vanish. For the most part, when Guerrero is written about, the serious allegations of fraud and FTC violations are mentioned in an aside, if at all. The conversation is now squarely about the validity of his methods.

Yet *Boston* magazine's Chris Sweeney has steadily, singularly sounded bells of alarm. After he broke the story of Guerrero's shady past, he added details. In one follow-up, he reported on the fact that TB12 had been under investigation from a Massachusetts state agency for operating without proper licensing. But even as Sweeney passed along that critical information, he included a testimonial from a woman named Amy Finsilver.

After surviving a serious car accident, Finsilver was suffering constant, debilitating headaches. Nothing the doctors at Boston's highly respected Brigham & Women's Hospital were doing helped. Then, someone recommended TB12.

"Guerrero got to work," Sweeney writes, "vigorously manipulating the muscles around Finsilver's jaw, head, neck, and face. It was unlike anything she had ever felt—he worked his strong fingers into the nooks and crannies under her jaw. It was an intense sensory experience, and not particularly enjoyable. 'It was very painful,' she says.'" But that began her revitalization. "Since that first visit to TB12," Sweeney writes, "her recovery has been nothing short of remarkable. Seven months after the accident, the daily headaches have vanished."

I know what I'm thinking: I'm thinking, I can't believe people buy this shit. But I also know that they do, indeed, buy this shit. Despite the swindles, despite the fake cancer cures—they really buy this shit. Before our time is up, I ask Guerrero: How do you gain someone's intimate trust? How do you engender such passionate belief?

"When you start to work on someone, on their physical body, there's a very strong connection that happens," he tells me. The patient "has to trust that we know what we're doing. We make commitments and then we begin to make breakthroughs. It's line upon line. Precept upon precept. And then you can't unknow this."

Suddenly, the patient "is going to bed without any pain for the first time in years, and he's waking up without pain for the first time in years. Those things are very real to him. He's not gonna forget that."

What is Guerrero, really? A kooky trainer? A cynical con artist riding a thoroughbred? A life-extension evangelist? His base of power is the quarterback; as long as the QB stays healthy, Guerrero's manifesto stays healthy. Guerrero, by outward appearances, has Brady hooked good and deep. And Guerrero worked hard to do it. Looking back, the singular image of the relationship that comes to mind is Guerrero at Brady's side, all day long, massaging that one injured finger.

What is he, really? There is not much indication that he is anything but a very, very good masseur. *Has an empire ever been built on a more humdrum skill*, we wonder. But we've never felt Guerrero's hands. By most accounts, once he has his hands on you—once he makes the headaches go away, once he heals that finger, once he gives you a few more years on the field—you are his.

Shouty critics, nosy media, all of the voices chipping away—at that point, they are helpless. The patient has been hooked. They are under control. "You can't unknow what you know," Guerrero says of the men and the women who have paid him a lot of money for his services, and will continue to pay him a lot of money—through the TB12 book and the TB12 certification program and the TB12 app and the TB12 powders and the TB12 method. "No one is gonna be able to convince them that this isn't helping."

CHAPTER SEVEN
The Cartel Rasputin

WITH ALEX GUERRERO, I felt like I was skirting the edges of illegality. But I wanted to push further. What does Rasputinism look like in the actual underworld? To find out, I go to a quiet suburban pocket in El Paraiso, a neighborhood on the north side of Tijuana, hard by the US–Mexico border.

Adela Navarro Bello has been the director of *Zeta*, an independent paper renowned here for its committed coverage of narcotrafficking, for more than a decade. In 1997, her predecessor and mentor, J. Jesús Blancornelas, was attacked by gunmen from the Arellano Félix cartel while in his car with his bodyguard, Luis Valero Elizalde. Blancornelas was one of the first journalists to report on the cartel's existence. The vehicle was shot 180 times. Elizalde was killed. Blancornelas was hit four times, but survived. He'd pass away in 2006, handing the reins to Bello.

The two men with whom Blancornelas founded *Zeta*, in 1980, have both been murdered. Héctor Félix Miranda—aka Felix the Cat, as his byline read—was killed in 1988, by shotgun. Sixteen years later, Francisco Ortiz Franco was killed while in his car with his two children. On the bright day I visit the lovely, quaint offices of *Zeta*, two Chevy pickup trucks marked POLICIA ESTATAL are parked out front. A loose pack of cops in body armor and strapped-on ARs spill out of the trucks, laughing and chattering and drinking takeout cups of hot coffee in the strong sun.

Across the street there are neat rows of houses representing a hodgepodge of architecture that pings between decades, from standard fifties ranch houses to strange Miami-esque eighties lairs.

Some of the shrubbery is shaped into meticulous giant teardrops; some of it grows wild and free. A car alarm goes off somewhere in the cozy neighborhood, but the cops don't mind. Their walkie-talkies squawk constantly, but they don't seem to mind that either. I hang around nearby until one of the officers notices me.

He asks in Spanish, then English, "What are you doing here?"

"I'm a reporter," I say quickly, waving my notebook around for proof. "A reporter!"

He nods and politely escorts me inside, where a front-desk secretary shows me where to trash my gum, then warns me with a big, foreboding smile, "Don't worry, I'm not gonna get your DNA!"

I sit in a dark-wood waiting room, taking in *Zeta* HQ. It's effectively a wide two-floor home that's been converted into offices with an excellent air of homey professionalism. There are big potted plants everywhere, and black leather couches, and every bit of wall and shelving is filled with some bit of memorabilia or another, from international journalism awards to Blancornelas's well-preserved typewriter underneath a photo of the man looking stoic but happy. Old framed *Zeta* covers blare things like "La Mafia Invade Baja California" and "Mujeres Contra El Crimen" and "Mas Narcos."

Bello, an elegant, unbothered woman in her late forties, comes to greet me. She's in low-heeled loafers and a perfectly cut, sharp, dark-blue suit. She has gold rings on her fingers and an air of calm focus.

"Are the police always here?" I ask.

"Just for the last two months," she says. "We received a threat." She continues in a mix of English and Spanish, searching for the right words. "Someone from the Arellano Félix cartel ordered a member to—put some bombs? Make an explosion? In the building?"

The Arellano Félix cartel, also known as the Tijuana cartel, is a longtime player in the region. Operational since the early nineties, it was once the dominant force in the region. The lore of the Arellano Félix brothers would inspire the characters of the Obregon brothers in the movie *Traffic*. They were beyond brutal. As the *Atlantic* has reported, "The cartel employed a crew of 'basebal-listas' who would hang victims from rafters, like piñatas, and beat them to death with bats. *Pozole*, the Spanish word for a traditional Mexican stew, was the [cartel's] euphemism for a method of hiding high-profile victims: Stuff them headfirst into a barrel of hot lye or acid and stir for 24 hours until only their teeth were left, then pour them down the drain." Relatively, these days, they're a smaller force. As such, they're currently allied with another cartel, Jalisco Nueva Generación, against the Sinaloa cartel, the criminal organi-zation led for years by the world's most famous drug lord, Joaquín "El Chapo" Guzmán. Since its founding, the Arellano Félix cartel has always been led by a member of the family. Over the 2000s, the cartel weathered a string of leadership disruptions—one brother after another was arrested or assassinated. The oldest brother, Fran-cisco Rafael Arellano Félix, was actually shot in the head at his own sixty-third birthday party.

The party was held at an opulent hall in Los Cabos and was well attended by both family and famous Mexican footballers. The assassin broke through all the security with audacious chicanery: He was disguised as a children's party performer.

Zeta acquired and released cell phone footage of the killing. It's a jumpy clip, a bit disorienting. But you can clearly see a man dressed as a clown walk past the frame. Then the camera dips. Then screams erupt. "It was the Sinaloa cartel" who sent him, Bello says, characteristically matter-of-fact. "The clown entered, the gunshots were fired, and the clown fled."

Throughout the nineties, the brothers Benjamin and Ramón were the head of the cartel. In 2002, Benjamin was arrested by the Mexican Army. In the same year, Ramón was killed in a shoot-out with police in Mazatlán, in the state of Sinaloa. Their brother Francisco Javier—aka "El Tigrillo," or "Little Tiger"—took over. That lasted until 2006, when El Tigrillo was captured by the US Coast Guard in flip flops and plaid shorts. He was out chasing marlin on his yacht, *Dock Holliday*; when the boat drifted into international waters, the American authorities swooped in.

That string of killings and arrests put one woman much closer to the spotlight than she'd prefer. Her name is Enedina Arellano Félix. She's Benjamin, Ramón, Francisco, and Francisco Rafael's sister. Some of the more colorful reports calls her something else: "Narcomami."

For many years her job in the cartel was perceived as something akin to mob consigliere. But that belied her actual outsized role in the operation. As her brothers played the part of cinematically flashy drug lords, she was an unseen force—an invisible decider. Enedina was understood as the financial brains, as well as a kind of spokesperson. "She has a great presence for negotiations with the government and police," Bello explains. "She has always had power. Always."

Verónica Calderón, a reporter who has written about Enedina for *El País*, told me, "She is quite a rare example. The narco society, the personalities—they are so in your face. 'We're, like, the toughest guys.' And she's—an administrator! The people I interviewed about her, and the many people in Tijuana who have investigated her, they all say: She runs [the cartel] like it's an organization of real estate."

As Calderón has reported, teenage Enedina aspired to be the queen of the local Mazatlán carnival, a simple, wholesome honor for a young woman. Later, she'd study to be an accountant. "I found it a little bit heartbreaking," Calderón says. "She was a regular girl. I'm not saying, 'Oh, poor woman, she's innocent.' But because of her family, she took this up." There was, Calderón is suggesting, a certain lack of agency in Enedina's life. She was always surrounded by the world of drug trafficking.

Reporters for *Zeta* began covering Enedina in the nineties, once they became aware that the business she ran, Farmacias Vida, was a cartel money-laundering front. They'd later uncover that the Arellano Félix brothers were also laundering money by purchasing houses and plots of land throughout Mexico, from Jalisco to Baja, California. Many of those entities would be registered in Enedina Arellano's name.

According to Bello, there's a tradition in Mexico of drug traffickers' wives colluding with their husbands but avoiding repercussions. Bank accounts and shell companies might be registered in a wife's name; money-collecting duties might fall to them while their partners are incarcerated. And yet, no heat. "The most important thing about Mexicans and their idiosyncratic nature—the way Mexicans think—is that they believe women should be protected," Bello says. "The authorities will never touch the wife."

Enedina purposefully plays into Mexico's unwillingness to prosecute female narcos. "She keeps a low profile," Bello says. "She isn't a very notorious woman. She does not have a warrant out for her. She is not being investigated. She is free because Mexicans believe that women have nothing to do with narcos. She protects herself from the authorities in that sense."

Throughout her dealings, Enedina prefers quiet and stability. Bello tells me about a previous threat of violence to *Zeta*, from 2010. As with most of the information about threats that *Zeta* is privy to, this one came via contacts with the US government (which in turn collects information via undercover agents or wiretaps. In the past, the cartel would reference *Zeta* so frequently that they had a specific code word, X-24, for the newspaper's offices, where we're sitting now). The threat, it turned out, was a false alarm. A representative from the Tijuana cartel actually came to the paper's office to tell them as much.

"He said he came on [Enedina's] behalf, to tell us that there is no problem," Bello recalls. "That *Zeta* would not suffer or receive a consequence." Enedina wanted *Zeta* to know that, at least at that time, there would be no danger to the newspaper. If it could be avoided, there was no need for drama.

WHEN I ASK Bello if she's seen the same model of shadowy control as Enedina's and the Tijuana cartel elsewhere in the world of narcotrafficking, she answers quickly. "Yes, absolutely," she says. "The Sinaloa cartel and El Mayo Zambada."

It's a surprising answer—anyone that's heard of the Sinaloa cartel would tell you it's El Chapo who's in charge. But for serious narco watchers, El Mayo—born Ismael Zambada García in the tiny village of El Alamo in 1948—has long been an object of fascination.

A US law enforcement official once told the L.A. *Times* that he considers El Chapo to be "the muscle" of the Sinaloa cartel and El Mayo to be everything else: "The brain. The logistics. Security. Everything." That list of duties includes, if necessary, physical force. Said the official, "Like Chapo, he will exert violence. Not in a whole-sale manner. He's a little more surgical. Because he knows it's bad for business."

While the media has largely been obsessed with Chapo and his outlandish prison escapes, the US government had long considered both men highly coveted. Before Chapo was incarcerated, the rewards on their capture were an identical $5 million.

Like Enedina, Zambada has carefully calculated his low profile, with one major exception. In 2010, Zambada sought out Julio Scherer García, the veteran reporter and founder of the magazine *Proceso*, for an interview. The meetup was arranged with tireless precaution: interminable drives, switched cars, long waits in safe houses. Eventually Scherer did meet Zambada face to face. They sat and and talked while enjoying, recalled the *Proceso* reporter, an arrangement of "milk, meat, beans, tostadas, cheese," and "sweetened coffee." (A few years later, El Chapo would famously try a similar maneuver with the Hollywood actor Sean Penn, then acting as a reporter for the magazine *Rolling Stone*.)

In the interview, Zambada didn't say much by way of confiding. He did claim that on four separate occasions he'd managed to escape forces of the Mexican government by disappearing into the landscape of Sinaloa, with which he's so intimately familiar. And he said that if he was ever to be captured, "I don't know if I have the guts, [but] I want to think that, yes, I would kill myself."

Michael S. Vigil is a former DEA agent who worked undercover in Mexico for years, often within the Sinaloa cartel. He told me that El Mayo is "probably the only remaining old drug trafficking capo that exists in Mexico."

Vigil clucks at the irresponsible partying of certain "narcos juniors." He recalls the 2016 kidnapping of El Chapo's son Iván Archivaldo Guzmán, who was nabbed while carousing in a high-end Puerto Vallarta restaurant named La Leche. The kidnappers were members of Sinaloa's rival, Jalisco Nueva Generación.

The ex-DEA man brings all this up to contrast with the unfailing restraint of El Mayo. "He is astute enough," Vigil says, "to never come down from the mountains."

Vigil himself has been up in the Sierra Madre range, inside of El Chapo and El Mayo's native Sinaloa. "It is desolate, rugged, isolated," he says. "And these guys play Robin Hood. They give the poor villagers money, they build schools, they provide medical treatment. If people see anyone they don't know, the narcos know within five minutes. And they can escape into the wooded areas and ravines."

El Mayo, Vigil says now, is in poor health, suffering from diabetes and high blood pressure. But he won't come down from the mountains for anything, not even medical care. "He knows that as long as he stays up there, he will be safe."

Maintaining this cloak of invisibility has netted Zambada untold rewards. As *Newsweek* has pointed out, "Zambada was listed as a defendant in a U.S. case as long ago as 1978, when Colombia's Pablo Escobar was just starting his trafficking career. Unlike Escobar, who was shot dead in 1993, Zambada has never been arrested and is still selling cocaine."

El Mayo's own son, Vicente Zambada Niebla, has not been as lucky: after an arrest in 2009, an extradition to Chicago, and a prolonged legal battle, the narcos junior copped a plea deal. As the *New Yorker* reported at the time, Zambada Jr. "confesses that he was a senior figure in the Sinaloa cartel and a 'surrogate and logistical coordinator' for his father. He admits to having smuggled 'multiple tons' of cocaine, using 'private aircraft, container ships, go-fast boats, fishing vessels, buses, rail cars, tractor-trailers, automobiles [and] submarines.'"

In the course of pleading guilty, Zambada Jr. revealed how preposterously lucrative the drug business has been for his family. "According to the plea agreement . . . the younger Zambada must surrender assets amounting to $1.37 billion—and Zambada did not contest the number."

Back in the *Zeta* office, Bello explained further.

"El Chapo was the executor of operations for the transportation of drugs. El Mayo was more of a moral leader that would say, 'Do this, do that, do this.' The low profile gives them the most impunity. It ensures them a greater capacity of life. When they lead a more active life, putting a face and a name to the cartel, one becomes easier to pursue. When they are moral leaders, they remain untouched. They aren't assassinating anyone. They are only giving orders. They tell people how things should be done—that's the most efficient way."

This is a strange and particular kind of Rasputinism. Traditionally, as we've observed, the Rasputin gains notoriety for being in the shadows. The more unknown something is, the more the public is denied access, the more entrancing it can be. But in the drug trade, a Rasputin isn't served well by notoriety. They still want power, money, control. But they also want anonymity.

Narcomami and El Mayo know what they're doing. They're avoiding the heat by pulling the strings from behind the scenes. They don't party, they don't kill (if they can avoid it). They let their frontmen do that. El Mayo has seen El Chapo carouse his way into international fame and, most recently, a cell in a max-security federal prison in lower Manhattan. Narcomami has seen her brothers terrorize Tijuana with their flashy ways. And then she's seen them end up dead or in jail—one of them killed by a clown at his own goddamn birthday party.

So the cartel Rasputins lurk behind, allowing the world to know as little of them as possible. They act the part of consiglieri, right-hand people, behind-the-scenes operators. But in the cartel, and for the careful cartel watchers, the truth is known. These Rasputins are kingpins, too.

BELLO WAS IN HER early twenties when she realized she wanted to cover narcotrafficking. At the time, she had planned on becoming a lawyer. She thought she wanted to defend people who were deprived. But this was the Benjamin and Ramón era of the Tijuana cartel, and the brothers were unavoidable. Stories of them carousing through Tijuana's bars and clubs—in leather jackets and luxury cars—were rampant, as were stories of them killing in public. "That consumed our society," Bello says.

Instead of law, she went into journalism. And she knew right away where to go: Blancornelas, and *Zeta*. She quickly understood the great responsibility she'd taken on. "As a journalist, you can't subtract yourself from the problems of a society," she says now. "You have an obligation to report on what is happening. If narcotrafficking is what is happening, then you must write about that."

In the room where we talk sits Blancornelas's old typewriter, carefully preserved. As we talk, the climate that enabled his shooting, and the killings of *Zeta*'s cofounders, continues unabated. Just before we meet, news of the killing of the reporter Javier Valdez Cárdenas breaks. "That was a massive blow to journalism in Mexico," Bello says. "We know it was the Sinaloa cartel. But who ordered the crime, and why are they not receiving judgment?"

Upstairs in the office, next to a sunny courtyard, *Zeta*'s small editorial staff has a lazy Friday afternoon meeting, broken up regularly with rolling laughter. Bello walks me toward the conference room, stopping for a second to give an errant soccer ball a good kick. We poke our heads into the room full of reporters, and they turn to look at us and smile and then they go on back to business. A small "Deportes" department—a few tubby dudes in backward baseball caps—hang out nearby, shooting the shit. Out front of the office, a phrase is punched into black steel—Libre Como El Viento. *Free Like The Wind.*

I ask the inevitable question: Aren't you people fucking scared?

"I don't know," she says. "Blancornelas, he taught me. We're a very small newspaper. I have a direct relationship with all the people working. I write, I investigate. I do. I invite them to do the same. Like he did with me." She stops, then picks up again. "My work is very passionate. I love it very much. And regrettably, we are accustomed to surviving in a hostile environment."

Bello also has to deal with something Blancornelas never did: unfounded doubts. "They said, 'She'll run it into the ground,'" she recalls with a smile, of the days she first took over *Zeta*. "But that was eleven years ago."

In a strange way, as a pioneering woman in narcotrafficking reporting, Bello has something in common with her subject, Enedina. "Back during the rise of narcotrafficking," Bello recalls, "women were used as drug mules that would transport drugs in their bodies. That's how they were most used. But as the years pass, in terms of business and politics, women have fought for the positions they want. The same goes for organized crime. There are [still] very few women who are given leadership positions in the world of drug trafficking. But there are women narcotraffickers."

Here, most notably, that means Enedina.

She hasn't inspired a wave of female narcos, at least not yet. But within the family, at least, her influence is being felt. A new generation of Arellano Félix men—the narco juniors—are now rising in the cartel. According to *Zeta*'s reporting, the sons of Ramón and Benjamin are operationally active and effectively steering the ship. But they avoid the flashy styles of their fathers in favor of the low-profiles of their aunt. There are no cars, no photos, no incidents, Bello says. Nothing about them is known.

And what about Enedina? I wonder. Has her success behind the scenes in the cartel afforded her any kind of personality cult here in Tijuana? Does she have fans, like El Chapo?

"No one knows where she is, no one knows what she looks like," Bello says. "No fans. She's regarded as a legend. She has become a myth."

CHAPTER EIGHT
The Radical Rasputins

AFTER MEXICO, I thought more about Rasputinism on the fringes of society. Kubrick, Lish: they used the tenets of Rasputinism to create art. Alex Guerrero: he used it to peddle hope and make money. Narcomami: she used it to move kilos of cocaine (and make money). There was a natural progression. The transgressions were getting more palpable, more practical. Where else did Rasputinism exist? How else did it do damage?

All over Europe, from Antwerp to Berlin, clusters have formed around Rasputinesque clerics. The *Sentinel*, West Point's counterterrorism publication, calls them "charismatic preachers." In Brussels, there was one such man named Khalid Zerkani.

Zerkani is serving a fifteen-year sentence in Belgium's Prison d'Ittre. Before his 2014 arrest, he operated out of the Molenbeek neighborhood of Brussels. In the 2015 Paris attacks, 130 people were killed in coordinated actions throughout the city. In the 2016 Brussels attacks, thirty-two people were killed. Several of the men behind both attacks, including strategist Abdelhamid Abaaoud and bomb-maker Najim Laachraoui, were from Molenbeek. In fact, according to Belgian authorities, they were former charges of Zerkani's.

"He established himself, firstly, mainly as a gangster," the journalist Hind Fraihi, who's written a book about Molenbeek, *Undercover In Little Morocco*, says on the phone from her Brussels home. "He had this kind of a gang. Young people who were mobilized to rob people, in the streets, in the metros."

He was a little chubby and known for doling out gifts. So, Fraihi says, "they called him Papa Noël. Santa Claus. The gang was called 'the Gang of Papa Noël.' They were engaged to do small criminal acts and they would see that as a good cause for jihad. So you had a combination of Islam"—his own manipulated, self-serving interpertation of Islam—"and, in some way, *Oliver Twist.*

"He didn't really have a theological or a scholarship background," Fraihi says of Zerkani, "so recruitment went in a very selective way. Just repeat some [Koran] verses—the particular ones that are about jihad." In his recruits' eyes he had credibility, which stemmed from his own criminal experiences; he knew enough to say the right things. "A little bit of Islam—just a one-sided view of Islam," Fraihi notes. "Whatever you did, even if it was robbery, it was for a good cause of jihad. These young people really believed it. They really believed they were doing it for a good cause."

Another of the "charismatic preachers" is Abu Walaa, also known as "the preacher without a face." Originally from Iraq, Walaa settled in Germany as a teenager in the early 2000s. Within a decade he was a starlet in the world of jihadist social media; he could rely on the support and attention of over 25,000 Facebook fans. In his videos he would promote war but also provide innocuous observations about married life. "Often times a trifling matter escalates into a big dispute," he astutely pointed out in one installment. He earned his nickname from filming his content, always, with his back to the camera.

When he was arrested in October of 2016, Abu Walaa was accused of sending at least twelve men to ISIS battlefields in Syria and Iraq. Prosecutors alleged that two of his recruits killed over 150 Iraqi soldiers in suicide attacks. His recruitment network provided lessons in Arabic and extremist ideology. They took recruits on long hikes with packs on—conditioning for the coming wars.

Like Zerkani's operation, the network raised money through burglaries. Walaa termed it *ghanima*: plunder from the infidels. There were other small-time rackets. Before men left for Syria, they'd be made to sign contracts for phones and tablets. The contracts would go unpaid; the devices would be resold. Walaa also owned at least one legitimate moneymaking operation, a clothing store named Dejavu Jeans and More.

In December of 2016, two months after Walaa was arrested, the Tunisian national Anis Amri killed twelve people by driving a stolen truck through a Christmas market in Berlin. Amri was a recruit of the Abu Walaa network. According to an informant to German authorities, two of Walaa's main subordinates were in touch with Amri. In their lectures they would speak about Germany as *darul harb*—a "land of war"—and encourage domestic attacks. When Amri himself expressed interest in such an operation, the informant said, they enthusiastically supported him.

HOW DOES THE recruitment of attackers work? "It's a little bit like market dynamics," Daniel Koehler, the founder of the German Institute on Radicalization, tells me on the phone from a conference in Norway. "You have someone seeking solutions and someone offering a product."

Those seeking solutions might be teenagers with a vague understanding of geopolitics. "I have met people who were assigned, as a school project, a presentation on the Syrian civil war," Koehler says of extremists he's interviewed, "and they start digging in and they see massive injustice and what they understand as the hypocrisy of the West."

That kind of process can begin what Koehler calls the "contrast society." A potential recruit is now in an "area of interaction," where radical groups seek out recruits with familiar imagery, mostly online. Recruiters might use "Hollywood movie posters" or "the GTA computer game" and "Photoshop it as jihadi propaganda. They actively incorporate pop culture elements in order to be more attractive" to young people.

Koehler describes to me a theoretical group of teenagers, still tethered to their Western societies but increasingly open to extremist language. "They might hang out and play basketball and in the meantime, when they would chill out, they would watch ISIS [videos] or follow tweets from their favorite ISIS fighters."

In this way, recruiters who are "actually doing the headhunting" find willing recruits already primed by propaganda. The final connection can happen in, say, a mosque with extremist leanings. But that's not a uniform situation. Khalid "Papa Noël" Zerkani met his recruits on the streets of Molenbeek. Abu Walaa ran pop-up seminars in towns throughout central Germany.

Despite largely targeting immigrant communities from the Middle East, most of the "charismatic preachers" are known to preach in German, not Turkish or Arabic. That's because they are specifically not targeting immigrants. They're targeting the *children* of immigrants, for whom German is the primary language.

According to Johannes Saal, a jihadism expert at the US Naval Postgraduate School, "They know their followers are young Muslims who grew up with two identities, two cultures." The preachers themselves "often come from this background. They have a good feeling for these people, for their personal problems."

Their messaging is blunt, effectively so, and delivered to a willing audience. Explains Saal, "They introduce them to this jihadi ideology which is black and white. They give simple answers to complex social problems." Next, "they address some kind of altruism. They say, 'Look what's happening in Syria—your Muslim brothers and sisters are suffering. You need to do something.'"

Many of the recruiters are in their early thirties. That's old enough to come off as impressively experienced, but young enough to establish genuine one-on-one connections with the teenagers or twentysomethings that are their targets. Like Zerkani, their knowledge of real Islam can often be severely lacking. But relative to their recruits—themselves often just becoming familiar with the Koran for the first time—they know enough to present as scholars.

Saal recalls an interview with an ex-ISIS member who was describing the process of his radicalization—how forceful the preacher that introduced him to extremist ideology was, how impossible it was to counter the point of view. "The foreign fighter said, 'This guy was just talking, and I couldn't say anything about it,'" Saal recalls. "The way he was presenting his arguments—he was so charismatic, I didn't even have a chance to bring forward a thought.'"

Saal notes that recruiters often attempt to establish a familial connection. They're not so much father figures as they are surrogate big brothers. In fact, one common tactic is to recruit family members together, and thus accelerate bonding. In 2017, a cell in Spain carried out attacks that killed thirteen people in Barcelona. The cell included three pairs of brothers and was linked by a Moroccan man named Abdelbaki Essati. According to the *New York Times*, Essati "sometimes wore jeans" like a "hipster," "was unfailingly courteous," and actively "targeted groups of brothers, perhaps because family ties make it harder for individuals to leave the group, even if they want to go to the police."

I'D READ A strange story about a man named Denis Cuspert. He was a German national, born in Berlin in 1975. But he'd first gained fame as the rapper Deso Dogg. By the time of his death, in early 2018, he was an ISIS propagandist stationed in Syria. I wanted to understand how this man had been pulled to this ignominious end.

As an MC, Cuspert was an obvious product of nineties American hip-hop. With heavy chains, coiled rage, and a lean, muscular frame often paraded shirtless in his music videos, he was clearly pinching a bit of Tupac (he named one album *Alle Augen Auf Mich,* a German translation of Pac's *All Eyez on Me*) and a bit of Mobb Deep.

In 2012, he left hip-hop behind. He moved from Berlin to the central-west German city of Solingen and helped create an organization dedicated to jihadist propaganda named Millatu Ibrahim, or Community of Abraham. In mosque sermons and media appearances, he spoke grandly of the plight of the Palestinians, the drone attacks in Pakistan, and the sins of American imperialism. He presented himself as a reformed infidel ("Deso" even was short for "devil's son") who'd embraced the light.

Though he left rap, Cuspert never abandoned music. He began instead singing songs in praise of the international jihad—what jihadists refer to as *nasheeds.* Traditionally, *nasheeds* are songs of uplift, largely a cappella, about Islam, its practices, and its history. But Cuspert's were songs about fighters-in-arms, about explosions, about mass murder. In one, a German-language adaptation of a jihadist anthem called "Qariban Qariba," Cuspert declared, "Enemies of Allah, we want your blood / It tastes so wonderful."

By the end of 2012 he'd left Germany and made his way to Syria, where he worked with the militia Junud al-Sham. Within two years, he'd moved up to the big leagues: he was now an ISIS propagandist. He became known as Abu Talha al-Almani—Abu Talha the German. He was on the front lines, cheating death, singing songs of war. In propaganda videos, he was seen marching past the bloodied and at times decapitated victims of his fellow fighters; his job was to praise the massacring, and he took to it with fervor.

"It comes as no surprise that even Abu Talha being rushed to the hospital after the air attack was captured on camera," noted the Middle East Media Research Institute in a report after an incident in the summer of 2013, in which he was nearly killed by shelling. "Few jihadi alive today are as photographed or video-recorded as Cuspert."

Isabelle Kalbitzer, a spokesperson for Berlin's Verfassungs-schutz, a state-level intelligence service, told me, "He was something like a pop star of jihad."

Cuspert's *bay'ah*—his oath to ISIS—was recorded and disseminated in early 2014. "My goal was to get famous with music," he says in the hour-long video, brandishing an AK-47 for effect. "And when there would have been a big musical event, like the Grammys, I would have stood at the stage, I would have said: 'There is no god but Allah! I hereby cancel my music career!'"

As he talks, footage from his old music videos is spliced in. There he is, young Deso Dogg, never smiling, throwing punches and headbutts toward the camera lens in cinematic black and white.

As Cuspert rails against his old world, we see photos of various vices seemingly plucked from a lazy Google Images search: music festival revelers; a close-up of pills and powders; a man pouring a beer at what might be an Applebee's. It's so clumsy as to be surreal. Then, Cuspert consummates his *bay'ah*. He sits on his knees in front of a green sheet, in camouflage.

"My dream has been fulfilled," he says. "Victory, or martyrdom. I will continue my work until a bullet or rocket shall hit me!" And as he's wrapping up, at this purportedly hallowed moment, you can clearly hear the distinctive whistle-chirp noise of an incoming message. Someone in the room has forgotten to mute their Samsung Galaxy.

After joining ISIS, Cuspert became a wandering mascot. Over and over, in propaganda footage from battlefields throughout Syria—wherever atrocities occurred—there was the man now called Abu Talha al-Almani. "He was like *Where's Waldo*," says Alberto Fernandez, a former counterterrorism specialist with the State Department. "He was popping up all over the place."

In 2007, before he began appearing at war zones, a Berlin-based rap journalist named Daniel Schieferdecker had interviewed

Cuspert. He described a confused man, one caught between hip-hop and his fledgling faith: "He said that he may have to leave the music business to get calmer, and that he tries to follow the lead of musicians like Cat Stevens, who make music the Islamic way. He said that this might be his way, too."

The man who pulled Cuspert in this direction was named Mohamed Mahmoud. They met in Solingen in 2012. He was an Egyptian by way of Austria. "He was a good friend of Cuspert's" at first, Saal explains. He "really had an influence on him. He radicalized him not just to Salafism, but to violence."

Cuspert's relationship to Mahmoud was atypical in that the two were roughly the same age. Generally, terror recruiters are a bit older than their recruits. But then, Cuspert was also older than the traditional recruit. And Mahmoud was a bit of a wunderkind.

He'd worked on behalf of Al Qaeda before establishing his ISIS connections; by his twenties, he was already an experienced propagandist. From 2007 to 2011, after being convicted on charges of "promoting a terrorist organization," he served a prison sentence in Austria. Of his propaganda work for Al Qaeda, he once said in an interview, "We were like a media organization; we just wanted to give people the opportunity to hear the words of the mujahideen."

Mahmoud was "not really a sophisticated preacher," Saal says. "Not super charismatic. Other German jihadis, they mock him a bit for not having sufficient knowledge."

Still, a series of lectures that Mahmoud gave in German was widely distributed and, according to Saal, "really made an influence on ISIS fanboys." Part of the simple appeal lies in the language. The vast majority of ISIS propaganda is in Arabic. To the German-speaking "fanboys," that stuff was useless. Mahmoud's native facility with German made him their guy.

Mahmoud would go on to marry a woman named Ahlam Al-Nasr. Together, they formed what the *New Yorker* called a "jihadi power couple." Al-Nasr is a poet. Her debut collection, *The Blaze of Truth*, compiled more than a hundred of her pieces: "elegies to muja-hideen, laments for prisoners, victory odes, and short poems that were originally tweets," explained the *New Yorker*. She was known as "The Poetess of the Islamic State."

Cuspert had found himself among professionals. They, in turn, knew how to utilize Cuspert—how to play off his former public image as Deso Dogg. By the end of 2012, Cuspert was pinging around Salafist mosques in Germany for seminars, providing emotional tellings of the story of his conversion. Still fumbling toward knowledge of Salafism, he came off as a peer to young audiences who were still learning themselves. He was a hit.

I GO TO Berlin to visit the home of MC Bogy, who was close to Denis Cuspert in the mid-2000s. I find a cramped studio apartment filled to the edges with dusty tchotchkes of Americana: a framed Big Pun triptych; likenesses of Ice-T; a string of still-in-the-packaging Tony Montana dolls complementing the Tony-Montana-holding-a-microphone tattoo that graces Bogy's soft white belly.

He's wearing cargo sweatpants and a camouflage durag. He has a Mike Tyson–like Maori face tattoo. And he is unfailingly polite, providing me with coffee, juice, and a plate of fresh watermelon. For the next few hours, he speaks with great passion in halting English of his good friend Deso Dogg. He calls their union "like Steven Spielberg meeting Stephen King"—two titans, coming together. "We made much music together," he says. "I'm very proud of that."

Cuspert wasn't, Bogy insists, an angry person. Once, during a recording session, a critter scurried through the studio and Cuspert jumped to its defense. "He said, 'It's an African mouse.' I don't know why he decided it was African mouse. He said, 'Stop, stop, don't kill the mouse. He's from Africa, like me!'" Cuspert got his way, and gently guided the mouse into the alley.

Bogy shows me one of Deso Dogg's old lyric sheets, with words written in a big sloping font across lined paper. It's signed Abu Maleeq. Maleeq is Cuspert's son's name—Cuspert was naming himself, in traditional Arab conventions, "Father of Maleeq."

"I slept with him in the same rooms," Bogy says. "We wore the same clothing. We went to other cities together—I went to the dope spot, smoked weed, took cocaine, fucked bitches. Look, I was addicted to drugs, and he always wanted to take me away from drugs. He helped me when I was sick, he always stood with me when I was drunk. I'm not seeing it with pink glasses on. He was always there for me."

Bogy converted to Islam as an adult and says he would at times pray with Cuspert. But he waves his and Cuspert's shared faith off as too intimate to discuss. "You love your dick, I love my dick," he says, grabbing his crotch while pointing to mine as emphasis for the analogy. "But that's private! That's yours and that's mine!"

To explain what happened to his old friend, he reaches instead to the comfort of American culture. "Maybe in Germany people would kill me for what I say, yes? But for me, it's a story like Anakin and Darth Vader." In *Star Wars*, Anakin Skywalker is a fallen hero: touched by the dark side of the Force, he becomes the treacherous villain Darth Vader.

IN 2009, A document titled "A Course in the Art of Recruiting" began to make the rounds online. It was originally distributed through Al Qaeda networks; later it would be embraced and adapted by ISIS propagandists as well. It is a guidebook for recruiters.

"To souls of the martyrs of the jihadi groups throughout history," reads the manual's dedication. "To the internet Mujahideen and the media Jihadi knights: we have created a graded practical program for recruiting."

The document is highly specific. It provides exact instructions on how to behave with your recruit: "Don't criticize the candidate's behavior"; "thank him for any help, even if it just a little"; "occupy as much of his time as you can"; "make a schedule for him to listen to at least one lecture daily." It even lists specific, particularly effective lectures to push on the candidate, including "The Condition of the Drowning People" and "I Saw Prophet Muhammad Crying."

It warns not to broach the topic of jihad too early "so as to not make the relationship appear as your recruiting him; he will say to himself, 'You are doing all of this with me, just to recruit me, etc.'" Another reason to hold off until the time is right: "Maybe this candidate loves the mujahideen but the media has distorted their image."

Categories of potential recruits are defined and evaluated:

- "The non-religious Muslims": The most preferred, according to the document, because "you will be the one to guide him to the right path."
- "Generally religious people": Good, except for anyone who fits these descriptions: "the loner," "the stingy person," "the excessively talkative person."
- "University Students": So-so, says the document: "The university is like a place of isolation . . . and is full of youths. However . . . it is also full of spies."

After your targets are identified, you move on to a stage that sounds, intentionally or otherwise, like the establishment of a budding romance. The manual instructs you to send "a religious sms message" to your target or to "invite him to lunch or breakfast, this, I swear by Allah, makes you become close to him." Afterward, you are to fill out a chart, scoring yourself on questions like, "Does he love to spend a lot of time with you?"

If you score less than ten, "start from the beginning." If you score over nineteen, carry on to the stage of deep bonding.

This one is estimated to take two months of intensive work, and is the time to really bore down. (At one point the manual asks a question directly of the recruiter: "Have you reduced the amount of unbeneficial time you spend on the internet?") Activities here go beyond breakfast; the manual suggests going on "a picnic to a nice place" or walking through a graveyard and "describ[ing] Paradise and Hell and Judgement Day."

Here, finally, you may casually, carefully bring up jihad.

By the final stage, "The Establishment of the Brigade," the candidate must be hammered into shape. The manual instructs the recruiter to close the deal with great force: "Bite down on it with your molar teeth," it demands.

"In Conclusion," the manual reads, "I ask our Lord to use us and not replace us; ask that He makes us a sword positioned to strike over the necks of His enemies. I ask Allah not to make us die until Islam is mighty." Set the recruit free to attack; he is now ready for war.

ABDUL KAMOUSS IS an imam who specializes in preaching to German-speaking Muslims like Denis Cuspert. Before Cuspert left Berlin, the two met at al-Nour Mosque. Their conversations, Kamouss recalls to me in a coffee shop in Berlin, felt aimless: Cuspert was clearly more interested in politics than religion.

Quickly, Cuspert grew frustrated with Kamouss and stopped coming around. "He started to drift, to look for something political," Kamouss says, adding with a self-deprecating smile, "not me. I am a *soft* Muslim." Kamouss is Cuspert's failed Rasputin. If things had gone differently, if Cuspert had been otherwise inclined, perhaps Kamouss would have succeeded in steering him away from his path.

Later, watching Cuspert's reinvention online as a prominent speaker and singer, Kamouss was horrified. "He was trying to be an image of himself, a persona," Kamouss says. "He felt entitled. He had a sense of being important. With his charisma and his background as a creative person, it seduced the uninformed younger generation. They would not even realize that he is not trained, that he is teaching about things that are too complex for him to even touch."

Cuspert was an ex-con who'd lost years to prison. He was estranged from his children and their mothers. His rap career, and the image with which he'd chosen to define himself, had stalled out. Then he met Mohamed Mahmoud, his final Rasputin. And suddenly, in his mid-thirties he found himself, for the first time in his life, influential. From the outside, the rise appears to have been swift and intoxicating.

In a way, Kamouss sees Cuspert's path as inevitable. He talks of Cuspert's "psychological problems," of Cuspert's thirst for a "new life." And yet, in imagining one last conversation, Kamouss lifts clenched fists as if to shake him by the collar. "I would speak to him pointed, directed, so that he would get it," he says. "I would sit with him and not let go."

WHAT COMES NEXT? Already, there are signs that the modes of recruitment that have been charted in this chapter are a thing of the past. Manipulators like Khalid Zerkani, Abu Walaa, and Mohamed Mahmoud may be less and less prominent. They were the Rasputins. They spread the message. Now, though, the message spreads not just through "charismatic preachers," but through all forms of media.

As I write this, New York City is a few weeks past a terror attack that killed eight people. On October 31, 2017, a twenty-nine-year-old man who'd immigrated to the United States from Uzbekistan rented a Home Depot truck in New Jersey, drove it over the George Washington Bridge and down the West Side Highway, then barreled it over a bike path in lower Manhattan. Analysts would later note his actions hewed closely to instructions laid out in an article from the November 2016 edition of *Rumiyah*, an ISIS publication.

The article, titled "Just Terror Tactics," specifically directs an attacker to use a load-bearing truck with a slightly-raised chassis. It reads, "Observing previous vehicle attacks, it has been shown that smaller vehicles are incapable of granting the level of carnage that is sought. Similarly, off-roaders, SUVs, and four-wheel drive vehicles lack the necessary attributes required for causing a blood bath . . . smaller vehicles lack the weight and wheel span required for crushing many victims."

The inset photo is a stock image of a U-Haul truck, one promoting tourism to Pennsylvania across its breadth. The caption of the photo says "An affordable weapon."

"An appropriate way should be determined for announcing one's allegiance . . . so that the motive of the attack is acknowledged," the article continues. "An example of such would be simply writing on dozens of sheets of paper 'The Islamic State will remain!' or 'I am a soldier of the Islamic State!' prior, and launching them from the vehicle's window during the execution of the attack." Papers found on the site of the lower Manhattan attack read "The Islamic State will endure."

Daniel Koehler, of the German Institute on Radicalization, says he's convinced that the most efficient approaches are still built on a combination of offline and online recruitment. But Rasputins can wield their power entirely in the latter way, too. In the same conversation, Koehler mentions one telling example: "I've seen a case where a sixteen-year-old boy in Germany was radicalized by a jihadi preacher in the UK all via Facebook chat."

Hind Fraihi, who studied Molenbeek, says, "You don't see recruitment anymore in the streets. It's all social media and the Internet. People just don't need a network, don't need a background, don't need safe houses, don't need expertise in dealing with weapons or moving money underground. Without any authority, without any network, with just some little notions about jihadism, you just do it yourself. You just take a knife and get a truck and just do it yourself."

DENIS CUSPERT WAS first reported dead in October of 2015. He'd been near death once before—in the summer of 2013, the Syrian Air Force shelled his location, leaving him with a serious head injury and temporarily in a coma. But this time the Pentagon was sure: While traveling in a pick-up truck on a road out of Raqqa, they reported, Cuspert was hit in a US airstrike and killed. "Cuspert was a foreign terrorist fighter who used social media to take advantage of disaffected youth," Elissa Smith, a Defense Department spokesperson, said at the time.

When new propaganda footage featuring Cuspert was released posthumously, the logical working assumption was that the footage was filmed before his death. Then, in the summer of 2016, working from undisclosed intelligence, the Pentagon changed its mind. In a new statement, they referred back to their 2015 announcement: "At the time, our assessment was the strike was successful. It now appears that assessment was incorrect and Denis Cuspert survived the airstrike."

In January of 2018, once again, Cuspert was declared dead. This time the source was Wafa Media Foundation, a pro-ISIS entity. They reported he'd been killed in fighting in Deir ez-Zor province in eastern Syria. They provided photos of his body. It seemed, this time, it had finally happened. Denis Cuspert had been killed.

After multiple false reports of his death, Cuspert arrived at what now can't help but feel like his inevitable end point. But there is no grand fate here; it wasn't destiny that put him on this path. He was put on this path by his Rasputin, a man from Austria named Mohamed Mahmoud.

CHAPTER NINE
The Shakespearean Rasputin

WE HAVE SEEN BY NOW that the relationships between the Rasputins and their subjects are extreme in their intimacy. On the surface, these bonds can be defined by common terms. Technically, they're friendships. Mentorships. Working unions. In practice, however, those phrases feel insufficient. Silly. Because in *practice*, these bonds are something far more intense. Denis Cuspert was led to his ruin by his Rasputin. Can it get more intense? More intimate? Well—there is intimacy, and then there is love.

I'd like now to discuss a specific iteration of Rasputinism. I'm calling it the Lady Macbeth Situation. It's a simple formulation: Whenever one's Rasputin is also one's romantic partner, you're looking at a possible Lady Macbeth Situation.

Before we go any further, let's revisit the source material. Based loosely on real events recounted in the 1577 history *Holinshed's Chronicles,* Shakespeare's *Macbeth* follows the titular Scottish general through a brief ascent and then an utter and complete undoing. The tragedy begins with Macbeth having recently acquitted himself well in battle. Then, in an odd forest, he runs into the Weird Sisters. They're witches, and they promise him life is about to get even better. They tell him he is destined to become the King of Scotland.

Macbeth is intrigued. He shares word with Lady Macbeth. And then everything goes haywire. Hearing the Weird Sisters' prophecy, Lady Macbeth doesn't sit idly by—she immediately plots to make it real. Soon enough, Macbeth and Lady Macbeth have murdered King Duncan, framed the king's own servants for the death— and then murdered them, too, as part of the cover-up.

Before the tragedy is all over, Lady Macbeth ends up guilt-racked and insane. "Here's the smell of the blood still," she says to herself, in a midnight reverie. "All the perfumes of Arabia will not sweeten this little hand." But before she crumbles? She's a force of nature.

Macbeth wavers and wobbles in his convictions. Lady Macbeth won't hear of it. First, she browbeats Macbeth into committing the regicide. After he slays Duncan, he immediately comes back to her—stumbling, fumbling, confused. She realizes that in his horror over what he's just done to the poor, innocent (former) king, he hasn't completed the frame-up. So she takes the dagger and heads back into the crime scene, and drips the blood on the servants and plants the weapon herself.

Several times in the play, Shakespeare toys with the cliché of female fragility. "Come, you spirits / That tend on mortal thoughts, unsex me here," Lady Macbeth says early in the plotting. "And fill me, from the crown to the toe top-full / Of direst cruelty! Make thick my blood." When the homicide is first discovered, Macbeth's rival Macduff tries to keep the bad news from the missus. "O gentle lady, / 'Tis not for you to hear what can I speak," he tells her. "The repetition, in a woman's ear, / Would murder as it fell." But the audience knows how preposterous this all is. Because we know that Lady Macbeth is a stone cold psychopath.

Technically, the Weird Sisters' prophecy sets the plot into motion. But for a play full of talk of destiny, it's remarkable how little happens until Lady Macbeth *makes* it happen. As the Shakespeare scholar C. H. Herford once wrote of *Macbeth*, "He is not fate ridden, nor irresponsible, nor the helpless sport of irresistible powers. He is no symbol of the destiny of man." What he is is a man beholden to his wifely Rasputin.

It's a perfect literary example of a familiar condition. From Eva Perón to Hillary Clinton, the tradition of the dominant first lady is proud and long. And all over the world, first ladies have followed their husbands into office. (In Argentina, Cristina Fernández de Kirchner directly succeeded her husband Nestor and ruled for eight years, until 2015.) But you don't have to *officially* take power to wield it.

IN 2016, A tragic Lady Macbeth Situation rose to the surface in Nicaragua. The president of Nicaragua is Daniel Ortega, a formerly beloved leader of the Sandinista guerrilla revolution. His vice president, Rosario Murillo, is also his wife and the mother of six of his eight children. And according to the former Sandinista guerilla Monica Baltodano, the position of VP didn't grant her power. It just officially gave her "the kind of institutional power that she already had de-facto."

Ortega first gained fame as a 1970s revolutionary. Nicaragua had at that point been ruled by the corrupt familial dynasty of Anastasio Somoza García since the 1930s. The Sandinistas were an armed communist insurrection; they captured not only Nicaragua, but the world's attention. As a leader of the Sandinistas, Ortega was both pragmatic—he believed in strategic alliances with all Somoza opposition, no matter their political bent—and bold. In 1967, he stormed a Bank of America in Managua with a machine gun. He wanted to help fund the revolution; he was duly arrested and imprisoned for seven years. In 1978, he helped orchestrate a violent takeover of the Nicaragua National Palace during a parliamentary session. Almost a thousand people, including national legislators and then-president Anastasio Somozoa DeBayle's nephew José, were taken hostage. A full-on armed civil uprising rolled on.

Rosario Murillo was by Ortega's side through all of his adventuring since the '70s. She was a true believer. A fierce ideologue. They met through the underground Sandinista network then active in Costa Rica. They lived together for a while in a safe house full of fellow guerillas operating under false names. She wrote revolutionary poetry. "Let me tell you that in Nicaragua we learned how to load and unload a rifle," one poem went, "how to put it together, how to take it apart, through songs."

In 1979, unbelievably, the Sandinistas managed to defeat Somoza and to take power themselves. Throughout the '80s, Ortega ruled the country, first as part of a coalition body and later as president himself.

In 1990, he lost his first election and lost power. For the next decade-and-change, he kept on losing elections. Then, in 2006, Ortega made a remarkable political comeback. Nicaraguan political observers said it was Murillo who helped Ortega finesse his way back into the presidency.

Once Ortega was back in office, Murillo quickly became a self-styled champion of the people. Part of the power she accumulated can be traced to her appearances on official government broadcast channels. These were fiery daily speeches, laced with revolutionary mantras and poetic flourishes and references to Catholic saints. Murillo would also announce populist government programs on these broadcasts: affordable housing, microloans, discounted school lunches, free pigs. It was always unclear if Murillo was the one actually coordinating the execution of these programs. But it was also irrelevant. Simply being the one announcing them was enough.

Ortega was reelected in 2011 and 2016. It was before that latter campaign that Murillo established herself as his vice-presidential candidate. Opponents were horrified at the blatant nepotism and consolidation of familiar power. But Murillo sold it, craftily enough, as a boon to feminism. As she said at the time, "This has opened the doors to the full participation of women in all spheres: political, social, and economic."

By 2016, an opposition politician named María Fernanda Flores was saying of Murillo, "I think she is more powerful than

[Ortega]. She's the only one who talks. You almost never hear Daniel. You forget what his voice is like."

IN 1998, ROSARIO Murillo's daughter, Zoilamérica Ortega Murillo, made a startling announcement. She revealed publicly that Daniel Ortega, her stepfather, had abused her for nearly twenty years. The abuse allegedly began in 1978, when she was eleven and the Sandinistas were still a populist rebel force. The sexual abuse ended when she got married to Alejandro Bendana, the Sandinistas' former envoy to the UN, but the verbal abuse continued for years. Bendana told the press at the time of Zoilamérica's accusation, "In the mornings I would get a call [from Ortega] asking me to do this and that, a special mission for the party. That same telephone would ring at night, and he would intimidate my wife with indecent sexual propositions."

At that point, Ortega had been out of power for eight years. After Zoilamérica's statements, contemporaneous news reports predicted his political death.

But then a sad, strange thing happened: Rosario Murillo denied her daughter's accusations. She called her a liar. She closed ranks around her husband. As Zoilamérica would say later, "I speak to her only to receive threats. She opted for an alliance of power."

Zoilamérica now lives in self-imposed exile in San José, Costa Rica. It's the same city where she spent her teen years. Then, she was with her family and their fellow Sandinista rebels, on the run from the ruling Somoza party. Now, she's once again choosing to live free of Nicaragua's leadership. When I spoke with her on the phone, I found her to be warm and quite funny. Later, through a translator, she told me about her life and about her mother.

Rosario Murillo was fifteen when she gave birth to Zoilamérica, her first child. They lived then in Managua, Nicaragua's capital city. As a young mother, Rosario Murillo relied on her family for help; Zoilamérica lovingly recalls her grandparents and her aunts and great aunts all raising her. Her mother "was this specific kind of rebel against her parents and society," Zoilamérica says. "She lived a bohemian life—an artist's life. Full of alcohol and parties all during the hippie movement." Effectively, Rosario Murillo was a part-time mother. Zoilamérica adds, "I was also formed by the revolution."

Zoilamérica was ten when Rosario Murillo moved the family to San José. She remembers reading her mother's poetry as a teenager. They were powerful stanzas full of hope. "Her poetry during the revolution was most beautiful," she says. "Very free and spontaneous."

"When did she change?" I ask. "And why?"

"She always had a strong impulsivity," Zoilamérica answers. "A strong presence. She always felt the need to have control over others. [But] she couldn't secure a high position during the years of the revolution. And that feeling of not having power fed her necessity *to* have it. Securing control was key to her life's mission." She adds that in 2006, when Ortega took back the presidency, Rosario Murillo "returned as if with a vengeance against everyone who had not given her the place she thought she deserved. She was converted into a woman with unlimited power."

Zoilamérica's relationship with Murillo was always contentious. Still, when Zoilamérica went public with her accusations against Ortega—at thirty years old, with children of her own—she had reason to believe that her mother would stand by her. Instead, the relationship fell apart forever. And cruelly enough, it was right then and there that Rosario Murillo began her ascent.

"One must remember that through her support of my outcasting, that became the greatest blackmail that she could ever have," Zoilamérica says. "Before I was shut out, she had not succeeded in securing that much power. Daniel [Ortega], according to his [own] words—he was going to be believed or convicted. The loyalty she showed with my denunciation—she guaranteed to him that she is the person who will defend him [no matter what]. With my exile, he realized that he needs her. And he realized that she always gets what she wants. "

In Zoilamérica's view, it was that betrayal that granted Murillo the greatest political capital of her life. In the years since, Zoilamérica has watched her mother work diligently to remove detractors and surround herself with loyalists. "She manipulates through empathy," Zoilamérica explains. "And truthfully, this has been evolving and reaching new levels of cruelty. She identifies people's weak spots and exploits that to form her attack. She exploits people through the fractures of their lives and their vices, such as alcohol. She will publicize stories, not with the only objective to express her own disdain, but to destroy the person and their dignity."

Of Murillo's famed public communiqués, Zoilamérica says, "It seems to me that it hasn't been her speeches that has allowed her to gain the influence she has, but rather, the way she uses symbols. It's an unoriginal form of rhetoric, but the politics combined with religion and New Age [spirituality]"—when all that came together, "at that moment, her message became astounding. Her power is through appealing to emotions."

Of Murillo's relationship with Ortega now, Zoilamérica says, "It's a relationship that acts as an alliance. It tells a story of love and affection apart from the myths that they themselves constructed. She wanted to feel as if she was the heroine of the people. Her objective was to show that she will be the salvation."

"Are they equals?"

"Before my denunciation, they were not equals. But since, she constructed her own power parallel to his."

"And now?"

"She has more power than him. He no longer makes decisions. If she's feeling kind, she will ask for his opinion or will inform him of her decisions. Maybe even discuss the decisions. But nothing more."

IN THE SPRING of 2018, student protests began to roil Nicaragua—tragic, bloody things. Protestors were met by Nicaraguan Army units armed with AK-47s. Scores of people died in the streets. A journalist, Ángel Gahona, was shot and killed while broadcasting live on Facebook. The spark was the Ortega government's attempt to pass an austerity measure reducing social security benefits. But as protesters told the media again and again, this resentment and this rage had been bubbling under for years.

Ortega's government is famously corrupt. According to a US diplomatic cable released by Wikileaks in 2010, "Ortega [has] regularly received money to finance electoral campaigns from international drug traffickers, usually in return for ordering Sandinista judges to allow traffickers caught by the police and military to go free." (In the eighties, that also included kickbacks from Colombia's Pablo Escobar.) In his second go-round as president, Ortega's government was becoming not just corrupt but largely undemocratic, too. He'd eliminated term limits and curtailed the power of the Supreme Court. Placing his own wife as his vice president was just another grand symbol of his illiberalism.

Many of the protestors were from the Polytechnic and Central American Universities. Once, long ago, similar student protests had helped launch the Sandinista revolution against the Somoza government. In the end, Ortega the revolutionary had become a power-hungry tyrant. The protesters took to chanting, *"¡Daniel! ¡Somoza! ¡Son la misma cosa!"* "Daniel! Somoza! They're the same thing!"

And all the while, Murillo convinced Ortega to brook no impudence—to never, ever waver. In one of her public broadcasts after the demonstrations broke out, speaking of the protestors, Murillo said, "Those tiny, petty, mediocre beings, those beings full of hate, still have the nerve to invent dead." (She was claiming that the protestors had purposefully inflated the number of casualties.) "For those crimes, we demand punishment."

When asked if she believes her mother and Ortega will survive the protests, Zoilamérica responds, "To survive implies being immune to death. I don't want to focus on what will happen with them. I prefer to tell you the story that Nicaragua will rise. But I need to tell you something. To be talking about Rosario Murillo today, that is very symbolic to me. Because I am feeling the ending of her power. It's coming."

"Can you imagine one day returning to Nicaragua?"

"Yes," she says. "These days, a lot more." It will be difficult, she explains. She'd have to rebuild a life from scratch. She means emotionally as well as practically—she'd need to find a source of income, a new home, a new car. "But I do imagine working on an educational project of some kind," she says. "Trying to help prevent this kind of free transfer of power from one person to another, and forgetting our own power within."

"What is the first thing you would do once you returned?"

"The first thing I would do would be to recover places in my memories. What I need to do is plant flowers. In other words, I need to be able to go to many places without fear. And second, I want to visit people that died during the time I was not there. People I wasn't able to say good-bye to."

The last time Zoilamérica and Rosario Murillo had a full conversation came soon after Zoilamérica's allegations against Ortega. "She proclaimed me guilty," Zoilamérica says. "She started telling me that I was responsible for affecting the lives of my children. She manipulated my maternal side to generate guilt. She tried to have me submit myself to her once more."

Zoilamérica did not budge, did not break. She's never wavered from her account of Ortega's abuse. And in the years after, she began to understand her new reality. "One abandons the fantasy that one day their mother will support them," she says. "To understand that she wasn't going to accept me anymore as a daughter—it was a process that was very complex, very painful. And after that I had to also accept that she is capable of anything."

"There was no returning to what it was like before. I accept that the person I am speaking to you about today is not the person that once I would have considered to be my mother. Today she has become someone else."

ROSARIO MURILLO HAS been ruthless in her pursuit of power. She not only denied the abuse of her own daughter—she exploited the denial. She was in the safe houses; she was there when they were building the revolution. If Ortega survives the protests, Murillo may well succeed him as president. So why did she always play a secondary role?

It's because of one hard and inescapable reality: For women in a patriarchy, the only path to power might just come through the husband. Technically, this is Rasputin Rule #7—"They must lack the abilities themselves." But in the Lady Macbeth Situation, the Rasputins don't necessarily lack the abilities—they're just not allowed to flex them. Clearly, Murillo is just as single-minded and power hungry as Ortega. Given the chance, she could be Nicaragua's dictator tomorrow. Many feel she already is. The lesson here is a bitter one, and one that ambitious women have long learned. You don't necessarily have to give up on your ambition to power. You just might have to seek it through your weak-willed husband.

By the end of Shakespeare's tragedy, Lady Macbeth has killed herself offscreen, leaving Macbeth alone to hold the throne against Macduff's impending charge. And Macbeth proves himself comically, utterly incapable. As Macduff advances, Macbeth stomps around his castle. He's put on his armor, pointlessly; he sputters and he rants. Eventually Macduff arrives, in a field before the castle, and duly slays him. Without his wife, Macbeth proves himself to be nothing.

CHAPTER TEN
The Korean Rasputin

THE "KOREAN RASPUTIN" SCANDAL erupted in the late stages of 2016 and brought out, week after week, hundreds of thousands of protesters in the streets of Seoul calling for then-president Park Geun-hye's ouster. On one Saturday alone, a peak of 1.7 million people took to the central Gwanghwamun Square and sprawled throughout the city from there. Protesters depicted themselves as puppeteers controlling the strings of Park marionettes.

As the news broke internationally, I was delighted and bewildered alike. There I was, hunting for stories of Rasputinism. And there, suddenly, was a perfect contemporary case study, screaming out for attention from six thousand miles away. I knew that our Rasputin's name, in this case, was Choi Soon-sil. But I had so much more to learn.

IT ALL STARTED with a tablet. A foolishly discarded Samsung tablet, acquired by the Korean news organization JTBC. It had belonged to Choi—that much was made clear by the smiling Choi selfie on the tablet's camera rolls. It also contained drafts of two years' worth of Park's campaign and presidential speeches—over forty altogether—marked clearly with Choi's edits in red. But Choi wasn't a speechwriter. In fact, she had no official government position at all.

In their attempts to fend off the storm, both women would offer apologies. Park would do so over the course of two somber press conferences. At that point, there still seemed to be a way out of the muck. Wasn't Choi really just an informal advisor? Wasn't this all being overblown? In her first press conference, Park humbly attempted to downplay the nature of their relationship. "During the presidential election, Choi played the role of expressing her opinions or impressions of how my messages could be delivered in public speeches or press releases," Park said. "It was done out of the purest intentions." Finally, she bowed to the camera and left without taking questions from reporters.

In a later statement, she would add, cryptically, "There have been claims that I fell for a religious cult or had [rituals] performed in the Blue House, but I would like to clarify that those are absolutely not true."

Park also offered condolences. She went beyond the boilerplate: she really sounded like she was pouring out her heart. "I find it very difficult to forgive myself. I feel gravely saddened. I can't sleep at night. I don't know what I could do to allay this anger from the public. And I wonder why I became president. I feel devastated."

But new and damaging information just kept on surfacing. Korean media revealed that Choi had used her influence over Park not only to edit her messaging, but also to shake down the massive Korean conglomerates known as chaebols. For years, chaebols like Samsung and Hyundai had been mysteriously moved to funnel major sums to Choi, in part by donating to sports and culture foundations she controlled. Estimates of how much Choi pulled in ranged from tens of millions to hundreds of millions of dollars.

The money and influence partly went to finance and support the equestrian career of Choi's daughter, Chung Yoo-ra. Hoping to win Choi's favor, Samsung even went straight to Chung, gifting her stables and thoroughbred horses directly. One thoroughbred alone, named Vitana V, cost $800,000. Choi would allegedly go so far as to fix equestrian competitions in her daughter's favor. After one such contest didn't go in Chung's favor, the judges were arrested. Chung had come in second place.

The specifics of Choi's Rasputin run are rife with more strange details. Choi owned a coffee shop in Gangnam, the famously upscale Seoul neighborhood. There, she'd host her retinue of lackeys. The crew included one K-pop music video director and a fellow commonly referred to as her "gigolo," a former national fencing champion turned handbag designer named Ko Young-tae. While he'd later deny carrying on an affair with Choi, he admitted that Choi had purchased hundreds of ostrich skin and crocodile leather bags from his brand, Villomillo. Once then-president Park started wearing them in public, the Villomillo brand took off.

At her Gangnam coffee shop, Choi would sit down with businesspeople and politicians and strike self-enriching, government-sanctioned deals. Critics would later see this as a facsimile, or an end run around, official Blue House policy.

Choi and Park's relationship appears to have been prickly and one-sided. After sending documents to her for approval, the president would ask specifically, "Did Choi confirm this?" In response, Choi would huff to her underlings that it was "tiresome to coach the president on every little thing." Evidently, though, Choi was providing Park with the emotional support that the president needed.

Choi also got Park on anti-aging supplements and injections like garlic extract, Chinese licorice extract, and Laennec—Japanese placenta extract. According to public records, the Blue House would order vials and vials of the stuff. Park also regularly had Choi travel with her on foreign diplomacy trips.

Perhaps most harrowing of all, some believe that Choi was instrumental in shaping South Korea's policy toward its nuclear-armed neighbor to the north. According to Woo Sang-ho, a representative in Korea's National Assembly, "Choi Soon-sil reportedly said North Korea will collapse within two years—if Park was captivated by her prophecy and implemented her foreign and North

Korea policies, this is a serious problem." One of the speeches that Choi was found to have edited was a high-profile 2014 address in Dresden, Germany, in which Park outlined her administration's path toward reunification with North Korea.

There was so much to parse in this relationship: so many accusations, so many sordid details. What seemed to infuriate the millions of Korean protesters wasn't so much the money, or the corruption, or the collective shame. Any given detail, perhaps, could be explained away. But the barrage was ceaseless. Their president had been thoroughly, completely compromised.

One damning piece of early evidence in the scandal was security camera footage showing Choi hectoring two presidential aides. It was leaked by Ko Young-tae, the former alleged gigolo. Choi and Ko's relationship soured at some point—"She treated me like a slave, swearing at me many times," Ko would later say in testimony to parliament. Feeling put upon by his one-time benefactor and possible lover, Ko decided to reveal what he knew. He leaked the security camera footage. As one blaring newspaper headline would put it, he was a "toy-boy turned whistleblower."

At one point in the clip, an aide humbles himself by cleaning his cell phone on his shirt before turning it over to Choi. This was seen as obsequiousness of the highest order. Said Ko, "[Choi] acted as if her underlings were subhuman." In a way, that included President Park herself.

It was a very *specific* bond that existed between these two powerful women. How and why did Park submit to the whims of her old friend Choi?

FORMER PRESIDENT PARK'S father, Park Chung-hee, was himself elected president of South Korea in 1963. An autocratic strongman, he was widely credited with modernizing the country's flagging post–Korean War economy. In 1974, his wife, Yuk Young-soo—Park's mother—was killed by an assassin with North Korean sympathies who was targeting the president. In 1979, he himself was killed by his own intelligence officer during a manic early evening meal full of errant gunplay at a dining room within the Blue House compound.

In the years between her parents' awful deaths, Park took over many of the ceremonial roles of the first lady. And it was then that the future president met her first Rasputin.

His name was Choi Tae-min, but he used many aliases. He was, he claimed in his newspaper advertisements, a "Messenger from the Spiritual World" here to help "religious leaders of all beliefs." He was, he told his followers, the messiah.

Messianic cults have long found Korea to be a fervent meadow. Some religious scholars credit the phenomenon to Korea's famously diverse religious traditions. Shamanism, Confucianism, Buddhism, and Christianity all flourish in the country. The devastation of the 1950s Korean War, in which the North invaded the South, is cited as a major factor as well. Perhaps in the wake of the war, the theory goes, a shattered, ambiguous society felt mainstream religious traditions were no longer offering solutions. So they decided to look past them. According to some estimates, in the 1960s there were roughly seventy individual Korean shamans who were able to boast of disciples who believed them to be the messiah.

Any given cult leader has their own unique, idiosyncratic practices, of course. But in Korea many of them share common beliefs and teachings: they say that the Second Coming of Jesus Christ will be Korean; they say that the Lord will pass down new scripture in Korean; they say that the new Chosen People exist right here in Korea.

Choi Tae-min was just one of many. How did he rise to such a place of prominence?

It was in the mid-seventies, while fronting an ostensibly Christian group called the Korean National Salvation Crusade, that Choi Tae-min worked himself into the confidences of the Blue House. He wrote a letter to a young Park telling her that he had spoken to her mother, who had been assassinated months before.

In later accounts, Choi Tae-min was said to have reached Park's dead mother after a serious bout of cave praying. He'd claim to one former confidant that Park's mother shared a secret only she and her daughter would know. In this account, after he sent his letter, he was fetched to the Blue House in a chauffeured car. There, Choi Tae-min shared the secret he'd heard from the ghost of Park's mother. Park duly fainted and entered a trance during which she met her dead mother, who told her to trust Choi. And the Rasputinesque bond between Park and Choi Tae-min—the bond that would eventually be passed down to Choi Tae-min's daughter—was formed.

Choi Tae-min died in the mid-1990s. Many years after his death, questions were still being asked. In 2007, William Stanton, then the American ambassador to South Korea, wrote a classified memo (later released by Wikileaks) in which he hit upon the outsized role of Choi Tae-min in the political discourse. Ahead of upcoming elections, Stanton explained, Park had been forced to explain her relationship "some 35 years ago with a pastor whom her opponents characterize as a 'Korean Rasputin'—rumors are rife that the late pastor had complete control over Park's body and soul during her formative years and that his children accumulated enormous wealth as a result."

JI-IL TARK IS a professor of divinity at Busan Presbyterian University. His father, Myeong-Hwan Tahk, was a religious scholar as well. They even shared a specialty: the shamans and cults of Korea. In the early seventies, Tark's father interviewed Choi Tae-min, just before the man entered the halls of power.

As Tark explains it, his father heard of Choi Tae-min through one of the shaman's hyperbolic newspaper advertisements: "Choi Tae-min introduced himself as a messenger by God, and he said he can cure any kind of diseases, and that he can prophesize what happened in the future."

Tark shares with me the original ad from his own archives. It's a strange, beguiling document:

A Message from the Spiritual World:

The Creator who is the master of the spiritual world has sent an Envoy to this region in order to achieve that which has been desired for thousands of years: "the Awakening from Buddhism," "the Advent from Christianity," and "the Innae-cheon from Cheondoism."

Those who are suffering from diseases which cannot be cured by modern medicine and those who face financial troubles should come immediately for consultations.

Tark's father spent time with Choi Tae-min and his followers during a private ceremony held in a small, rented wedding hall near Gyerongsan, a place many shamans' disciples believe will be a place of safety and salvation during the inevitable end days. Tark shares with me with his father's direct account of what he saw: "On the walls, [Choi Tae-min] had drawn multicolored circles. He stared at them intently as he continuously chanted 'Namu-jabi-jo-hwabul,' which he claimed would cure all diseases and bring one to enlightenment. The ritual was very simple: people stared in the circles and repeated the spell." Tark offers me a loose translation of the spell, Namu-jabi-jo-hwabul: "Obey-mercy-harmony-Buddha."

In attendance during Choi Tae-min's speeches and his ceremonies were other shamans. The following is from Tark's father's original reporting: "A shaman who worships minor spirits cringed and trembled before [Choi Tae-min]. Even a shaman who met him for the first time prostrated himself before [him]." Apparently, Choi Tae-min was the shaman's shaman. The scene was so bizarre, so powerful, that Tark's ultra-rationalist father briefly questioned his understanding of reality. "Seen in this light, one might say that [Choi Tae-min] . . . was possessed of some kind of spiritual power."

Then he shook it off with sarcasm: "Of course, this was probably not the work of the Holy Spirit."

In May of 1975, Choi Tae-min reinvented himself as the leader of a mainstream church, the Korean National Salvation Crusade. His following blossomed; he developed friends in high places. Tark's father warned his colleagues: *'They try to change their mask but they have the same face,* Choi Tae-min is not a Pastor. He is a shaman!"

That's when the KCIA, the Korean equivalent of the CIA, came calling. Lee X-Gyu, then employed as the KCIA chief of religious affairs, sent a message: He told Tark's father to "tread carefully."

"They urged my father to stop talking about Choi Tae-min," Tark tells me. "To *stop* research on Choi Tae-min."

"Urged?"

"Threatened!"

Choi Tae-min engendered powerful reactions from his fellow men of faith. Years later, a pastor named Jeon Ki-young would recall an outlandish tale. "When I looked at Choi with the eyes of the spirit, I saw that his eyes were black and hollow, and he looked like he was possessed," Jeon told Korean media. "Just then, I said to Choi, 'Hey, you freak—I'm a servant of the Lord!—what are you really?' Then his face twisted and contorted. His eyes went bloodshot, and his body trembled. I still remember vividly how he looked at that time."

But neither criticism from scholars nor from the religious institutions could stop him. By the summer of 1975, Choi

Tae-min was organizing massive rallies in the name of the Korean National Salvation Crusade throughout the country, including the 20,000-capacity Seoul Stadium. Choi Tae-min had tempered his rhetoric. He'd sanded down some of the kookier bits. But just like the old shaman days, he readily whipped up an existentialist fervor.

"Conscience is being corrupted," he bellowed at one rally. "The ideals of humanity are being buried. [We] vow to come together and give [our] hearts and souls to the mission of defeating the communists and saving the country!" In attendance, behind her tight phalanx of bodyguards, was the young Park Geun-hye.

When the Choi Soon-sil scandal broke in 2016, Tark went into his archives and found his father's old materials: his father's primary research, along with piles of Choi Tae-min's old ads from his messianic shaman days. These are quoted previously in this chapter. "When Korean people realized our president was influenced by a religious cult leader and his daughter, that made us very angry," Tark says.

Tark explained the nature of Choi Tae-min's control: "He was interested in political power but also financial success. He was able to achieve both. He might have had some kind of mind control over former President Park. And I have no doubt that Choi Soon-sil was the successor of Choi Tae-min. She influenced Park Geun-hye. Surely Choi Soon-sil knew what to do. Because she saw how her father had controlled Park."

Internationally, the names Choi Tae-min and Choi Soon-sil will not enter lore. But their tale is quite possibly the most dramatic example of true-blue Rasputinism that we've seen since the Mad Monk himself.

It's rare enough to see one person yanked to and fro by two separate Rasputins. But this was two *generations* of Rasputins playing games, beating back all enemies and critics and manipulating a person for their own gains.

The Chois could never be president. A former shaman? The daughter of a former shaman? Of course they couldn't. But why would they want to be president, anyway? Playing mind games with President Park made them plenty rich and powerful enough.

It's not just one of the most elaborate and longest-running tales of Rasputinism to present itself. It's also, possibly, the most callous and coldly calculated. Outwardly, the elder Choi shared Rasputin's religiosity. But did he really believe in the holy cures he was peddling? Or was he there just to make a buck? And what about his daughter, Choi? Did she believe in the Japanese placenta extract she prescribed to her friend Park? Or was she playing her for a fool the whole time?

Say what you will about our friend Grigori, but never doubt: He was a true believer.

IN LATE 2016, as realization of the breadth of Choi's corruption first swelled, the protests and critiques against Park swelled as well. Park was moved to apologize a second time. Again, she found herself struggling to explain, *really* explain, the strange nature of her relationship with Choi.

"My fellow Koreans, since I took office and became president, I was always concerned with whether there were any issues arising from my personal relations," she said. "I even detached myself from my family." It was true; Park was estranged from her siblings. At one point that was seen as boosting her electability: Past Korean presidential corruption scandals had centered around family members, something Park would theoretically be immune from. "Living by myself, I didn't have many people who could help me with my personal affairs. And so I maintained a close relationship with Choi Soon-sil, who helped me out. Yes, it's true that I had lowered the barriers between us, because she stood beside me in the most difficult times."

It was perhaps an implicit reference to an incident that had occurred in spring of 2006. While attending a campaign event for her Grand National Party, Park was attacked by a knife-wielding assailant. The man slashed a four-inch gash into the right side of her face; the injury required sixty stitches. Just ten days later, Park returned to active political life. Following that display of remarkable resilience, she gained some of the best press of her career. And after the incident, it was Choi that tended to Park's healing. That hinted at the kind of familial intimacy these women shared.

When Choi spoke to reporters after the scandal broke, she kept it simple enough: "I committed a sin that deserves death."

It was all part of the intensely heightened environment of the scandal. Addressing the country's Constitutional Court, Park's lawyer attempted to portray her as a victim of a mania. "Socrates was put to death, and Jesus crucified, in mob trials," he said. Now, "our democracy is in danger because of so-called majority opinion instigated through demagogy."

It wouldn't make any difference. Park would end up impeached. And both women would end up convicted on separate charges including bribery, corruption, and abuse of power. At first they were held at the Seoul Detention Center; eventually, Choi was transferred to another facility in Seoul. Said one report, "Concerns have been raised about the possibility of . . . psychological discomfort should they encounter each other."

Choi was sentenced to twenty years in prison. Park was sentenced to twenty-five. At sixty-six years old, Park was given a veritable death sentence. The former president of South Korea has denied the charges but has given up on appeals.

CHAPTER ELEVEN

All the President's Rasputins

THE EXTREMITY OF SOUTH KOREA'S response to the Choi Soon-sil scandal startled me. It started with millions in the streets. It ended with a president not only impeached, but imprisoned. Seoul revolted. How would the American public respond to a president being similarly played? Would they also find the Rasputinism to be so repugnant?

In a lesser way, America has its own case study with Steve Bannon, Trump's former chief strategist. But Choi Soon-sil had palpable influence for decades, not months. Trump's history with Bannon and his other Rasputins is much more—*schizophrenic*. Inside Trump World, from the days of the campaign and on through into the White House, it has been Royal Rumble all the time. Leaks, factions, ad hominem bashings. The most delectable assassinations of character—anonymous or otherwise! A lot of metal chairs have been swung by a lot of people into a lot of other people's backs. It has been a surreal, unprecedented social experiment: Let a bunch of crappy Rasputins loose in the world's greatest halls of power, and let them go to town on each other.

As Trump's scandal-riddled former advisor Roger Stone has said, "The administration is like the French Revolution. You never know who will be beheaded next."

To understand what it's like to try and Rasputin Trump, I meet Sam Nunberg, as instructed, on a street corner on the Upper East Side on a weekday afternoon. Within minutes we're in a near-empty bar enjoying a tall plastic pitcher of domestic beer as "Stayin' Alive" pumps over the speakers.

Nunberg, who is in his late thirties, was already an established Trump World character at the time of our sitdown. But months after our meeting he'd gain infamy via what was invariably, and perhaps correctly, referred to as a "meltdown." It was a Monday, March 5, 2018 and it started with a subpoena from Special Counsel Robert Mueller's investigation into Russian interference with the 2016 election. Nunberg had worked on the Trump campaign. Mueller wanted to have a chat about that work in front of a federal grand jury. But Nunberg didn't want to play along; as he told the *Washington Post*, "Let him arrest me."

For the rest of the day, Nunberg would ping around various MSNBC and CNN news shows, rambling and ranting about how stoked he was to be ignoring a federal subpoena. "It would be really, really funny if they wanted to arrest me because I don't want to spend eighty hours going over emails I had with Steve Bannon," he said on live TV early in the day. Then, later: "Mr. Mueller can send me to jail, and then you know what I'm gonna do? I'm gonna laugh." At one point while interviewing him, CNN's Erin Burnett interjected with this aside: "Talking to you, I have smelled alcohol on your breath. I know it's awkward. You haven't had a drink today?" Nunberg assured her he had not. By the end of the day, he told the Associated Press, "I'm going to end up cooperating with them." It would be a bizarre, pointless, beautiful kind of performance art. For one day, at least, he would be all everyone wanted to talk about.

When I meet Nunberg, however, a few months before Subpoena Day, he's calm and engaged and happy to chitchat. He was born and raised just a few blocks away, he tells me as we walk south; in fact, he still lives in his childhood home, with his parents. "I pay utilities and stuff," he explains. He also points west, down toward a *shul* a few avenues away: "That's the synagogue where Ivanka converted." He's wearing a pastel polo out of which pops a bit of chest hair and a thin gold chain. In one hand is a Blackberry plugged into a mobile charger. In the other is a silver vape on which he absentmind-edly chews. He is smiley and boyishly chubby. His hair is cut Tintin spiffy. He is one of Donald Trump's original would-be Rasputins.

Millions of New Yorkers grew up seeing Trump's name splashed across the covers of the *New York Post* and the *Daily News* and were never convinced to care. Nunberg, though, bought in to the Trump tabloid mystique early. He personally encountered the man for the first time in 1989, with his father, at Wrestlemania V. "I'm like, [a little kid], and we were literally sitting right behind Ivana and Trump," Nunberg says, relishing the memory.

The '89 Wrestlemania was held at Trump Plaza in Atlan-tic City. As Sam remembers it, sitting behind the Nunbergs was Thomas Kean, then New Jersey's governor. Trump saw it as an opportunity: He had young Sam and his dad moved to the first row on the other side of the ring. He wanted to be photographed block-ing the governor's view of "Macho Man" Randy Savage. There's actually footage of the future political aide in attendance: panning the crowd, the cameras caught Nunberg rolling his arms up and down over his head in loyal mimicry of WWE tag team duo the Bushwackers' trademark move.

The other major influence in Nunberg's life is Roger Stone. A long-time Republican tactician, Stone got his start on Richard Nixon's Committee to Re-Elect the President (or CREEP) and went on to infamy for running oodles of proudly scruple-free campaigns. Stone has Nixon's face tattooed on his upper back; sports a head full of entrancingly strange (and admittedly transplanted) white hair; and sometimes dresses like a steampunk movie villain.

Stone, Nunberg's hero, would also become his mentor.

In 2010, Nunberg, who was then working for the American Center for Law and Justice, testified during hearings for Park51, a proposed project for an Islamic community center two blocks north of the former Twin Towers site. Republican critics used the proposed plan to whip up Islamophobic outrage and eventually managed to turn the center into a sticking point in that year's midterm elections. It was referred to as the "Ground Zero Mosque."

At public hearings over the project, Nunberg railed, "This'll be like taking a ship from Pearl Harbor to erect a memorial for the kamikazes killed in the attack." The clip was "spliced everywhere," Nunberg says with pride. "And that brought me to Roger."

Stone, who's known Trump since the eighties, had been trying to convince him to run for office on and off for years. "I was like a jockey looking for a horse," Stone has said. "And [Trump's] a prime piece of political horse flesh." In 2010, while advising Trump unofficially, Stone brought in Nunberg. And after Nunberg came on board, Trump quickly took the Park51 issue as his own.

Around then Nunberg floated ratcheting up tensions around the issue, he says, by parking a truck across the street from the proposed site of Park51—meaning, blocks from Ground Zero—with a fake missile on top.

He smiles as he tells me the story. "Like, sick shit. Sick political stuff." Exactly in line with Stone's M.O. "Ratfucking" is a DC term, credited to a Nixon campaign manager, for sleazy political gambits. Roger Stone has been called "the Godfather of Ratfucking."

Nunberg worked for Trump on and off from 2010 to 2015, a period of time during which Trump's political operation—always lean—was comically skeletal. Nunberg was in meetings and on the road and everywhere else with the candidate, watching as Trump the politician oozed forth into being. And now, with certain hyperbole, he takes no small chunk of the credit for forming that bizarre character.

Nunberg and Stone have been credited with pushing Trump to amplify the racist, paranoiac "birther" claim that Barack Obama wasn't actually born in Hawaii. Nunberg says he found the whole thing to be "bullshit," but agreed with Stone that it had value as a "political issue."

At the 2011 White House Correspondents' Dinner, Obama famously bashed Trump, who was in attendance. Days before, Obama's birth state of Hawaii had released his longform birth certificate, killing the last remaining shreds of doubt over the validity of the "birther" claims. Obama took the opportunity to do some roasting.

"Just recently, in an episode of *Celebrity Apprentice*, at the steakhouse, the men's cooking team did not impress the judges from Omaha Steaks," he cracked. "And there was a lot of blame to go around, but you, Mr. Trump, recognized that the real problem was a lack of leadership, and so ultimately you didn't blame Lil Jon or Meat Loaf—you fired Gary Busey. And these are the kinds of decisions that would keep me up at night. Well-handled, sir. Well-handled."

Trump could be seen glowering through the bit. Later, pundits would theorize this was the moment he began plotting his presidential ascent in earnest. But it was also the moment that, for the time being, paused his political career. "Obama probably did stop him with that dinner," Nunberg recalls. "It pissed him off. My idea was this—you should hold a press conference at Trump Tower demanding $5 million for *all* of his records. I said, let's go one step further! Let's keep it going!" Nunberg wanted to keep twisting the knife. It didn't matter that it didn't make sense—records of *what*, exactly? Just keep twisting the knife.

"But then the fucker killed bin Laden." That's true: The day after that 2011 Correspondents' Dinner, Obama announced that US Special Forces in Abbottabad, Pakistan, had conducted a raid that culminated with the assassination of Osama bin Laden. All while riffing on Trump, Obama knew SEAL Team Six was advancing toward bin Laden. "He's so lucky," Nunberg smiles.

Still, Nunberg was convinced that Trump had presidential potential yet unfulfilled. He recalls seeing him that year at the Conservative Political Action Conference, a major GOP event. "Trump goes to CPAC and I saw something—I saw cameras clicking, *click click click click click*. These are conservative people! They believe in political philosophy! They think Donald Trump's a liberal!" It didn't matter; they were fawning, and they were clicking. "He was like a rock star. He was, like, our own Obama."

Nunberg brags that he and Stone also began Trump's weaponization of Twitter. He recalls the first Trump tweets to get attention as a clapback to some kerfuffle Trump had gotten in with former Utah governor Jon Huntsman, who was then running in the 2012 Republican primaries.

One read, "Jon Huntsman called to see me. I said no, he gave away our country to China!" Another read, "The lightweight, @JonHuntsman, used my name in a debate for gravitas—it didn't work. Sad!" Surprisingly for Trump's team, as Nunberg recalls, they were picked up by political and entertainment outlets alike. Nunberg and Stone pushed him to keep going. "We would send him suggestion for tweets," Nunberg says. "He started to see the publicity. He started to see it as this great medium."

Nunberg even claims it was he and Stone that first convinced Trump to start his defining campaign promise: a security wall along the southern border. "I wanna be careful," he says. "I'm not responsible for Donald Trump's actions. But did I come up with the wall? The answer is yes."

Nunberg says that, at the time, Stone and he were concerned with getting "a little meat on the bone" of the fraught campaign.

"I used to call it the Donald Trump Variety Show," he says. "He only wants to talk about current events, and himself. Fine. OK. How do we get him to talk about policy? How do we get some substance on this variety show? Let's tell him we'll build a wall. It's like a real estate deal. He'll talk about it. Because *nobody builds like Trump*."

In his time attempting to push forth Trump the politician, Nunberg learned other lessons in controlling and cajoling Donald.

Some were simple, or predictable, like avoid being the one who has to tell Trump bad news—he has a slight tendency to shoot the messenger. Never interrupt him, never lecture, never scream. Also: "If you can compare things to real estate, that's always good for him. I said at one point, 'I know this sounds so clichéd when I give you these real estate analogies' . . . he said, 'No, no, it's good, keep doing it.'"

Plus: "You have to approach him and tell him you're taking the bigger, bolder, more exciting position. That's how we got to the wall." And of course, "Tell him, 'You'd be the first. You'd be the only one.'"

Some lessons were a bit stranger. Nunberg would on occasion approach Trump with a folder of information he wanted Trump to use and say something to the effect of, "You're not gonna believe it. I got you manna from heaven." According to Nunberg, this would be a good way to get Trump to snap to attention. "I'd say, 'I don't *knoooow*—should I give this to you? You may actually *wiiiin* and have to be president if I give this to you!' And he'd say, 'Oh, just give it over.'"

The question of how not only to get information to Trump, but how to get him to pay to attention to it, has been a central issue in his administration. As Politico wrote in early 2017, Trump is a president "notoriously influenced by the last person he has spoken to." In *Fire and Fury*, Michael Wolff's infamous book on the early Trump administration: "It was one of the key elements of [internal] understanding of Trump: The last person the president spoke to ended up with enormous influence."

Strangely enough, the phrasing was an incidental echo of something from Rasputin's days. They used to say that the most powerful people in Russia were Tsar Nicholas and whoever the tsar had spoken to last. As one joke went, "Tsar Nicholas is like a feather pillow. He bore the impression of the last person to sit on him."

NO ONE MAN SHOULD HAVE ALL THAT POWER

It didn't take some master manipulator to figure it out: In the Trump administration, controlling the flow of information might just mean controlling the most powerful man in the world.

The early days of Trump's presidency were a chaotic free-for-all. One person close to Trump, but not employed in the White House, would tell me that he heard of people "flooding the zone" with Trump—meaning, a like-minded group of aides coordinating to all tell him the same thing at the same time in hopes that he'd actually listen. "If they can get multiple people suggesting something," the friend explained, "they feel they have a better chance of getting it accomplished."

While the ineffectual Reince Priebus was chief of staff, he'd huff and puff about all the various ways aides were trying to slip Trump information that was often completely unvetted. The best-known story from those days concerned a piece of strange content slipped to Trump by K. T. McFarland, then the deputy national security adviser. It was a printout of a *Time* magazine cover from the 1970s warning of an imminent global warming–induced ice age.

It seemed to be clear proof of a long history of media histrionics around the issue. It incensed Trump, as McFarland well knew it would. The problem: It was a fake. Staff members were deployed to grab Trump and stop him before he inevitably tweeted about it.

As 2017 rolled on, senior government employees would learn the various tricks and tactics that Nunberg had picked up long ago. A source would tell Reuters that Trump was getting only "single-page memos" and "visual aids like maps, charts, graphs, and photos" in part because "the guy's a builder. He likes to visualize things. He has spent his whole life looking at . . . floor plans."

That self-aggrandizement that Nunberg had long observed (and exploited: "You'd be the only one") was echoed in that Reuters report, as well. According to another source, "National Security Council officials have strategically included Trump's name in 'as many paragraphs as we can because he keeps reading if he's mentioned.'"

When former Marine Corps general John Kelly replaced Priebus as chief of staff in the summer of 2017, he successfully executed a simulacrum of military order. He became obsessive over the information that Trump received and the people that Trump gave an audience to. He forced all meetings with Trump to be scheduled through him; even Ivanka was no longer allowed to just waltz on into the Oval Office.

Staffers took to calling Kelly "the church lady." And soon enough, reports trickled out that Trump was still placing calls to old friends and long-fired loyalists—late at night, when Kelly couldn't catch him.

Roger Stone predicted it wouldn't last. "General Kelly is trying to treat the president like a mushroom," he said after Kelly's takeover. "Keeping him in the dark and feeding him shit is not going to work. Donald Trump is a free spirit." And yet, compared to the earlier chaos, Kelly's presence was demonstratively calming. The Rasputin carousel had been, at least temporarily, taken out of commission.

SAM NUNBERG WAS employed long before John Kelly came on the scene. He was around Trump's political world when it consisted of a few guys in a backroom, screaming at each other, neck veins bulging. And of all that time, Nunberg is proudest of helping Trump survive his summer 2015 faceoff with the late Arizona senator John McCain. It was a garishly unabashed execution of a mantra usually credited to Benjamin Jowett, a nineteenth-century Oxford academic: "Never apologize, never explain."

At that point in the 2016 election cycle, Trump and McCain had already been feuding. McCain had struck first by saying Trump was "fir[ing] up the crazies" on the campaign trail. Then, at an Iowa event called the Family Leadership Summit, Trump was asked about his new enemy, former POW John McCain. "He was a war hero because he was captured," Trump spat out. "I like people who weren't captured."

During the Vietnam War, McCain spent over five years imprisoned. He was captured in the fall of 1967 when his bomber was hit by a surface-to-air missile over Hanoi. He ejected from the aircraft and landed in Trúc Bạch Lake, where he nearly drowned; during the ejection, he broke both arms and his right leg. Upon landing he was taken into custody by the North Vietnamese, who bayoneted him and beat him with the butt of a rifle. In a prison called "The Plantation," McCain was kept in solitary confinement for two years. He was initially denied medical treatment and was later tortured—his left arm broken again, his ribs cracked. For the rest of his life, he was unable to lift his arms above his head.

At that point Trump had already avoided blowback from a string of his wayward comments. But this one seemed sure to stick.

"Us getting out of the McCain thing was the *best* thing," Nunberg recalls. "OK, let's go through the lineage. Trump gives this speech on a [Saturday] in Arizona, an amazing speech. Says we're gonna take our country back. Says 'We're the silent majority and we're not silent anymore,' which Roger"—eternally the Nixon fanboy—"had been trying to get him to say for forever.'

Then came Iowa, the McCain comments, and a barrage of cable news outrage.

Charting the course, Nunberg pushed Trump to hold ground. Juiced up by the Arizona speech, he felt the momentum was firmly behind them. "I said, it's irrelevant if he's a war hero! Make that clear distinction and just say *fuck you* to everyone."

Nunberg felt a basic fact was being overlooked: "McCain lost"—in 2008, against Obama. "He's a fucking loser! That's what Roger and I said. And he really, really listened to us. I said to 'em,

'Fellas, logically, the easiest thing to do is apologize. But we gain nothing. Let's keep what we have here, and fight.'"

Apparently, Trump listened. No explicit mea culpa was ever offered. And what many thought would become a campaign-killing moment became—nothing. As Trump would later tell the radio host Don Imus, when pressed on the scandal: "I like not to regret anything. You do things and you say things. And what I said, frankly, is what I said. And, you know, some people like what I said, if you want to know the truth. You know, after I said that, my poll numbers went up seven points."

The logic of Benjamin Jowett became fully internalized— elemental to Trump's very being. As president, it's how he governs. Whether it's a cockeyed defense of homicidal white supremacists or loose talk with a nuclear-armed rogue state: *Never apologize, never explain.* Every time this happens, somewhere in the back of his mind he might just remember how he trashed a POW and then watched his poll numbers go up seven points.

"We said, 'Fuck you,'" Nunberg recalls. "We're not apologizing for *anything.*"

Trump first fired Nunberg in 2014, after BuzzFeed published a negative Trump profile; Nunberg had set up the piece, granting the BuzzFeed reporter access. Trump rehired Nunberg months later, then fired him again after a year, when a series of racist Facebook posts from Nunberg came to light. Nunberg had referred to Obama as a "Pan Arabist Marxist Muslim" and fretted about America being forced into "Kenyan socialism." He'd also written, right after Obama's election, that there were "still tickets available for the Hip Hop Inaugural ball."

"I don't understand this," Nunberg says to me, about those Facebook posts. I assume he's about to express contrition or offer mitigation. Instead, he says, "I sat there one day, deleting everything, until nothing was there. So I don't know why those didn't show up on my thing! To delete it!"

And then he quickly pivots to the *real* root of the problem, as he sees it: his feud with Corey Lewandowski, the campaign manager Trump hired in January 2015 and fired in June 2016. Yet another would-be Rasputin who came and went and, like Nunberg, remained loyal to Donald.

Nunberg and Lewandowski were viciously territorial toward each other from the very beginning of Lewandowski's tenure. "The fucking interloper," Nunberg spits. He blames Lewandowski for leaking the Facebook posts. Afterward, Nunberg recalls telling Lewandowski, "You scumbag piece of shit, by the time I'm done with you, your family will be eating out of the motherfucking garbage."

Lewandowksi was taping the conversation. He turned the audio over to Trump, and summed it up as a threat by Nunberg to kill his family. Nunberg is aghast at the lack of nuance in the interpretation of his words: "I didn't threaten to kill his family! I said I was gonna ruin his career!" Then he adds, "Corey will tell you I had a drinking problem. That guy's a fucking alcoholic. I don't wanna hear about drinking problems."

At this point, Nunberg and I are on our second pitcher of beer. In an aside, he gets up out of the booth, turns his body in profile toward me and says, "Do I look fat to you? I've been drinking too much. Do you think I need to lose weight?"

"No way," I say.

He ponders this for a moment. And we go back to drinking, both of us thoroughly enjoying our impromptu afternoon beers.

I think about the naked, blunt self-concern. I think about the unbridled rage. There are some unmistakable echoes here of his one-time benefactor. "Something I learned from Mr. Trump," Nunberg says, taking a long, joyful drag on his pint glass, "is that revenge is very important."

CHAPTER TWELVE
The Ivy League Rasputin

TRUMP'S EARLIEST POLITICAL RASPUTINS were Roger Stone and Sam Nunberg. From birtherism to the wall, they fueled Trump with his early, inciting fodder. But they were never idealistic Rasputins. As Nunberg himself admits, he didn't really believe in the substance of many of the ugly things he was convincing Trump to scream. It was a cynical calculation. A way to get close to grand power.

The next candidate for Trump's Rasputin was Nunberg's arch-nemesis, Corey Lewandowski, the ex–campaign manager. But Lewandowski never aspired to life as a puppeteer. His operating principle was "let Trump be Trump."

After the election victory, Trump's daughter Ivanka was hailed as an influencer, most often by liberals who saw her as a potential stabilizing force. She was known for her support of paid family leave and LGBTQ issues. Trump was known for his special, particular dotage on Ivanka over the years. A direct quote: "You know who's one of the great beauties of the world, according to everybody? And I helped create her. My daughter, Ivanka. She's six feet tall, she's got the best body." (Not mincing words, *The Daily Show* would put together a segment titled "DON'T FORGET: DONALD TRUMP WANTS TO BANG HIS DAUGHTER.") Could she be the one to pull the strings? By the fall of 2017, she'd already thrown in the towel. "Some people have created unrealistic expectations of what they expect from me," she told a reporter.

As the vice president, Mike Pence was the most obvious candidate for Rasputinesque behavior. But he seemed happy enough

NO ONE MAN SHOULD HAVE ALL THAT POWER

spending his days smiling thinly in public. Counselor Kellyanne Conway, a crafty DC lifer, surged forth for a bit as a possible controller but would end up wasting her talents in empty, inane cable news surrogacy.

Reince Priebus, Trump's first chief of staff, appeared mild-mannered but was actually known for a touch of behind-the-scenes ratfuckery. He reportedly deputized his ally, former White House press secretary Sean Spicer, to protect his image by barking at various national reporters. It would not save Reince, months into the presidency, from getting the chop.

Then, for ten swaggering days as interim communications director, Anthony Scaramucci made a run at the Rasputin championship belt. He kicked the door down. He swore that he'd sort out this mess come hell or high water. And then he gave the *New Yorker* a fiery diatribe of an on-the-record interview in which he castigated his enemies with the passion of a thousand burning suns. There are many moments from that interview that should be cross-stitched on pillows and chiseled into plaques, but my personal favorite is, "I'm not Steve Bannon, I'm not here to suck my own cock."

It became instantly infamous; it got him fired days later. Inside the White House, they took to calling the Mooch a "suicide bomber."

Later, Scaramucci would describe the White House as a "kill or be killed" environment. "The first pill you take is the 'anti-friendship' pill," he said during a speech at a Hanukkah party hosted by the pro-Trump rabbi Shmuley Boteach (author of *Kosher Sex: A Recipe for Passion and Intimacy*). "You can be my friend for thirty years, but I'm gonna stab your eyeball out with an ice pick if it gets me more power. The second pill you take is the 'power is aphrodisiac' pill. Students of history know that power corrupts and it corrupts absolutely."

It was just before Scaramucci's exit that Kelly came in as chief of staff and began implementing some semi-convincing simulacrum of exacting order. With that kind of control, you would think, would come a grand potential for influence. But outside of hardline views on immigration, Kelly has no overt taste for Rasputinism. He wanted to close the borders. And he wanted to make the trains run on time. By the time he departed, just before the second Christmas of the Trump administration, it was tough to pinpoint what, exactly, his influence had amounted to.

Above and beyond all our aforementioned candidates, then, two would-be Rasputins have shined brighter and stronger: Steve Bannon and Jared Kushner.

Bannon spent one eventful year, nearly to the day, employed by Trump. He came on as campaign manager in the late stages of the presidential election; he was fired days after the ugly and violent 2017 Charlottesville riot. Before the election, Bannon called Trump both a "blunt instrument" and an "imperfect vessel." But he was Bannon's *own* instrument-y vessel. Unlike Nunberg and Stone, Bannon wasn't in it for proximity to power. He wasn't in it for the games. He had a true dream of an isolationist, anti-immigration America. And he was working feverishly, endlessly to execute it.

Kushner has been with Trump longer than anyone. He married Ivanka in 2009. He stayed mostly quiet through the whole campaign, until it was in the bag. Then he sat for a cover story with *Forbes* where he was celebrated, with gushing corroborating quotes from Peter Thiel and former Google CEO Eric Schmidt, as the secret Silicon Valley–informed mastermind of the campaign, Grinningly, and with no jargon spared, he took credit for it all. "We played Moneyball, asking ourselves which states will get the best ROI for the electoral vote," he told the magazine. "I called some of my friends from Silicon Valley, some of the best digital marketers in the world, and asked how you scale this stuff."

In the annals of Rasputin studies, the case histories of Jared and Steve are two of the best. In their short, messy histories, there is much to learn—about how to be in position to achieve wide Rasputinesque control, and how to fritter it all away.

Kushner is our fake Rasputin, and still at it.

Officially, he's juggling a preposterous workload, from disrupting government through the Office of American Innovation to improving job training in federal prisons to working toward a Middle East peace deal to reforming Veterans Affairs to solving America's opioid epidemic. Is there any evidence that any progress has been made toward any of this? Is there any evidence that Kushner controls Trump, or ever did? It doesn't really matter. As we'll see, as long as he looks the part, that might just be good enough for Kush.

Bannon is our failed Rasputin, and long gone.

"I am Thomas Cromwell in the court of the Tudors," Bannon gloated right after the inauguration. It was a wild, great, chilling line—Cromwell, an influential minister in King Henry VIII's court, was a proto-Rasputin. Clearly, Bannon was making a threat. Was he also, perhaps, foreshadowing his certain fate? Steve is a well-read dude. Surely he knew that in 1540 Cromwell ended up, at King Henry's order, with his head axed off and, according to the more colorful histories, popped onto a spike on London Bridge.

MUCH LIKE HIS father-in-law, Jared Kushner made his money through nepotism and real estate. Charles Kushner, Jared's dad, built the family fortune with four thousand New Jersey apartments (which, incidentally, Charles inherited from his own father, Joseph, a Holocaust survivor from Belarus). Charles had four kids and a loving wife with whom he kept a prominent Orthodox Jewish home; some summers, they'd host Israeli prime minister Benjamin Netanyahu. Then, in 2005, a scandalous face-off with his brother-in-law, William Schulder, blew up in Charles's face.

Schulder was cooperating with federal investigators who had tagged Charles with illegal campaign contributions. At the height of the blood feud, Charles hired a prostitute to seduce Schulder in hopes of landing *kompromat* on his nemesis. When everything shook out, Charles found himself convicted of witness tampering and sentenced to two years at Federal Prison Camp in Montgomery, Alabama.

It was at this point that Jared officially took over the Kushner Companies' operations. But nearly every single weekend while Charles was imprisoned, he'd fly down from New York to visit his dad in jail.

It's a wild tale, with a telling footnote. The US Attorney who aggressively prosecuted Charles Kushner was future New Jersey governor Chris Christie. In the early years of his governorship, particularly after his spirited response to 2012's Hurricane Sandy, Christie was a beloved national figure regularly bandied about as a possible "populist" presidential candidate. By 2016, however, his administration was proven to be endemically, dangerously corrupt. And Christie's once grand dreams had been dashed.

The prodigal son of New Jersey had one last move to attain national relevance: latch on with stiff fingers to the longshot, upstart campaign of Donald Trump; hope it all panned out with a seemingly impossible victory; assume a cabinet position. Amazingly, parts 1 and 2 went to plan. But after Trump's inauguration, Christie got disappeared. The same *Forbes* article that led Kushner to crow over the victory he'd masterminded called Kushner and Christie's battle a "knife fight" that had ended in a "Stalinesque purge."

Looking back now, Christie's demise is the last competent thing Kushner has been publicly credited with.

Months into the administration, Kushner's fecklessness had become a running national joke. Every time Trump did something joyously, potentially world-sabotaging—like pulling out of the Paris Agreement to combat climate change—it'd be a safe bet that "unnamed sources close to Jared" would pop up in national newspaper explaining how hard Jared had tried, and failed, to convince Trump not to do that thing. Seemingly the only thing Jared was hard at work doing was trying to repair his reputation.

From afar, Kushner looked like the part of an ideal Rasputin. A Harvard-educated, New York City–reared sophisticate who'd triumphed in business before incorporating the manifold reach of Silicon Valley into his quiver. A telegenic patrician in a well-cut blazer. By contrast, Trump was a baggy suit babbling catchphrases. The secret to getting his attention was as simple as . . . repeating his name a bunch. Shouldn't Kushner have been able to dominate this man?

But it turns out Kushner's great strength was just that—looking the part.

Kushner first became a public figure in 2006 when he bought the *New York Observer*, a once-venerable tabloid. Early, he was hands on, eager to shape himself as a budding media mogul (perhaps in the vein of another one of his father figures, News Corp mogul Rupert Murdoch). In multiple conversations with former *Observer* employees, I hear the same thought: Kushner was little more than a thin, good-looking shell.

One *Observer* writer explained that there really wasn't that much to say about him. "He was very defensive about us writing about his brother's VC firm," the writer recalls. "He gave a speech at a company party once where he said we were going to step on the gas and take it to the next level, and I remember thinking it was the lamest speech ever. He was happy they got a staff writer for $25K (me, my starting salary). That's my whole file."

"He just had no gravitas," another writer said. "He's tall. Handsome. Rich. Low affect. Not super articulate. Not a charismatic person. Not super memorable. I don't know—usually great managers or whatever, they have something. And Jared—there was very little *there*."

When I ask one high-level editor who worked for Kushner about any "Rasputin-like" abilities, he politely scoffs.

"It's hard for me to picture him in that light," the editor says. "If anything, his father may have been that for him. Like, when his father was in prison, you could never tell if Jared had the power, or the access to the money, that he would theoretically have. One or two times I would ask him flat out: Can you make a decision? Or is this a family decision? I got the sense that he had to have these family dinners, and it's not like they cared [about the newspaper], but they'd fuck with him. 'Oh, what's going on? You're still losing money?'" The infantilism was audible: When Charles would visit the office, staffers would note Jared calling his father Daddy and greeting him with kisses.

Looking back, the editor feels that Kushner was "conniving," but only in the sense that he'd "promote this idea that he has power, whether he had it or not. The whole thing with Jared was about self-promotion, about keeping an appearance. He wanted to appear to have a plan when it was really, really clear he did not have a plan. He wanted to seem decisive. Like an adult. Like he'd mastered these issues."

The editor recalls how Kushner changed the *Observer* from a broadsheet print format (like the *New York Times*) to a tabloid print format (like the *New York Post*), then back to broadsheet, then again to a modified tabloid format. "And that was all in six years! That's completely insane! And every time he was decisive, he was forceful, he seemed knowledgeable, he was excited. And every one of those times he was totally clueless."

The editor further remembers that in personal conversations, Kushner was "very soft spoken. Maybe a little bit oily. He would just be like, '[name redacted]—what you're giving me—it's a plan. I've heard this plan before, though. What I'm looking for is a *vision*.'"

NO ONE MAN SHOULD HAVE ALL THAT POWER

Foster Kamer, a former writer and editor at the *Observer*, had one specific, elaborate dalliance with the man. Kushner tried to get Kamer to put together a hit piece on Richard Mack, a real estate rival of his. As Kamer tells it, Kushner's grudge with Mack sprung forth when Mack declined to enter into a deal that would help Kushner restructure a hefty bit of debt he was saddled with. Kushner eventually figured out a way to do it without Mack's help. But he never let go of the slight.

So one day, Kamer alleges, Kushner sat him down and told him that he had it on good authority that Mack had been essentially defrauding the real estate trust he was running by keeping good deals for himself and shunting less-promising deals to the trust.

Adding a strange twist to the tale: several employees of the paper recall Kushner claiming that Mack and his wife were engaged in what, effectively, were dueling affairs. At least one employee recalls Mack and his wife's alleged paramours, according to Kushner, being fellow boardmembers of the 92nd Street Y. The 92nd Street Y is a cornerstone of New York Jewish high society; it holds events and gatherings and lectures on, say, the late fiction of Isaac Bashevis Singer. Not exactly the kind of place you'd expect to find steamy dueling affairs. But who are we to underestimate the steaminess of Jewish New York high society.

It turned out that Kamer had been the third or fourth reporter that Kushner had tried to sic on the story. All of them had failed to find anything. Kamer, hoping to avoid their fates, asked Kushner straight up: Who's your source? And can I talk to him? Eventually, Kushner agreed to the meeting with the source, and it proved to be comically pointless; the source provided none of the dirt that Kushner insisted he had.

"And I go, 'Well, Jared, if this guy knows about Richard Mack's improprieties, why won't he talk about it?'" Kamer recalls.

"And that's when he puts his feet up on the desk and he says, 'Because he's not sleazy like us, right?' And then he laughs."

Kamer, too, would echo what others have said. You look at him and all seems right; you hang around and listen to him talk for a few minutes and it all falls apart. "Superficially, there's a lot to be jealous of," Kamer says. "He has a lot of money. He's a good-looking dude. He has a pretty wife and ostensibly really sweet and charming kids. Who are not terribly guilty of anything. Yet."

But what's happening on the inside? Hard to say. "He cares if he gets his way," the high-level editor says. "It demonstrates that he's in charge. As far as what he really wants—what's his belief, at the core—I think he may have none. I don't know. He *probably* cares about Israel?"

Kamer believes he has one other animating principle: vengeance. "Donald is essentially Jared's adopted father. And Donald hasn't served time in federal prison for blackmailing his brother-in-law with a prostitute. But to understand the kind of Rasputinesque genesis of this character—it all comes from Charlie. There's a continued theme of enemies. Of revenge. Of us and them."

And that's why, Kamer says, that when he was employed at the *Observer*, "I literally had nightmares about Jared being this powerful. Like I'd wake up in the middle of a nightmare where he'd be the king of some place, some faraway distant land."

To Jared's credit—if there's one thing he *has* accomplished so far, it's outmaneuvering enemies. That list starts with Christie; continues on to the Reince Priebus–Sean Spicer axis; and is topped, most famously, with Bannon.

He has attained some kind of surface presence. As one anonymous White House official told the press, "When you complain about Gary [Cohn, the chief economic advisor] or Dina [Powell, the former deputy national security advisor], you're really complaining about Jared and what he's doing, because you're not able to complain about Jared around here." The criticism is allowed. Just not explicitly. Because appearances must be kept.

You can credit his survival entirely to the fact that he's technically family, and many have. But at least at one point, even the lawyers that Trump hired for the Russia probe suggested pushing Kushner out. Between his presence at the Trump Tower meeting with lawyer Natalia Veselnitskaya, who in June 2016 offered Don Jr. damaging information on Hillary implicitly on behalf of the Russian government, and his repeated failure to disclose contact with foreign officials, he was deemed too messy.

He went nowhere. So he must be doing something right. Because Bannon is gone. And Kushner still, technically, runs the Office of American Innovation.

In the summer of Trump's first year in office, a photo of Kushner at a forward operating base in Qayyarah, Iraq, speaking with a US military official made the rounds. The official, gesticulating seriously, is, as you would expect, in army fatigues. Kushner, listening with care, is also wearing what you'd expect: khakis, a blue oxford, a well-cut blazer. And all that is stuffed inside a tan bulletproof vest. Sharpie and duct tape have been used for a makeshift ID. The only bit of the ID showing in the photo reads "KUSH."

There's a world in which that photo is soberly, warmly received. Kushner has been charged with handling the Israel-Palestine portfolio. He is the American president's tacit liaison to the Middle East. Why wouldn't he be in Iraq, doing as much personal reconnaissance as possible? And sure, yes, it did look a bit silly, that outfit. But is it that wild for Kushner to want to protect himself with a bit of body armor over the civvies?

The world in which that photo is soberly, warmly received did exist, briefly. It was the one in which Kushner gets to pose on the cover of *Forbes* magazine, smiling as widely as humanly possible, his dimples shining obscenely. That's the world in which Kushner gets to keep his mouth shut until it's time to take credit.

But that world is not ours, not anymore. That photo was scratched into our retinas, and Kushner was roundly, savagely mocked for it.

He always wanted to leave us with an image. In the first year since entering the White House he spoke publicly twice, for a total run time of just over five minutes. The plan was to pop up, later on down the line, smile that smile, and gesture vaguely toward all that he had done. He never wanted to Rasputin anything. He just wanted to look the part.

CHAPTER THIRTEEN
The Alt-Right Rasputin

FOR YEARS, long before America knew his name, Steve Bannon had aspired to transmit his ideology through a candidate of his choosing. There was Sarah Palin, John McCain's former running partner; Jenny Beth Martin, the Tea Party personality; the senators Rand Paul and Ted Cruz; the celebrity neurosurgeon Ben Carson. It wasn't talked about much, but Bannon had had dalliances with them all. He courted them personally and endorsed them on the alt-right news platform, Breitbart.com. As Kurt Bardella, the former *Breitbart* spokesperson, once said, "Steve is, and has been, someone looking for a political figure to attach himself to." For Palin, he even made a glowing documentary (called, strangely enough, *The Undefeated*). If circumstances had been different, it could have been one of these people above whom Bannon rode into infamy. But it wasn't. Because in the end, along came Donald Trump.

Bannon's philosophy should not be underplayed. He believes America is fundamentally a Judeo-Christian country and that Islam is fundamentally a force of jihadist extremism, and he believes the two are destined for epic war. He is a nationalist and a hardliner and a true ideologue; it is at the very core of his being, the life force that animates him. But when it comes to how to get his message across, he has been flexible. When you're actively aspiring to become a Rasputin, you have to be.

From the beginning of Bannon and Trump's doomed pairing, the fit was awkward. In private conversations, Bannon would say, "I don't know whether he really gets it." Eventually, publicly, Bannon would embrace his vessel, his instrument, in totality. "He's an expert in communications, in a much more sophisticated level than anybody I ever met," Bannon would say after washing out of the White House. "He is literally providential." Providential, as in opportune, or brought forth by God.

Bannon's celebrity arc is strange and inimitable. He was sixty-two years old when Trump named him campaign manager and launched him into national prominence. Before that, to most of the country, he was a nobody. He grew up with a large Irish family in Richmond, Virginia. Later, he'd dubiously claim, "I come from a black working-class neighborhood. I know what they want." He served for seven years in the Navy, got his MBA from Harvard, and spent years as an investment banker at Goldman Sachs. He has three kids and has been married and divorced three times; he's also a devout Catholic.

In the book *Bannon: Always the Rebel*, a fawning 2017 quickie biography, Bannon explains how he quit drinking cold turkey. It was 1998, and he'd enjoyed a rough few days of international bingeing. He was at Goldman at the time; he'd partied with clients in London the night before, then had pounded flutes of champagne and Bloody Marys on the flight back to L.A. In the fridge at his California beach home, a six-pack of St. Pauli Girl awaited. He says he opened the fridge, stared down the sixer, drank five of the beers, left the sixth— and then never drank again.

Since, he's maintained his sobriety with scripture-informed meditation based, in part, on a book called *Zen Catholicism*. Every day, once in the morning and once at night, he does the "examen," a spiritual exercise promoted by Saint Ignatius of Loyola, the sixteenth-century founder of the Jesuits. It helps one, Bannon says, to "become aware of the presence of God in your life."

In the 2000s, he reinvented himself as a filmmaker and started making low-budget conservative agitprop documentaries. One of his earliest appearances in the national media came in a *New*

York Times piece about the lesser-known conservative part of Hollywood. It is a splashy, auspiciously insane national-media debut:

> *"Look at Feb. 25, 2004—a watershed week for the Hollywood right," [Bannon] said in his Santa Monica office while scribbling a circle around the word "Lord" on his whiteboard. "On Ash Wednesday, 'The Passion of the Christ' is released theatrically, and on Sunday, 'Lord of the Rings'—a great Christian allegory—wins 11 Academy Awards. So here you have Sodom and Gomorrah bowing to the great Christian God, and did you guys notice? No, because 99 percent of the content in the media's sewage pipes is the culture of death."*

In 2004, a Bannon-directed documentary, *In the Face of Evil: Reagan's War in Word and Deed*, screened at small conservative-leaning film festival in Hollywood. After the screening, Andrew Breitbart—the eponymous founder of Breitbart.com, now deceased—excitedly rushed up to the filmmaker. As Bannon proudly recalls in *Always the Rebel*, "He squeezes me like a grape. He's a man's man, he grabs me like my head's going to blow. And he goes, 'You get it, culture's upriver from things. You're Leni Riefenstahl.'" That'd be Riefenstahl, as in Hitler's favorite filmmaker and the darling of the Third Reich.

After Breitbart's death, Bannon would become Breitbart.com's new chief. Officially, his title was executive chair. In practice, he was the warlord. "I found him petrifying to work for," a Breitbart columnist would write. "He's like the eye of Sauron: He sees everything and exists on Diet Coke and no sleep." (This was intended as a cheeky compliment.) Bannon saw all as bloody carnage. Not the glory and valor of honorable war—like, Cormac McCarthy shit. In his lexicon, victories that Breitbart had ostensibly engineered, like John Boehner's 2015 resignation as speaker of the house, were "scalps."

It was while working as an on-air personality for Breitbart that Bannon first wooed Trump. In a series of radio interviews the two conducted before Trump hired Bannon, you can actually hear Trump being pulled in one direction or the other. After Trump's victory, the *Washington Post* would point to telling examples:

> *Bannon told Trump, "I know you're a student of military history." Then, he laid out a case for questioning the U.S. alliance with Turkey, a member of NATO since the 1950s.*
>
> *Wasn't it true, Bannon asked, that the situation was a bit like the web of treaties that connected European countries before World War I?*
>
> *"People were locked into these treaties. . . . It led to the beginning of the bloodiest century in mankind's history," Bannon said. He said that Turkey had changed since it joined NATO, turning to Islamism under President Recep Tayyip Erdoğan. What if Turkey was drawn into a broader conflict in Syria, perhaps with Russia?*

By the end of Bannon's spiel, Trump was happily nodding along: "This is not something, Steve, that you want to end up in World War III over."

In *Always the Rebel*, Bannon boasts how, exactly, he'd created the victorious version of Trump. When Bannon came in, Trump's deficit in the polls was around 15 or 16 points. Bannon fine-sliced that deficit: Trump's approval among Republicans was in the 70s; they needed to get that to the 90s. So he said, "Put enough Republican stuff in there about the courts," meaning promises to fill federal court vacancies up to the Supreme Court, with conservative judges. Dry, down-the-line, relatively uncontroversial stuff—the kind of stuff Bannon didn't really care about. "Put all that stuff that they would say, 'Hey, Donald Trump's terrible, but he's not Hillary—give people permission to vote for Trump."

"On trade, on China, on the military—basically, he already had pretty well-formed his mind," Bannon says. "Already, America First. Now, on the social issues and immigration"—there, in Bannon's estimation, Trump was not hardline enough. And so when he took over the campaign, Bannon says, he made sure to pull Trump along into his own extremist views.

WHEN BANNON WAS fired as White House senior advisor in August 2017, it was a blow to his nationalist base and a boon to those repulsed by his virulent anti-immigration worldview. It was also, in a way, the end of a golden era for the Trump administration. Because no one did more than Bannon to imbue the Trump White House with its all-consuming backstabby paranoia.

His wars for Trump's attention with Jared and Ivanka—"Javanka," as he christened them—are legendary. They were also deeply fucked up. One of his go-to moves was to outflank Kushner on the Israel issue—to be more hardline than the proudly, devoutly Jewish son-in-law. According to Michael Wolff's *Fire and Fury*, "Bannon could bait Jews—globalist, cosmopolitan, liberal Jews like Kushner—because the farther right you were, the more correct you were on Israel . . . For Kushner, Bannon's right-wing defense of Israel, embraced by Trump, somehow became a jiu jitsu piece of anti-Semitism aimed directly at him. Bannon seemed determined to make Kushner appear weak and inadequate—a cuck, in alt-right speak."

But Bannon's wars went everywhere in the administration. Some battles were obscure: He bragged about pushing out a publicly little-known State Department employee named Susan Thornton that he deemed soft on China. (It never happened.) Some were high-profile: He took to dismissing National Security Adviser H. R. McMaster as the leader of a "globalist empire project." (McMaster survived him by seven months.) He also reportedly tried to undermine the hiring of Anthony Scaramucci before it happened, afraid that Scaramucci's casually friendly relationship with Trump would imperil his own chumminess with Donald. (Once in the job, Scaramucci undermined himself perfectly well on his own.)

There *were* moments when Bannon's war-all-of-the-time mentality seemed to serve him well in the administration. It quickly became clear that what Trump valued above all was blind fealty. And who better to respect a chain of command than Steve Bannon? As Ken Cuccinelli, the president of the Senate Conservatives Fund, once put it, "If the whole White House is backed up against the wall facing a firing squad, Steve will stay there. The other guys will run."

As Robert Mueller's investigation was first ramping up, Bannon relished the fight. He wanted to establish a War Room chock full of advisors just as pugnacious as him. That inchoate War Room even had a colorful catchphrase nicked from *The Godfather,* meaning, more or less, get ready to fight: "Go to the mattresses." But the War Room never actually came to be.

That's how it happened, again and again: Bannon would flit in and out of relevance, his efficacy constantly hitting brick walls. Bannon took credit for convincing Trump to pull out of the Paris Agreement. But in the months after the decision was made, the *New Yorker* reported that Bannon knew Trump was already leaning toward pulling out of Paris—and that his big strategy for securing the decision was *not speaking to Trump* for the three days before the announcement was officially made.

There *were* public moments when Bannon's puppeteering revealed itself clearly. Trump's infamous inauguration speech— grand talk of American carnage—seemed spilled right out of a Bannon fever dream. When Trump spoke in Warsaw in the summer of 2017, Bannon's voice again appeared to echo through him: "Heroes remind us that the West was saved with the blood of patriots,"

Trump bellowed, "that each generation must rise up and play their part in its defense, and that every foot of ground, and every last inch of civilization, is worth defending with your life." (An aside: The official White House transcript of the speech would make sure to note, six separate times, that the Warsaw audience broke into chants of "Donald Trump! Donald Trump!")

The Warsaw speech is a minor moment in the history of the Trump administration. But it has wide and telling overtures. A populist firebrand for proud xenophobes—a bogeyman for the left—how *did* Bannon manage to worm his way into the grand imagination of a nation?

His greatest trick? Seeing the world as constantly nearing the breakout of apocalyptic war. For Bannon, the barbarians are permanently at the gates.

His former news organ, Breitbart, does all it can to portray a world beset by bloodlusting foreign hordes. So who will save us? Someone that understands. Bannon can explain exactly why all this chaos is happening—he can do so with pseudoscience and fringe sociologists and long-ago-discredited historians from his vast archives. Nary a Bannon profile doesn't mention how crazily well-read the man is; a handful of articles have tracked the specific strange texts on which he's built his ideology. Dedicated Bannon watchers know them by heart: *The Fourth Turning*, from Neil Howe and William Strauss; the writings of the far-right-beloved philosopher René Guénon; *The Camp of the Saints*, a 1973 novel that imagines France embroiled in a race war triggered by the arrival of an armada of Indian immigrants. (An English translation bills it as "a chilling novel about the end of the white world.")

So he can tick off battles from the Punic Wars and passionately rattle on about bonkers historical theories and tell you, with certainty, that *this* moment in time is just like this *other* moment in time, where Carthage was on the rampage and nearly all was lost for

Rome. Yes, he can just about *convince* you that the world is ending and that there is only one path for salvation—and it is to listen to Steve Bannon. You can see why that'd be so appealing to nativists, to have their distrust of foreigners justified not as ignorance and small-mindedness, but as part of some predestined grand fight for the soul of their country. And you can see why it'd be so frightening to lefties, to hear a race-baiting nationalist suggest that he alone understands our historical course, and that he alone can affect it.

It's simple fear-mongering on an epic historical scale. But to credit Bannon with any actual, unique insight into our modern condition—let alone actual pull—is foolish. As a fictional character, the hyper-referential, juiced up, raving, and blustering Bannon is a strange delight. As a real-life strategist, he's a thin joke.

ONE OF BANNON'S most infamous moments of influence came in the wake of the 2017 white supremacist riot in Charlottesville in which Heather Heyer, a thirty-two-year-old antifascist protestor, was run over and killed. At the corresponding Trump Tower press conference, Trump famously declared that "both sides" were at fault for the violence. It quickly surfaced that Bannon had been a vociferous supporter of this extremist tack. Even better for Steve: Kushner himself had lobbied Trump to retract or modify the comments and had heard back, "Forget it."

But Charlottesville was the beginning of the end. Every time Bannon was hailed as "the Great Manipulator"—*Time* magazine, February 2017—we'd hear how angry this made Trump. Internally, Bannon was suspected of self-aggrandizing leaks about how he was winning the war on the direction of the administration. Reince Priebus once told him, "You've got to get people to stop writing this shit—people know it's you."

The publication of reporter Joshua Green's *Devil's Bargain*, about Bannon and Trump's relationship, pushed the situation into the red. Anti-Bannon forces knew Trump hated the book—that he couldn't stand the attention Bannon was getting. So they mentioned the book every chance they could.

To the *New York Post*, Trump would say, "I like Steve, but you have to remember, he was not involved in my campaign until very late. I had already beaten all the senators and all the governors, and I didn't know Steve. I'm my own strategist." In a subtweet, he'd add, "I love reading about all of the 'geniuses' who were so instrumental in my election success. Problem is, most don't exist. #Fake News! MAGA . . ."

Unbeknownst to the public, Bannon had preemptively submitted his resignation a few weeks before Charlottesville. He'd read the writing on the wall. Days after Charlottesville, the resignation was accepted. He was officially out. It had all ended as everyone had predicted it would. Trump got sick of hearing about Bannon's shadowy control.

In the spring of 2017, when Bannon's grand Rasputin project was still on track, he took a photo with Rabbi Shmuley (he of *Kosher Sex* fame) that the good *rebbe* then posted on Twitter. "With @SteveBannon in the White House," it read. "Steve is a great, stalwart friend of the Jewish State." Behind the two smiling men was a whiteboard crammed full of small, ominous text. It read things like "Build the border wall" and "Cancel all federal funding to sanctuary cities" and "Suspend the Syrian Refugee Program." Next to the items deemed completed, there were big, proud checks. This was Bannon's master plan.

In the summer 2017, when Bannon left the White House, the whiteboard was left behind in storage. There'd be no more items to check.

Bannon's immediate pose was of fiery defiance. In his one-note style, he declared "war" on the establishment Republican party and told anyone who'd listen he had his hands back on his "weapons." "I was just a staffer, and I'm not a good staffer," he told *Vanity Fair*. "I had influence, I had a lot of influence, but just influence." Now, "I have power." On *60 Minutes*, he boasted, "the media image is accurate—I'm a street fighter." His elemental purpose was to "support Donald Trump," to "make sure his enemies know there's no free shot on goal." Of his role in the Trump orbit by the end of his White House tenure, he insisted, "I had the same influence on the president as I had on day one."

For a few weeks there, it seemed like perhaps Bannon was right. Reports out of the White House were that Trump, true to form, was still sneaking late-night phone calls to Bannon. Meanwhile, Bannon claimed victory while propping up the far-right Alabama Senate candidate Roy Moore, who defeated the incumbent Luther Strange in the Republican primaries. Moore was supposed to be the cusp of a wave. After him would come scores of Bannon- and Breitbart-supported candidates—unconventional names baptized in the fiery lake of #MAGA. They would be on Capitol Hill first and foremost to swear undying allegiance to Trump and his agenda. And they would be Bannon's people. Their puppet strings would be firmly in his hands.

Eventually Moore was outed as an ephebophile at best, a sexual abuser at worst. But Bannon stuck with him. In one last campaign rally—held in a barn and co-headlined by a former *Duck Dynasty* cast member—Bannon trotted out his old populist bits.

Mainstream DC thinks you're "a pack of morons," he told the Moore supporters. "They think you're nothing but rubes. They have no interest at all in what you have to say, what you have to think or what you want to do. And tomorrow, you're gonna get an opportunity to tell them what you think of the elites who run this country!"

The next day Bannon watched Moore lose Alabama, a staunchly red Senate seat, to the mild-mannered Democrat Doug Jones.

STEVEN BANNON'S DEATH knell was Michael Wolff's *Fire and Fury*, the blockbuster book on the first hundred days of the Trump administration. After its release in early January 2018, the veracity of much of Wolff's juicy unsourced reporting was doubted. In one representatively nutty section, Wolff claimed fact checkers for the *New Yorker* contacted Bannon directly to get a comment on Scaramucci's claim that he self-fellates.

But Bannon's quotes in the book were on the record. Bannon said Donald Trump Jr. and Jared Kushner's infamous 2016 mid-campaign Russia meeting at Trump Tower was "treasonous." He said, "They're going to crack Don Jr. like an egg on national TV."

Trump quickly released a statement on Bannon: "When he was fired, he not only lost his job, he lost his mind." Even worse for Bannon, he was gifted a sobriquet by Trump: "Sloppy Steve." Bannon then lost his benefactors, the deeply pocketed father-daughter donor team of Robert and Rebekah Mercer, and his position at Breitbart (in which Rebekah has a minority ownership stake). And against all known Trump World protocol, he released a quasi-mea culpa and a defense:

"I regret that my delay in responding to the inaccurate reporting regarding Don Jr. has diverted attention from the president's historical accomplishments in the first year of his presidency—I am the only person to date to conduct a global effort to preach the message of Trump and Trumpism; and remain ready to stand in the breach for this president's efforts to make America great again."

It was too late. Bannon had blinked. He apologized. He explained.

As the drama was unfolding, Trump sent senior advisor Stephen Miller on CNN, where Miller duly eviscerated Bannon: "It's tragic and unfortunate that Steve would make these grotesque comments so out of touch with reality and obviously so vindictive."

Bannon and Miller were extremely close once. And they were perfectly ideologically aligned. According to one Breitbart employee, their partnership was a "sponsor-client relationship from what I can tell, or mentor-mentee." Of Miller, Bannon had said, "You could not get where we are today with this movement if it didn't have a center of gravity that was intellectually coherent . . . and Stephen Miller was at the cutting edge of that."

Inside the chaotic Trump White House, Miller had actually proved uncommonly disciplined. He was obsessed with one thing—fighting immigration into the United States—and he worked diligently to execute his vision. In one of his most infamous moments, he seemingly helped quash a Department of Health and Human Services study that indicated, according to the *Times*, that refugees brought in $63 billion more in government revenues over the past decade than they cost. The information wasn't helpful for Miller's mission. And so the information died.

The harsh truth was that for all of its dysfunction, the Trump administration had succeeded in closing border doors. For one, by its second year, the administration had capped annual refugee admittance at 30,000, a record low, and a far smaller number than the 110,000 the Obama administration had accepted in its last year in office. At one point, speaking of American immigration policy, Miller boasted, "We have taken a giant steamliner barreling full speed, slowed it, stopped it, begun to turn it around, and started sailing in the other direction." He was being creepily, gleefully hyperbolic. But he wasn't necessarily wrong.

Bannon's tenure would prove to be more impactful than originally imagined. The original travel ban, the policy move he was most closely associated with, sputtered through a series of legal challenges on its way to the Supreme Court. In June of 2018, the Supreme Court upheld it. Around the same time, Trump began rolling out one of Bannon's most treasured strategies: a trade war with China.

And in a way, Bannon could take credit for Miller's machinations, too. Leaving a man behind to advance his hardline anti-immigration plans—*that* was influence. But that man Bannon left behind then went on national TV to excommunicate the grand Rasputin. So that was it—the last gasp of Bannon's Rasputinism.

The lessons are simple: Don't self-promote. If you're too well-known, you're doing it wrong. It's Rasputin Rule #5 he's breaking: "They must operate from behind the scenes." It's supposed to be *shadowy* control. Stay in the damn shadows.

Bannon never really got it. Even after leaving the White House, according to reporters who visited his home in DC (what had once been known as the Breitbart Embassy), there were copies of *Devil's Bargain*—the book that had so angered Trump—piled up for perusal.

All in all, depending on how you count, the run had lasted roughly sixteen months. Trump hired Bannon in August of 2016. They won the White House together a few months later. By August of 2017, he was back out in the wilderness with his "weapons." By January of 2018, he was excommunicated from Trump World altogether. As his ties to American politics frayed, he increasingly went abroad. In search of relevance, he popped up with proud nationalists in power in Italy and budding president-demagogues in Brazil. But he was little more than a far-right gadfly. It was, to be sure, a remarkable chain of events. For his whole life he was a well-paid obscurity. In his early sixties, he became, for some, a national nightmare, and, for others, a salvation. We believed he had the power to change the country. And then, poof. It was all gone.

At the end, he was a joke. In the wake of his downfall, the satire site Clickhole summed it up nicely: "A Master Strategist: Steve Bannon Has Completed His Yearlong Plan to Become Increasingly Irrelevant before Eventually Getting Fired."

CHAPTER FOURTEEN
Obama's Rasputins

DAN PFEIFFER FIRST BEGAN WORKING for Barack Obama in 2007, during the Illinois senator's longshot presidential campaign. He'd stay with the president for nearly two full terms, first as communications director, then as senior advisor.

"The President gets inaugurated and you get on a bus and they drive you to the White House and you wander the hallways until you find a desk with your name on it," Pfeiffer recalls, of those early, early days. "12:01, *you're* in charge. It's hard to have great conviction about whatever course of action you're recommending—you just discovered where the bathroom was two minutes ago. You really do feel the weight of where you are. When you're working on a campaign, the stakes seem really high. And they are! But it's really hard to start a war or crash the markets. And you can do that in the White House by saying the wrong thing. You can pretend you're super cool. But the Oval Office is the Oval Office."

Those first six months, Pfeiffer says, were a blur—no one *really* knew what the hell was happening. Nonetheless, some insisted on playing the part. "People would go in and speak with *great* confidence. And Obama, he could tell if you were . . . *overcompensating*." From those early days, the tone was set for the rest of the Obama administration: There wouldn't be any playing around with the facts. "You'd have to give your best advice while knowing what you really don't know."

Briefings were not the Trumpian "diagrams and pictures"— Obama would want "all the information." He liked to whip the room up into a debate club. "This is the former *Harvard Law Review* president in him—the bulk of the team of advisors would be advising Course A, and he'd argue Course B," says Pfeiffer. "In his mind, what he was doing was pressure-testing the preferred position. But if you don't know that, you could leave confused. Sometimes people would leave meetings *very* worried he'd do something crazy."

Obama would "seek out dissent—the higher the stakes, the more he wants dissent. I have known him to invite people to meetings in particular because he knew they'd disagree with where this was going. Sometimes he'd invite the smartest people who would not otherwise, based on pure rank, have the have status to be in that room."

Pfeiffer adds that the president was also testing his advisors: "If you hear Obama making the case for Course B and then you flip to Course B, he'd take a mental note of that." And pretty much no one could get away with staying neutral. "There's something called 'backbenching.' You're in the Roosevelt Room, and the deputies for the cabinet heads are sitting in a back row. Obama is famous for calling on the people who are backbenching. And you better have something to say when you get called." Again, it's "law school—you can get called on at any moment."

With all that sparring, would it get testy? "I mean, people would get perturbed at each other," Pfeiffer says. "Sometimes he'd get perturbed at us. But Obama has a calm demeanor, and he expects that from people around him. He likes people calm and collected."

For all of Obama's internal pushback, word of dissension rarely spread. As the Israeli newspaper *Haaretz* has reported publicly, there were only a few "key moments when Barack Obama took important decisions against the advice of his most senior advisers." One came in February 2011: In the wake of early Arab Spring protests, Obama decided to push Egypt's Hosni Mubarak to resign. The other came in September 2013, when, after Syria's totalitarian leader Bashar Assad used chemical weapons, Obama decided not to seek reprisal.

I ask Pfeiffer if Obama had vulnerabilities. Was there something you could do to push forth *some* kind of manipulation? Well . . . among the closest advisors, Pfeiffer admits he had *one* small advantage to get Obama to pay attention. I lean in, more than a bit intrigued.

"I was always the one to do his interview and press conference prep, so I had the best sense of his body clock. I knew the cues. 'OK, he's gonna give us four more minutes before he moves on to something else.' So you wanna be able to say, 'Here are the three things—one, two, three.' To speak in a clear, linear sense that doesn't go on and on." Hmm. *Speak clearly and he'll probably listen.* Not quite a sharp yank of the puppet strings.

WILLIAM J. ANTHOLIS is a presidential historian and the director of the University of Virginia's Miller Center. In the history of the American presidency, he says, the concept of the overly influential aide goes all the way back to the beginning. "You can certainly play out Alexander Hamilton"—the iconic, hyperactive, and doomed Secretary of the Treasury—"as George Washington's Rasputin. But you can also play him out as the kind of wise counselor that any leader needs."

Hamilton was a visionary; he created the precedent for what an ambitious White House advisor could be. No one would quite achieve his renown. But many in his vein would come close. The most famous to date are Henry Kissinger, Richard Nixon's secretary of state, and Dick Cheney, George W. Bush's vice president. To link them is to dabble in an easy oversimplification: they were different men, acting in different eras. And Cheney's power in particular has been somewhat misunderstood—by Bush's second term, he'd been largely sidelined for more moderate voices like Condoleezza Rice's. But at his peak he did cajole Bush into the Iraq War, undoubtedly one of the greatest calamities ever engineered by a second-in-command. Watching him at his peak, the former Bush speechwriter David Frum once said, was like watching "iron filings move across a tabletop. You know there is a magnet down there. You know the magnet is moving. You never see the magnet."

What Dick and Henry had in common were explicit, well-defined worldviews and the steely, unblinking will to execute them. Not uncoincidentally, both would be accused of fomenting the worst in American warmongering. The backing of the murderous Pinochet regime in Chile; obstructionism in early Vietnam War peace talks; the mass bombing of Cambodia: Kissinger's crimes are almost too manifold to enumerate.

But beyond Cheney and Kissinger, there are many ex–White Housers in the Rasputin mold. Antholis easily rattles them off. "Harry Truman had John Steelman. LBJ had Marvin Watson. James Baker and Michael Deaver, they were a sort of tag-team Rasputin for Reagan. FDR had Eleanor Roosevelt." And then there's the former First Lady, Hillary Clinton, a fierce political force in her own right. Her input wasn't always desired, Antholis says, but the people in Bill Clinton's White House "just had to get used to the fact that this is the last person he talked to at night and the first person he talked to in the morning."

Then Antholis reminds me of a deeper cut from Clinton World: the ignominious tale of the consultant Dick Morris.

"Morris," Antholis says, "was the evil whisperer. As the story goes, Clinton would be going about his business during the day and Morris, at night, out of the formal chain of command, would fax him a memo—this was back in the days of the fax machine—and Clinton would change course." In September of 1996, an issue of *Time* magazine featured Morris superimposed on Clinton's right shoulder. The headline read "The Man Who Has Clinton's Ear." Underneath the headline, the cover read, "An exclusive look at the elusive Dick Morris and how he helps the President define himself."

In the article, one of Morris's former media consultant buddies says, "He's like a cult leader. The client has to get in there, drink the Kool-Aid, and look him in the eye, get the whole mystical connection going." According to *Time*, he was "Clinton's secret agent, bypassing the hierarchy and talking privately with the President on the phone and after hours . . . for a while he was known only as Charlie—so named by Clinton—the unseen force that hijacked speeches and made policies change course."

And then, just days after his *Time* issue dropped, Morris would be embroiled in a scandal that sidelined his career. Antholis recalls: "Morris ends up getting caught with a prostitute at the Jefferson Hotel! Up the street from the White House!"

In an exclusive report from the tabloid *Star*, a sex worker named Sherry Rowlands recounted how she'd meet Morris nearly weekly, and how at times during their trysts he'd volunteer confidential information like how NASA had discovered evidence of life on Mars. (Sherry also mentioned that Dick liked to suck toes). And so the very next week, he was back on the cover of *Time*. This time the headline read, "After the Fall."

There was no direct evidence that one of Morris's many political enemies had engineered the scandal. But there was a sense that Morris's love of the spotlight (and, yes, right, of course—of extramarital affairs with verbose sex workers) had led to his demise. As the *Time* article succinctly puts it, "The rule among campaign consultants is 'Don't put your head above the bunker.'" Morris was soon out of the Clinton administration. His days as a Rasputin were over.

It's just one story out of scores regarding White House aides who, at least for a little while, dominated and domineered the presidents they were meant to serve. At the Miller Center, Antholis is overseeing an ongoing presidential study called the First Year Project. "We're studying how presidents staff up their office," Antholis explains. "And sometimes the big personnel mistakes are in hiring, you know, rock stars, white knights—people who are visible, who are public. What you really need is a quiet person behind the scenes who knows the president's mind and has their back. The most successful aides shared a vision with the president of where they wanted the administration to go."

And always, Antholis points out, "When there were presidents that didn't have a vision, someone provided one for them."

THROUGH EIGHT YEARS, no one ever quite rose to the role of Obama's Rasputin.

The phrase *was* thrown around here and there. Sometimes it was character assassination; one article from the conservative publication *National Review* pointed to former Obama advisor Valerie Jarrett, stating she "appears to exercise such extraordinary influence she is sometimes quietly referred to as 'Rasputin' on Capitol Hill, a reference to the mystical monk who held sway over Russia's Tsar Nicholas." Sometimes it was a nerdy joke; on NPR's "Wait Wait . . . Don't Tell Me!" David Axelrod, Obama's former campaign strategist, was jokingly called "the Rasputin in this kingdom." But in the larger, popular imagination, no Obama employee rose to the role of true, proper Rasputin.

I ask Pfeiffer why. He points to Obama's devotion to rigorous, sober information analysis and reminds me it's the kind of thing that prevents manipulation pretty well. He adds one more reason: "You'd have to engage in a fair amount of self-promotion to become that person, and that was frowned upon. If you were that kind of person, you wouldn't last in our world. Those people"—the would-be Rasputins—"are drama. They wouldn't even make it to the hiring process."

I ask Pfeiffer why he thought there'd been so *many* would-be Trump Rasputins. "When I was leaving the White House, I said I was gonna avoid being critical of future White House staff, because it's a really hard job," Pfeiffer answers. He pauses. "I have failed."

In Pfeiffer's view, the White House staff—"every one of them"— knows Trump is "dangerously unfit for the job, and they are aiding and abetting him in that. And that's why everything leaks— they are trading on it to try to increase their celebrity, their earning potential in the market. We liked each other, and we cared about Obama more than we cared about Maggie Haberman"—the *New York Times*'s ace White House reporter—"thinking we were cool."

"These people are all out protecting their own brand. The transgender thing happens"—Trump's since-scuttled announcement banning transgender servicepeople—"and there are seventy-five stories that Jared and Ivanka didn't support that just so everyone in New York knows and so they'll still be invited to cocktail parties or whatever. Steve Bannon—he's good at creating the legacy of Steve Bannon. But he was a guy who was running a mediocre media property out of the basement of his house a few years ago. I am not persuaded he is some genius of American politics."

Pfeiffer is dismissive of the powers of Kushner and Bannon directly, but he's also dismissive of the very idea of the powerful aide. "I think we overstate the role of people like myself or David Axelrod or Steve Bannon," he says. "These aides, these consiglieres, these Rasputins if you will. The thing that matters is the president."

That has been more true at times than others. Interestingly enough, it seems to be quite true for both Trump and Obama. Obama fended off the rise of Rasputins with rigor and discipline. No one man or woman was given the last word, no man or woman was given undue sway. The only thing that mattered was the idea.

With Trump, it's more counterintuitive: It is precisely *because* he seems to prone to manipulation that he has not fallen under any one manipulator. There have just been far too many aspiring to the role. And whether inside or outside of the Trump White House, inside or outside his own family, where they've all ended up is in the same big, sweaty pit, fighting each other to the death. Just as you climb up to the lip of the pit, toward safety, someone is ready to drag you back down.

Christopher Ruddy is the CEO of Newsmax Media and one of Trump's old friends from his Florida country club, Mar-a-Lago. "I've never known Donald Trump to have one key advisor," Ruddy tells me. "I mean even Roger Stone, Sam Nunberg—they had close relationships, they had influence. But with Trump, he's very open to ideas. He's eclectic in his ideas. He has business associates, childhood friends, political people that he listens to. He's just constantly open. When I hear somebody has his ear over another, I take it with a grain of salt." It's a polite way of saying what his critics happily shout—Trump *is* utterly willing to be yanked forward by the last person he speaks to. But the key here, of course, is this—the last person he speaks to is constantly shifting.

In style, in demeanor, in ideology, Obama and Trump are on the far, far opposite ends of the spectrum. Strangely, though, they do have this one thing in common: They both appear immune to Rasputinism.

CHAPTER FIFTEEN
The Russian Rasputin

I'D EXPLORED POP MASTERMINDS, nefarious fiction editors, dogmatic film directors, and suspiciously powerful sports trainers. I'd heard about Rasputinism in the politics of DC and of Seoul. I'd learned the effects of the criminal and murderous Rasputins in Berlin and Syria and Tijuana. What I still wanted was to speak with a Rasputin who believes, just like *the* Rasputin, that he is sent by God. And so I needed to travel far.

I go to Moscow to meet the self-professed philosopher Aleksandr Dugin. It's nearly December, and a dome has been plopped down on the great city. Even in the hours of alleged daylight, there is nothing but shades of dull gunmetal gray. The Muscovites won't likely see real sun again until spring.

In the lobby of a heavy-stone building in central Moscow, I'm greeted by a friendly young woman in a pantsuit who, she explains, is working "in the field of geopolitics." She takes me to the security desk, where my passport is carefully, minutely inspected before I'm granted access. As we head upstairs the woman slowly whispers a joke: "This is what will save us from the terrorists."

We walk down a long, high hallway that looks or bare or unfinished or forgotten, like maybe someone was planning on shutting down this wing of the office but never got around to it. There are linoleum floors, cracking and peeling, and bits of mismatched tile in the style of sixties Americana. Rank-and-file office clerks shuffle through, and no one pays attention to a faint buzzing emanating from somewhere near.

We stop in front of a heavy wooden door. Inside is Dugin.

The man is an ideologue with a convoluted, bizarre, unsettling worldview. He believes the world is divided into two spheres of influence—sea powers, which he calls Eternal Carthage, and land powers, which he calls Eternal Rome. He believes it has always been so. Today, those spheres are represented by America, the Carthage, and Russia, the Rome. He believes that Carthage and Rome are locked in a forever war that will only end with the destruction of one or the other.

In Western media, he's become a dark character worthy of obsession. He quotes and upholds long-forgotten scholars with anti-Semitic leanings like Julius Evola, who critiqued Mussolini's Fascism for being too soft. (Evola is a deep-cut favorite of Steve Bannon's as well.) He's been linked with ultra-right movements internationally, from supporters of Marine Le Pen in France to supporters of Viktor Orbán in Hungary. Some read his writings hoping to suss out some linchpin of Russian domestic and foreign policy.

As the Russian American journalist Masha Gessen wrote in *The Future Is History*, her celebrated 2017 examination of modern Russia, "Dugin enjoyed a period of international fame of sorts as a Putin whisperer—some believed he was the mastermind behind Putin's wars." Others called him "Putin's brain," or even "Putin's Rasputin."

He sits at a plain desk, thick texts piled up in the bookcases behind him. His hair is brown and streaked with gray and parted floppily down the middle. He wears a dark-blue suit, no tie, and a lightly pinstriped shirt. There is a mole just to the left of his nose. His lips are buried in a big, bushy gray beard that, as *Bloomberg* once happily noted, "gives him a passing resemblance to the Siberian mystic who bewitched the last Tsar's family."

As the manifesto from one of the many political organizations he'd founded over the years once put it, Dugin's worldview is "built on the total and radical negation of the individual and his centrality." As one of his young followers once said, "Obedience and love for one's leaders are traits of the Russian people." And as Dugin himself once said, "There is nothing universal about universal human rights."

From the second I walk in the door, he is locked and ready to engage. "Western Christianity and Western modernity and Western global elites try to oppose artificial intellect over the natural human liberty—that is a kind of a doom of the West that we rejected always." He speaks in entrancingly accented, rapid English full of strange, unlikely phrasings rooted equally in the language of academia and his own far-flung and oblique obsessions—the occult, black magic, the hidden forces of history. He's also really hung up on the West's promotion of artificial intelligence. (Looking back now, I like to imagine that he was trying to tell me, if I'd only listened, that Skynet—the evil sentient world-destroying computer network from the *Terminator* series—was real.) If I let him, he'll go on all day.

But I'm not here to get the stump speech, the full spiel. I want to know: How has he spread his message? How has he infected President Vladimir Putin—and Russia at large—with this worldview?

THIS BOOK HAS been filled with those who influence and control and do not shout about it. Many take credit, but only to a point. Many do not want their control to be clearly explicated because they do not want it to be perceived as unseemly; it would compromise the efficacy of their project. Gordon Lish only claimed Raymond Carver after his work with him was done. Alex Guerrero is careful not to boast too openly about Tom Brady's devotion. But Aleksandr Dugin believes his influence is of a divine kind. And so he happily accepts the accusation of influence.

When I first ask him the question on influence he cuts me off, brusquely. I worry at first he's going to end this conversation prematurely. Instead, he immediately monologues on the topic; it turns out he was cutting me off so that he could get to his turn to speak faster. "I could recognize that I am responsible for imposing my world vision over others," he tells me. "And what excuse do I have for that? My excuse precisely exists in my own philosophy. I am not creator of the thought. It is a kind of angelic or demonic dialect that I'm involved in. I am but transmitter of some objective knowledge that exists outside of myself—*beyond* myself."

The arc of Dugin's life has been unlikely. In the eighties, he was an obscure, mild anti-Soviet dissident. In 1983, USSR authorities noted the trifling incident of Dugin playing the guitar at a party and singing what were, in his own words, "mystical anti-Communist songs." He was deemed a real threat by no one. But in the nineties, after the fall of the USSR, he became a national figure.

His writings began to gain currency, primarily his major work, *The Foundations of Geopolitics*, which became particularly popular with military elites. In 1993, he hosted the television program *The Mysticism of the Third Reich*, during which, as Gessen writes, he "hinted at a Western conspiracy to conceal the true nature of Hitler's power."

In *The Future Is History*, Gessen charts the rest of Dugin's rise. How Moscow State University's sociology department brought Dugin on board, implicitly legitimizing his theories with an elite institution's stamp of approval. How every one of Russia's national and international crises seemed to bolster him further.

In the summer of 2008, Russia invaded neighboring Georgia. Ostensibly, they were supporting South Ossetia and Abkhazia, two Russian-leaning Georgian enclaves with long-held dreams of independence. Effectively, Russia had invaded a sovereign state. For years, government officials had been issuing Russian passports to Abkhazians and South Ossetians; now Russian forces had advanced deep into Georgian territory. This was the real deal, the

Dugin-encouraged expansionist destiny. Russia once again had its guns cocked.

Dugin shined. Photos of him in South Ossetia circled. He stood in front of a tank, an AK-47 in his hands. As Gessen writes, that summer also "marked the first time he had seen one of his slogans catch on and go entirely mainstream, repeated on television and reproduced on bumper stickers. The slogan was *Tanks to Tbilisi*," the Georgian capital. "Dugin had written 'those who do not support the slogan are not Russians. *Tanks to Tbilisi* should be written on every Russian's forehead.'"

From 2011 to 2013, the "snow revolution"—a series of peaceful protests against Russian election fraud—burbled in Moscow. The Russian government's position was that the activists were paid agitators being supported by the US State Department. (As Putin declared in the early stages of the protests, "We are all grownups here. We all understand the organisers are acting according to a well-known scenario and in their own mercenary political interests.") In the winter of 2013, Dugin spoke at a massive government-organized counter-protest in front of a crowd of tens of thousands.

"Dear Russian people! The global American empire strives to bring all countries of the world under its control," he bellowed. "To resist this most serious threat, we must be united and mobilized! We must remember that we are Russian! That for thousands of years we protected our freedom and independence. We have spilled seas of blood, our own and other peoples, to make Russia great. And Russia will be great! Otherwise it will not exist at all. Russia is everything! All else is nothing!"

Internally, Putin answered the snow revolution with a crackdown. Externally, he answered with a show of force.

In 2014, again ostensibly answering the call of popular will, so-called "little green men"—Russian soldiers with no identifying insignias—took over the Crimean peninsula in the name of the Russian government. Crimea was a quasi-independent entity of Ukraine with a prominent ethnically Russian population. In the eyes of the international community, it was a brazenly illegal act. Once again, Russia was practicing expansionism.

Dugin was overjoyed. He had been pushing for a Crimean takeover since the nineties. He believed that it was just the beginning. Russia should go further and co-opt Eastern Ukraine (the traditionally Russian-speaking half of the country) as well. But for now, it augured great things. He saw it as a bolstering of the Russian sphere of influence. Eternal Rome was again strengthening itself.

During one major televised interview, Putin explained the Crimean invasion by saying "a Russian person—or to speak more broadly, a person of the Russian World—thinks about the fact that man has a moral purpose. These are the deep roots of our patriotism. This is where mass heroism comes from in war."

Now even Dugin's literal phrasings were being echoed back to him. As Gessen writes, "The phrase 'Russian World'—the vision of a civilization led by Russia—was Dugin's." This was, effectively, the real-life execution of Dugin's worldview.

Dugin did not talk to Gessen for her book. Possibly, he was familiar with Gessen's place as an outspoken Putin critic and decided to stay away. I can only assume that Dugin agreed to an interview with me because he'd never heard of me before. I assume that he felt comfortable he would dominate the interaction.

"I BELIEVE IN ideas that could well exist without man," Dugin tells me. "Angels are ideas without bodies. I'm a believer. I believe in angels. I believe in God. I believe in Revelation. I'm Christian Orthodox. And for me, the existence of angels, as well as the existence of ideas, is the *fact* of experience—not only narrative."

As Dugin sees it, he has stayed put, espousing these ideas that were given to him by the Lord. It's the world that has moved around him. Sometimes it's drawn to him. Sometimes it's repulsed. "I put myself in the center of all the society of history. It's not ego-centric. It's completely opposed to egocentrism. I put myself in the center of the world by precisely *liberating* myself from the individual. It is some other in myself that is the center."

Are you following? He is at the center because his truth is the true truth. But he is also opposite the mainstream. He stands, alone, against a great force. "Mass media, education, politics, social relations, class, economy—that is society," he says. "It is mechani-calized. A kind of social mechanics."

Dugin, however, is part of something else—the "revolution-ary elite that is coming to replace the elite." He is counter-elite. And not only in Russia, but "on a global scale—I awaken these peoples. I'm awakening these collective consciousnesses. Using the term of Carl Gustav Jung, I transform these peoples from the sleeping mode to the waking mode. From the drunken mode to the sober mode."

(He really does say the whole name: "Carl Gustav Jung." In the course of our conversation, he also name-checks Vilfredo Pareto, Louis Dumont, Hegel, Heidegger, and Charles Krauthammer, almost always quoting them directly, almost always prefacing said quote with some variation of the phrase "In the words of . . .")

He goes on: "That is the operation that I am leading. My influ-ence is *very* special. I would say, a *revolutionary* kind. That is why I am called, by some American figures, the most dangerous man in the world. I would gladly accept that as labeled. I hope that it is true."

His power and influence, he says, are of a slippery kind. "We could not measure for example, who is more popular, Michael Jack-son or myself," he says, chuckling softly.

Because Michael Jackson, or pop music as a whole, exists in the mainstream—inside the traditional flow of information. And despite his history of television appearances, Dugin claims that "the traditional ways to promote ideas are completely closed" to him "and were closed from the very beginning." Therefore, "in order to exercise, to fulfill this influence, I am obliged to seek, to search new ways. So I'm a kind of a, *mmmm*, metaphysical hacker. I try to find the backdoors of the program of globalization in order to make it explode." His work, he says proudly, is a "a kind of terrorism."

And despite this self-perceived singular place in the center of history, he says, "I'm not lonely Russian stranger. I am the most Russian man that we could imagine. I am Russia spirit. I *am* Russia!"

In conversation, as he makes his points, Dugin's hands move constantly. Not just one or two swipes; it's a wild, unceasing symphony of gestures. He swings an open palm, slams fingertips straight down on the tabletop, points an index finger in the air and his other hand's middle finger straight down. The fingers and palms move in synchronicity and also alone, every single one on a mission. He interlocks and breaks apart and throws out his hands and brings them back together. Some of the moves he repeats. Some come just once. I begin to believe that if I stay here long enough, he'll keep inventing ways to emphatically gesticulate forever.

His is a kind of intimate, anti-charisma. I realize that it's the surety of his purpose that compels. As in so many other situations, pure, unadulterated bluster is carrying the day for Dugin.

"People like myself reflect the liberty of mankind. Man is an entity that always can choose. It can say *yes* to globalization and to this artificial intelligence, to the so-called progress, to the individualization—*yes* to the global agenda. But the man can say, 'No, *no*! It's *not* me!' And that is the salvation of mankind. We need to liberate everybody. We need a global revolution. And I am conscious that I am fulfilling this role."

I ASK DUGIN about a man he's friendly with, to whom he's often been compared: Steve Bannon. Is it correct? Are they some kind of analogs?

"As long as I understand Bannon, I think that the comparison could be legitimate," he says. "Bannon suggested to Trump how to find the backdoor in the system. Absolutely, to be a kind of revolutionary—not from the right or the left, but a revolutionary against this world." But "Bannon is a PR specialist dealing in ideology. I am a philosopher, trying to transmit through art, special art, my historical mission in front of Russian people.

"Maybe the difference exists precisely in the different nature of our societies. American society is much more based on public relations. Pragmatism. If something works, it is already accepted. Technical efficacy is much more appreciated than, for example, ideological coherence or truthfulness. In the political public relations, the propaganda is a means to trick people. I am not using ideology. I am used *by* ideology."

Dugin is skeptical that Bannon ever had the mandate to be a true, pure ideologue. He recalls Trump once, way back on the campaign trail, skewering Bannon for reading too much. "I think that you *cannot* read too much. If you understand the weight of ideas, this accusation is a proof of some limited mind."

Arguing his point, Dugin falls into a minor reverie. "So many beautiful texts!" he says. "So many profound authors and philosophers . . . so many languages! The real richness, the real treasury of human wisdom amassed is infinite. The only blame should be, you are reading not enough. If you always, reading, reading, reading, it's nothing at all. Everybody of us should read more. More and more! If you think you read enough, you're *wrong*! You don't read *nothing!*"

Before his fall from relevance, Bannon and Dugin did have interesting parallels. Like Bannon's now-squandered power, Dugin's lies in his ability to portray all world events as part of a plot he's already seen. The sheer grandiosity of his speech is calculated to overwhelm. *I know it all*, he insists again and again, until the listener either accepts him as ridiculous or sublime.

But Bannon never had Dugin's air of historicity. Intentionally or otherwise, Dugin has been able to cloak himself in dark mystery.

Perhaps Dugin would prefer an example closer to home, then—Grigori Rasputin?

He's not offended. Not in the slightest. Soberly, he analyzes the pairing.

"So. The figure of Rasputin is misunderstood. He had influence over our tsar, personal influence. He was against the modernization and Westernization. He was in favor of Russian people instead of the corrupted Russian elite." So far, more than a few points of overlap between Aleksandr and Grigori. Certainly, Dugin is Rasputinesque.

But! "Rasputin wasn't philosopher. He didn't conceptualize anything. He's a kind of hypnotizer, a kind of a trickster, something like that. So the comparison is a little bit limited. He built his influence on the personal charm and on his individual influence on the tsar. That was a very special case. This was person-to-person, without some ideology. Some philosophy."

Who, then, is a closer peer or antecedent? For an answer, Dugin has to go beyond contemporary politics, beyond Russian history— and into the realm of the fantastic. "I compare myself much more to Merlin." The great wizard Merlin, the mythical one, the son of an incubus. King Arthur's advisor. "The image of the intellectual that is engaged in supra-human contemplation, in the secrets, that tries to clear the way for the secular ruler to create the great empire.

"Merlin. The founder of King Arthur's empire. That is my archetype, I would say."

I ASK DUGIN, "What comes next?"

"Some of the ideas that I defended from the ages—they have won. They are accepted by the government and realized in the

Eurasian union and Russian foreign policy and military strategy. The anti-modern, anti-Western, anti-liberal shift of Russian politics and ideology has been realized."

But "the other half is not yet fulfilled. That is the problem. The second part of my ideas, of my projects, of my visions of the Russian future is still waiting. It is suspended, I would say. It waits it's own time."

The problem, says Dugin, is that Putin has not institutionalized the bits of Dugin that he's borrowed. The Dugin worldview has not reached the point of "irreversibility." Here, Dugin is critical of Putin: "He pretend to be the ruler, pragmatic and not controlled by nothing, including ideology. He pretend to be the absolute sovereign instead of being the sovereign fighting for the mission.

"It is a kind of simulacrum," he says. "It is a kind of imitation. It seems more and more that it is a kind of very dirty play. A game they try to hijack. The real tradition, the real conservatism—they try to use that as tools and means for their rule."

He's careful not to point fingers too directly. This is modern Russia, after all. "Maybe not Putin himself," he says, "but the people around Putin."

Fundamentally, Dugin's disappointment is that Putin did not go far enough. That he did not push past Crimea and into Ukraine with the Russian Army. That he is not creating a "Russian world" beyond the borders of modern Russia—that he's not birthing a new Russian empire. In Gessen's analysis, this revealed the true nature of Dugin's influence. Putin wasn't being manipulated by Dugin's ideology; Putin was borrowing it, for his own ends.

So was Dugin influential? Or was he a stooge? Again, that old question: Where does the Rasputin end and the Rasputin's subject begin? Where do Putin's own volitions end and where do Dugin's prophecies begin?

One neutral observer might observe that Dugin's dark influence was great once, but has waned now. Yet another might observe that it was always transactional.

But Dugin doesn't have to control Putin, only and directly, to have influence on the culture. Igor Vinogradov, the editor of the magazine *Kontinent*, once said of Dugin and his disciples, "They are undertaking a noisy galvanization of a reactionary utopia that failed long ago—for all their ineptitude, they are very dangerous. After all, the temptation of religious fundamentalism . . . is attractive to many desperate people who have lost their way in this chaos." That was in 1992. Since, Dugin has published endlessly and spread his missives incessantly. Both in English and in Russian, the Internet is rife with his manifestos.

Andreas Umlaund is a Ukrainian political scientist who has studied Dugin at length. Perhaps inevitably, Umlaund's research into Dugin made Umlaund a target. As he explained to me in an interview from his home in Ukraine, Dugin's minions write articles that allege that he is "an anti-Russian agent paid by the [US] State Department" and that he's been "kicked out of universities for [sexual] harassment." According to these reports, Umlaund says, "German officials were looking for me because I was involved in child pornography. Allegedly, I'm a pedophile!"

Umlaund's greatest sin, in Dugin's supporters eyes, was exposing Dugin's explicit Nazi leanings. "I digged out these old quotes where he praises the SS and Reinhard Heydrich, the original SS officer responsible for the organization of the Holocaust. And they didn't like that, because by that time Dugin had already become part of the Russian establishment. And these old quotes, from when he was still a lunatic fringe actor, were an embarrassment."

I ask Umlaund what it's like, being targeted as the number one nemesis of a man like Dugin. With historically informed equanimity, he shrugs it off. "This is not an unusual campaign," he says. "Also in Soviet times, they were using pedophilia allegations against dissidents and of political enemies. It's from the KGB playbook."

Umlaund has continued his work, writing that the explosion of Dugin content, which begins around 2001, "has become difficult to follow. The number of Dugin's appearances in the press, television, radio, World Wide Web, and various academic and political conferences has multiplied." Dugin's aim, Umlaund argues, is to "radically transform basic criteria of what constitutes science, what scholarly research is about, and to permit bodies of thought such as occultism, mysticism, esotericism, conspirology, etc. into higher education and scholarship that would bring down the borders between science and fiction."

There's a classic *Simpsons* episode that I love, "Homer vs. Lisa and the 8th Commandment." It's from 1990, the early golden era of the show. It starts off with Homer spotting Flanders fussily rejecting a cable guy's illegal, tantalizing offer: fifty dollars for bootleg cable. Sensibly, immediately, Homer drags the cable guy over to his own home and readily accepts. But as the man is finishing up his installation, Homer has a twinge of morality.

"So . . . this is OK, isn't it?" he asks. "I mean everybody does it, right?" Coolly, the cable man hands him a pamphlet full of justifications for his actions ("Fact: Cable companies are big faceless corporations"). The evocative title: "So You've Decided to Steal Cable."

It's a wild oversimplification, to be sure, but the danger of someone like Dugin (and Bannon before him) is wrapped up in that pamphlet. You *can* make someone hate. But it's easier to find someone who already hates, and to give them justification—historical, epic justification—for their hate. People naturally drift toward doing bad things. But they'd also love a pamphlet explaining why it's all OK.

AS *BLOOMBERG* HAS pointed out, in 2014, Dugin lost his place at the Moscow State University "after activists accused him of encouraging genocide. Thousands of people signed a petition calling for his removal after a rant in support of separatists in Ukraine in which he said, 'kill, kill, kill.'" But he no longer needed an institution like Moscow State to have influence—he'd already become a prominent enough member of the establishment on his own.

During his time in the center of Russian politics, while the vagaries of the real world turned, Dugin tended to the ur-mission. Now, perhaps, he's back on the outs of his country's mainstream political thought. But his words have left his mouth and have been received. And he will continue talking and talking because he is playing a long, long game. "Some things are being realized that I have foreseen and foretold thirty years ago," he tells me. "Now I am foretelling and foreseeing what should come in the future."

As Dugin sees it, "The most highest point of American influence as universal power is behind us. Because America tries to go beyond the normal and the natural borders and tries to influence Middle East, Africa, Eurasia—and fails everywhere. America export chaos, bloody chaos. Everywhere America is, there is corpses. They have turned into a nihilistic force. The real greatness of America is not in continuation of this exporting of this bloody chaos."

Dugin suggests that America ask itself some hard questions. Like "What is victory? What is glory? What is real highest position in history?"

Dugin's vision is clear: America for Americans, Russia for Russians. And while Russia builds itself back up, it stays a closed society. "Being weak, we should stay closed from any influence," he says. "From the West, from the East, from China or Islam or Europe or America or Africa, we should stay *closed*"—he bangs a fist on the table—"in order to return to our force."

Through an open window, gray daylight pours in. Behind us, two women walk back and forth, mugs of coffee in hand, consulting texts and each other. They, presumably, are in the "field of geopolitics" as well. Here, in this room, in this massive building, Dugin quietly plots Russia's revival and sends out his warnings to Russia's enemies. The grand project rolls on.

America, declares Dugin, must follow the way of Trump into cynical and callow isolationism and avoid its once-upon-a-time fate as a shining beacon on a hill. Otherwise, Carthage and Rome will do battle. "When the United States tries to be unique, to be universal, a norm for all humanity—that creates the basis for inevitable conflict," Dugin says. "Then the final war is inevitable."

CHAPTER SIXTEEN
The Real Rasputin Redux

I LEAVE MOSCOW and its high-rise cocktail lounges and high-end coffee chains and take a quiet train through a vast and snowy countryside. I arrive in St. Petersburg, the one-time seat of the fallen Romanov dynasty and the last home of Grigori Rasputin. The city is grand and old and absolutely littered with massive chunks of opulence. St. Isaac's Cathedral and its towering Corinthian columns. The Church of the Savior on Spilled Blood with its iconic Technicolor onion domes.

And all around that opulence, the modern world noisily clatters about. Men and women in fancy Tsarist-era costumes mug around the tourist sites posing for pictures—the St. Petersburg version of Times Square Elmos and SpongeBobs. Surly vendors push novelty coffee mugs, many of them featuring Trump and Putin, at least one of them featuring both, shirtless, co-riding a galloping horse, the words "Not Gonna Get Us" splashed lovingly behind them.

I take a bus out of town to Tsarskoe Selo, the "Tsar's Village," where the Catherine Palace sits, pristinely preserved. This was the favorite home of Nicholas and Alexandra; this was where they spent most of their time with their friend Rasputin. On the bus, a woman with bleach-blond hair and a strong fragrance of perfume and cigarettes sidles up next to me, happily making conversation. I try to explain where I'm from, what it is I'm doing, why I came here. But nothing quite makes it through the language barrier. Nothing makes sense.

Cheerily, she shrugs it off and offers me a swig of a water bottle full of bubbly beer. Her boyfriend, sitting to her right, is aghast at her impropriety; to demonstrate as much, he swings a balled-up fist into her side. Between the fact that the woman is swaddled in winter clothes and has seemingly downed a good bit of the aforementioned beer, the punch doesn't have much impact—she smiles and shrugs him off, too.

Upon arrival, I slide through the elegant, gilded halls of the palace with the mandatory booties on my shoes. I walk past crowds of screaming schoolchildren in tiny suit jackets and try, and fail, to imagine Rasputin here, tending to little, sickly Alexei Nikolaevich.

I walk out into the gardens and then push forward into a strange and denuded forest. It's not like this place needs anything else to make me feel like I'm in a creepy gothic fantasy, and especially not at this time of year, with the suffocating grayness enveloping us in full. But just for good measure, the only other person around is a woman pushing a rickety—possibly empty?!—baby stroller. She keeps pace twenty or so feet behind me, and I start to daydream that she has come here, to this nightmare forest, to murder me, possibly with the baby stroller.

Finally, I arrive at a clearing in the woods where a path of frozen dirt leads to a small semicircle of black, barren trees. Tucked into a base of rocks is a large wooden cross. It's fashioned in the Russian Orthodox style, and so features an additional horizontal crossbeam, slashed at a slight angle, across the bottom half of the vertical pole. At first glance, it appears as if a traditional Latin cross has been planted upside down.

According to legend, for a little while, this was the last resting place of Rasputin. As the story goes, after the revolution, Bolshevik soldiers came here, dug up the body, and burned it in secret, in hopes of eviscerating any sites of future homage. I try to think of something to say to him, something profound. I breathe deeply and sigh and ponder. I can't think of anything. Later, the Rasputin biographer Douglas Smith informs me that the cross is a Rasputin

memorial constructed by local admirers. Rasputin was actually
originally buried in a church built by Anna Vyrubova, one of his last
disciples. Smith himself "went out past the park to look for traces
of the original church, but nothing seems to have survived. It's now
an empty field."

Back in the city I go to a banya—one of Russia's famous communal spas, with its saunas and baths. Rasputin loved the banyas;
he'd spend hours there with his male and female followers. Before
hitting the facilities, I sit in a fluffy white towel in a wide, central
lounge with high ceilings and dark wood benches and framed photos of Dolph Lundgren. I order what everyone else appears to be
having, which is beer and a small dried fish called smelt. As I sit,
pointlessly struggling with the smelt's tough, rubbery skin, my
friend on the adjacent bench takes notice and intervenes to help. His
name is Alexei, and he is a big, ruddy-faced man in his early forties.

First he says a few words in Russian to the waiter, who takes
the smelt away, to my sadness. I hadn't given up yet. Alexei suggest a different dish: "You should try horse sausage." I insist on the
smelt and it returns but, at Alexei's doing, chopped up for more con-
venient consumption, and with an accompaniment of thick black
bread. The smelt, it turns out, is delicious.

I chat with Alexei for a while, drinking my beer. We talk
about what American cities he's been to, what I'm doing in Russia,
and where else in the world we'd both like to visit. Soon enough, we
get to our two nations' preeminent modern connection.

"Tell me," he says. "This thing with Russia and Trump—
you believe it?" I try to demur politely, try to say some things about
how we should let the Mueller investigation take its course. Alexei
doesn't buy it. With a hearty chortle, he explains to me, "There no
proof! They say Russia, Trump, Russia, Trump—there no proof!"

Next he wants to slag off Hillary, and in hopes of changing
the subject slightly I ask, "What about a female president? Do you

think it's important? For Russia and the US?" He considers the question for a little while, then says, "You know—this thing with women freedom—maybe it go too far?" Between this and my smelt being finished, I decide that's my cue to leave. With a tight smile, I bid Alexei farewell and head into the insane heat of the sauna. Not much has changed in this banya in a hundred or so years. I imagine Rasputin here, his dick out like everyone else.

After a few minutes, my friend Alexei appears with bunched-up tree branches in his hands. You're supposed to lie back and have a masseur smash you all up with the branches. It's called a *banny venik*; it's a very common technique. I haven't paid for a masseur or anything, though. I was just planning on hanging out a bit. But at Alexei's insistence, I lie back and put on a funny little white sauna cap and let him bash me around a bit. My eyes closed, I have to admit: This feels incredible. When he's all done, I reach out for the branches and offer to give him a turn. Smiling, Alexei declines.

Out on the city streets, on the bank of the Moyka River, I go to the Yusupof Palace. This was the stately place that Prince Yusupof—who was said to have a family fortune contending with that of the tsar's—called home. It's also the site of Rasputin's death. Perhaps more than anything, it's the details of this death that continue to burnish his fame. Because Rasputin was said to be unkillable.

After making the decision that Rasputin had to die, Yusupof laid the trap. In order to gain Rasputin's trust, he played out a long and involved sham friendship. And so, when the night came, and Yusupof asked Rasputin to come, past midnight, to the Yusupof Palace to tend to his ailing wife, Rasputin readily agreed.

In his memoirs—*Rasputin: His Malignant Influence and His Assassination*—Yusupof lays down the scene. He told Rasputin that Mrs. Yusupof was otherwise engaged and would be down soon, then led Rasputin into a decadent basement. There was an "open fireplace of red granite" and "gilt cups and old Majolica plates" and "a large Persian carpet" and a "labyrinth cupboard and crucifix" and "a huge white bearskin."

Yusupof continues: "On entering the house I heard my friends voices"—an assemblage of coconspirators, waiting impatiently upstairs—"and the sounds of a popular American song on the gramophone. Rasputin stopped to listen." The song was "Yankee Doodle," then as now a solid jam.

Laid before Rasputin on a table were an array of petit-fours laced with potassium cyanide. There was also potassium cyanide–laced Madeira wine, Rasputin's favorite. Yusupof encouraged him to eat and drink. At first Rasputin demurred, but eventually, restless and bored, he agreed. Then, to Yusupof's horror—nothing happened. The poison had had no apparent effect. An increasingly fidgety Rasputin cajoled Yusupof into singing him songs. "I sing another. I sang again," Yusupof wrote. "My voice sounded strange in my ears. Time passed. This nightmare had lasted over two hours."

Unable to wait any longer, Yusupof dashed upstairs and grabbed a revolver from one of his coconspirators, Grand Duke Dmitri Pavlovic, and then stomped back down and impulsively shot a completely unaware Rasputin. The first bullet, he wrote, went through Rasputin's heart: "There could be no doubt about it. He was dead."

And yet! After confirming to the group upstairs that the deed had been done, Yusupof went back just to make sure. And in proto-horror-movie tradition, the villain came back for one . . . last . . . scare.

"Suddenly the left eye half opened," Yusupof recalled. "An instant later the right lid trembled and lifted. And both eyes of Rasputin fixed themselves upon me with an expression of devilish hatred. My blood froze in speechless horror. I was petrified. I wanted to run, to call for help. but my feet would not move, and no sound came from me. I stood riveted to the floor as if in a nightmare."

"Then the incredible happened. With a violent movement Rasputin jumped to his feet. I was horror stricken. The room resounded with a wild roar. His fingers, convulsively knotted, flashed through the air. Like red hot iron they grasped my shoulder and tried to grip me by the throat. His eyes were crossed and obtruded terribly. He was foaming at the mouth. In a hoarse whisper he constantly repeated my name."

In Yusupof's account, Rasputin broke free and made his way to the courtyard. There, as he attempted to scuttle away on all fours, he was shot again, two more times, by Vladimir Purishkevich, another coconspirator. Finally, *finally*, the body dropped for good. Now truly subdued, Rasputin was picked up and driven to a bridge on the northern outskirts of town. There the conspirators took Rasputin's body and dumped it into the Malaya Nevka River. That's where it was discovered later that day, as the sun broke, frozen in ice.

Maria, his daughter, would later write of having to identify the body. It was a horrid sight. "His face smashed in at the temple, clots of dried blood matting his beard and hair. One of his eyes dangling against his cheek held there by a slender thread of flesh. There were deep raw marks on his wrists, showing the struggle he had undergone to free himself when he was revived by the cold water beneath the ice."

One of the enduring peculiarities of Rasputin: Allegedly, he had water in his lungs indicating he was *still alive* when he was dropped in the icy river. Poisoned repeatedly, shot repeatedly, and finally drowned. The other enduring peculiarity, according to Maria: "His right hand lay upon his breast, its middle finger bent so that in combination with the index finger it formed the classical symbol of the cross."

The Yusupof Palace is a museum now. It treats the scene of the grisly world-shattering crime like a good opportunity for life-sized diorama action. Upstairs are mannequins representing Purishkevich and the other conspirators; they hang around, peeking out of windows, furtively smoking, furrowing their plastic brows, looking vaguely murderous. Downstairs in the basement, two more mannequins sit around a spread of fake poisoned treats. Plastic Rasputin glares at Plastic Yusupof, a hand stroking his long dark beard in suspicion. This is it: the place where Rasputin took his last conscious breaths. It feels like a bizarre bit of Epcot.

ONE AFTERNOON, IN the last apartment Rasputin would call home, I find what I'm looking for: some unvarnished, unperturbed trace of the man. This place isn't open to the public. But ask the right people and you'll get here.

The gatekeeper is a tall man named Dmitry. He owns the apartment. He grew up in the city, just a few minutes from where we are now. His sister Natalia explains: "We always knew about this apartment. Many people just, you know, *whispered* about this. It was Soviet period. People didn't want to talk about this."

A few years back, a chance to own the apartment presented itself, and Dmitry jumped. He's since made it a desirous word-of-mouth location for Rasputin obsessives—historians and writers and priests and nuns—from all over the world.

I follow Dmitry and Natalia off the street—a crowded drag with an arts theater and a samovar shop and an outpost of the dessert chain Vaffel & Wine—and through a courtyard. We walk into a dusty old building made of hard stone and good tiles and big, thick, chipped wood doors. A sullen teenager walks past us, headphones in, sharp emo bangs swooped over her eyes, annoyed that we're in her way. Then Dmitry and Natalia, with pleasure, do their part to take us back to 1916.

"They were *here*," Natalia says, pointing at the stair landings. "A lot of people here. A lot of people walking around here. All the way up to the third floor. They came to see Rasputin." This is where the supplicants would wait for an audience with the man, for a chance to feel his healing powers.

Dmitry points to the landing between the second and third floors. "The police sat here, like this, watching his door," he says. By the end of his life, Rasputin was tailed everywhere. One official report notes Rasputin hitting the banya with the wife of a fellow named Sazonov, then praying at the Church of the Savior on Spilled Blood, then making the acquaintances of sex workers named Kozlova, Petrova, and Botvinkina. And when he was at home, the police would sit here, right here, and watch him. "Not regular police," Dmitry adds. "*Secret* police."

We climb the last flight, swing open the last heavy and bolted wooden door, and enter the apartment itself. It's in a confusing liminal state; in the front hall there's construction materials and pairs of paint-splattered Adidas shower slides. Dmitry, slowly, is fixing the place up himself. He shows me the parquet on the floor: "Original." He knocks on the wall: "Original!"

"There was a big table here," Dmitry narrates, pointing into one room. "A lot of talking about God and these things. Rasputin was here, and it's a *very* important room." He points into another: "Here, usually he put children on the chair in front of him, and put his arms on children's shoulder and prayed. They came to Rasputin to heal their psychological illnesses, and he really did it. After his healing, these illnesses *never* came back to these children."

A year back from the day when we're talking, almost exactly, was the hundredth anniversary of Rasputin's death. "We were expecting some people to come and pay respects," Natalia says. But the flow, and the fervor, was beyond their expectations. "There were hundreds," she says. "Hundreds and hundreds and hundreds . . ." Despite it being the middle of winter, she says they carried with them the flowers of a willow tree—a staple of Russian Orthodox religiosity—that were in full bloom. "I didn't believe it," she said. "It's very strange. But I saw it!"

They came and crowded the apartment and began performing their own private religious services. Chants and prayers were heard. Candles were lit and, in these crowded halls, left burn marks on the walls. "They prayed for him because they believed he is saint. And this door, this original handle"—she jiggles it as she talks— "you can touch because Rasputin touched here. But on December thirtieth, many people *kissed* here." One woman, overcome, looking for mementoes to take home, began ripping out chunks of the wall. "She just grabbed this," Natalia says. "I told her, 'Listen, please, please, you're not the only one who wants this . . .'"

I ask the siblings what they themselves think of the Mad Monk. To own this place, to cultivate it like this—they must, perhaps, be some kind of true believers in his power? They assure me that they know how to separate the myths from reality. But they *are*—naturally, understandably—drawn to something that they do not quite understand.

"I was a kid in Soviet period," Natalia says, laughing. "Very *deep* Soviet period. My grandfather, he lived in Rasputin time. He told me, 'Grigori Efimovich Rasputin, ohhhhh, he was terrible! Oh, oh, oh, he was terrible!' He was person number one in that period. Then, after Revolution—information was closed." For nearly a century, you couldn't talk about him openly, and you certainly couldn't study him in school; he just didn't fit into the messaging of the Communist state. So he was a secret, and naturally intriguing.

Now, for Dmitry, the legends of Rasputin roll off his tongue. He tells us about how Rasputin prophesied his own death and the fall of the Romanovs, and how he prophesied the return of the Germans in World War II and the inevitable fall of the USSR, too. "He said famous words about the future. He said that the government that will come after the Romanovs, they will be a government of antichrists. They will have no church, no religion. And he said that in three times twenty-five years, they would be gone, too."

SO WHAT WAS Rasputin? Really, what was he?

Douglas Smith has done more than anyone to establish the historical realism of the man. "There are readers who say stuff like, 'Well, this isn't the Rasputin that I want,'" Smith says of his masterful 2016 biography *Rasputin: Faith, Power, and the Twilight of the Romanovs.* "People don't like to let go of what they think is the truth. The older biographies told stories of how evil he was—the Holy Devil. My research was more thorough and shows that's an empty construct. It has no validity."

In Smith's reading, Rasputin "truly was a man of great intelligence, great charisma, a certain undeniable magnetism. It was something he cultivated in his years as a holy pilgrim, wandering Russia in search of enlightenment and that kind of thing."

As for "his hold over people and his demonic power"—a myth.

"At that time, people in Russia were fascinated by the devil. People really believed dark forces were moving among them. They sensed that they were on the verge of an apocalypse"—he chuckles, nodding to the imminent February and November Revolutions— "and in that sense, they were very correct. But in another way, it was a fulfillment of a death wish."

Was Rasputin unkillable? Smith's own telling of the death relies on Yusupof's account. But Smith also reminds us that there are no other sources to corroborate a story told by a man hoping to justify a cold-blooded murder.

As for Rasputin's medicinal touch, Smith says, "People really thought that he had special powers to heal. But that's as much about people seeking things as it is his abilities."

Indeed, there are practical explanations for it all. In one rumor, one of the aides of the tsarina was loyal to Rasputin and was quietly poisoning Alexei with, Smith writes, "a powder [made] out of the antlers of young Siberian stags and ginseng root that in small doses would revive the flagging sex drive of old men, but in high doses could cause internal bleeding." It was through this well-placed aide, supposedly, that Rasputin controlled Alexei's yo-yo-ing health.

A simpler explanation makes even more sense: Rasputin's presence really was calming, and that calming had medical impact. As Smith explains, the royal doctors' "persistent examination" of the kid "only served to worsen the internal bleeding, since this inhibited the formation of the necessary clots. In hindsight, the best thing they could have done for Alexei was simply leave him alone. The rituals of medical care were echoed in Rasputin's calming words. Alexei fed off the calm of his mother, he relaxed, his blood pressure most likely dropped, his pain eased, and his body mended."

Of Rasputin's wider influence, Smith tells me, "His position at court was greatly exaggerated as a way of suggesting the bankruptcy of the entire Romanov political system. Rasputin was a sign of the degradation and decay of a once-proud imperial house." Strictly speaking, Rasputin helped lead the way for the February Revolution primarily by making the tsar look weak.

Smith offers a rigorous, sober, scholarly examination of Rasputin. It's the closest thing we have to an objective truth. It renders Rasputin less powerful than our wildest imaginations, but also kinder and smarter. As Smith points out, "My Rasputin *is* very visionary"—Rasputin fought against Russia's entry into World War I, which did prove to be disastrous. So his influence was not necessarily ill-begotten, and it was not necessarily devilishly used. He loved the tsar and the tsarina, and he didn't want his beloved Russia to suffer.

No matter; the world—most importantly, those who killed him—saw him as evil. And it does not change the facts. It wasn't magic, no. But one way or another, it *was* Rasputin who healed the tsar's child. One way or another, it *was* Rasputin that brought down the Romanovs.

Writing at the peak of the man's fame, the *New Sunday Evening Newspaper* declared, "Rasputin is a symbol—He is not a real person. He is the characteristic product of our strange times. . . . when the twilight descends all around, and in the half-light strange figures come crawling out from their cramped lairs—ghouls, bats, the undead, and every kind of evil spirit."

Since his death, and perhaps even before, Rasputin has been that symbol. And all of the Rasputins that have come in his wake—in part, they are symbols, too, of our fears and of our hopes both. We are terrified by those who secretly control—and yet we are drawn, inevitably, inexorably, to their dark powers.

There are those who manipulate to make art. There are those who manipulate to make money. There are those who manipulate in the name of their sworn ideology. There are those who do all three. Are they "true Rasputins"? No, of course not. Even Rasputin wasn't a true Rasputin. But it is the nature of their work—its shadowy ways—that makes them loom larger, ever more nefarious, in our imaginations. This is about the people who exist in the half-light, the ones who embody truths and lies they themselves do not fully understand.

When the Romanov family was murdered by Bolshevik guards in the basement of a makeshift prison known as the House of Special Purpose in the town of Yekaterinburg in 1918, it is said that the dead were carrying small trinkets memorializing Rasputin.

In his daughter Maria's telling, on the day of her father's death, "several Mothers Superior from various convents related some unexplained incidents in their various communities. Priests, for no logical reasons, had become insane, creating havoc and destruction and any number of the good nuns had become sex-crazed, offering themselves to the priests in wanton abandon."

How much of it is true? In the half-light, it all is.

AT THE APARTMENT, Dmitry and Natalia and I begin to make our exit through a back servants' entrance. It was the staircase Rasputin and Yusupof walked down, surreptitiously, that very last night in St. Petersburg. Yusupof led the way; he didn't want to be seen by the police or by the potential hordes of Rasputin supplicants, waiting there on those steps for healing.

"They escaped from here," Natalia says. "This was the last way. He never came back."

She goes on, lowering her voice, trying her best to take us back again to the winter of 1916. "Can you imagine Felix? He came and rang the bell. He raised this"—she gives the security chain a hard rattle—"and he *knock*." She says the word, a few times over, with a long, hard "k."

"Kkkkkah-nock, Kkkkkah-nock, Kkkkkah-nock."

Dmitry picks up the tale. "There are no light. Felix search for the door in the dark. And when they walk out, Rasputin grab his hand to go with him into . . ."

"Into darkness!" Natalia interjects with a yell. Hushing her voice again, she throws herself back into the tale. "He kkkknocked, he open the door, he take Rasputin, and he said—'Now we are going into darkness."

I stand here, in the still of an old and weathered St. Petersburg apartment that has survived the USSR and has survived Putin and looks to survive whatever comes next. I stand in the quiet chill with a pair of siblings as obsessed with Rasputin as I am. Why have I gone so far? What is it I'm still trying to understand? What am I doing here?

I am here to know the truth—to know who is behind the machinations of our culture, of our drugs, of our politics, of our lives. That's a worthy pursuit: to try to find the secret, hidden levers of power; to open my eyes to those who have real influence over me. But I am also here to know that I cannot know the truth—not all of it. That's the ineffable nature of these Rasputins—they live forever in the darkness. We want to shine a light. But we never fully can, can we? Their potency is forever obscured.

And potent they are.

I look at Dmitry and Natalia, my new friends, my sisters-and-brothers-in-arms in Rasputinism. Here we are, a century after his death—a century full of Rasputins, marching on happily behind us—and the three of us are here, soaking up the last moments of his life, trying to understand.

What *was* it about him?

Natalia, with fists clenched, answers in a calm, bold voice. She isn't so much looking at me as looking past me. Once, there lived a man named Grigori Rasputin. Forever, there will live the symbol of that man.

"The question *why*?" Natalia asks.

"Yes," I say. "Why?"

"Why people *believe* in him? Because he show the *power* of one person. One person *can* move the history. One person *can* move Russia to the end of empire. One person *can* destroy a country. He could! He could!"

EPILOGUE

AFTER RUSSIA I CAME BACK HOME to Brooklyn. My journeys in Rasputinism were over. I would have loved to live in Grigori Efimovich's strange world for just a bit longer. But I had to get on with the real world.

My girlfriend and I had recently bought an apartment. We'd been looking for a long time, and had made the simultaneously terrifying and thrilling decision to stay in New York, a city we'd both adopted as adults and loved deeply. With teeth-gnashing anxiety, we set about figuring out how to make it work.

I had enough panic attacks for the both of us; steely-eyed, she pushed us through our fears. At one point, after much consternation and many missteps, I managed to win amnesty on some ancient debts and raise my credit score up the fifty points I needed to enter the zone of respectability where lenders won't laugh at you. Believe me when I say I nearly cried. (My girl was pretty happy, too.) At the end of it all, between every cent of our collective savings and money awkwardly borrowed from our parents and a little chunk of credit card debt on top, we had enough for a down payment, and we were able to secure a bank loan.

Two weeks after we moved in, the roof leaked in the middle of the night. A fire-system sprinkler head malfunctioned, leading to an increasingly fluid indoor rain situation. The water was dark and coming out of the whole goddamn ceiling, and I was convinced at first, as we sprinted through the muck trying to salvage our earthly possessions, that a septic tank had burst—that we were literally being rained on with shit. It turned out to be just regular-old weird, dark fire-system pipe water. But it still felt like a horror movie where the home develops evil sentience.

The alarm blared. The fire department came. They popped out the busted sprinkler head and turned off the water main, but there was still water left in the pipes themselves. Along with seven big dudes in full firemen gear, we stood around, wet in sweat shorts, staring as the last leftover gallons poured out of a hole in the ceiling.

We were out of the place for six weeks. We spent it bouncing around Airbnbs and hotels and pleading and yelling with various flat-affect-voiced representatives of various insurance agencies. Eventually, after our waterlogged apartment was torn up and repaired, we moved back in. I was hugely relieved. I was also now pathologically afraid of water.

I understood that these were the kind of challenges that would face me, a human adult, going forward: bank loans, insurance payments, creditors, debts, late-onset aquaphobia. When I was younger, just the thought of that stuff made my eyes glaze over. But after we pushed through, I felt a bit of electricity. No, it wasn't endless Russian winters and epoch-defining manipulation. But perhaps my life wasn't destined to be lived only in the shadows. And that was OK. There was a thrill in keeping an apartment from falling apart, too.

Then I learned something. Now that all the drama had been dealt with, now that we were settled back in alongside all the building's other tenants, it was time to form an HOA—a Homeowners Association. This is the collective body that pays for insurance in case the whole building burns down, and also makes very important decisions like "should we get a communal grill" and "should we get new trash cans" and "should we put in bird spikes so the weird pigeons don't keep landing above the stoop." An HOA board had to be formed with a secretary, a treasurer—and a president.

My mind started racing. *Wherever there is a seat of power,* I whispered to myself, *there are those who seek to control it.* My neighbors were all sweet people; at least two were warm-hearted, trustworthy schoolteachers. And I was a reporter with an only-as-of-very-recently-improved-and-still-very-much-tenuous credit score. I knew what my place would be.

For the the HOA to be officially formed, the sellers of the building had to transfer insurance funds and legal docs to us, the tenants. The sellers' representative was intent on actualizing this transfer-of-power ritual on a weekday at a lawyer's office in Manhattan—a place where, clearly, none of us lived. To be honest, I didn't care much about a nonsense daytime task. (I work from home! I don't talk to anyone all day!) But *instinctively,* I knew this could be my cudgel.

I emailed the seller's rep, cc'ing everyone: "Why don't we do it in Brooklyn?" No response.

A few days later, I tried again. Nothing.

In the meanwhile, one neighbor—one of the schoolteachers and the mother of an adorable little girl—asked, *Had I heard anything from the seller's rep?* "Because with the kid," she said, "it really is hard to get into the city during the week." It was all rolling out very nicely. I played it cool, but I told her I would take care of it.

Behind the scenes, my email drips became a barrage. And finally, one lovely Thursday morning, there it was—capitulation.

Responding to my latest email, the seller's rep had written, "As to not delay this further, and force a trip into Manhattan, we suggest we meet locally . . . is that acceptable?"

I had demonstrated my powers. My *special arts.* The tenants had seen what I could do. And the rest, I knew, would be inevitable.

Eventually, another neighbor, a trustworthy, all-business operations manager, took over the presidency of the HOA. I took no official position. One does not need an official position to pull the damn strings. I would be the one to bend and manipulate the poor, helpless HOA to my every last whim. *Yes* to the new trash cans. *Yes* to the communal grill. *No* to the spikes—let the weird pigeons roam!

I would be our very own in-house HOA Rasputin. I could not wait. Let the dark days begin.

ACKNOWLEDGMENTS

I GOT MY FIRST BYLINE at the *Michigan Daily*. They also, if I'm remembering correctly, once let me review a U-God solo album?! My first real job was at *New York* magazine, where I started out as an intern. My first editorial task was . . . picking up shirts for the office basketball team. I met a lot of smart people and got better at writing. My second real job was at *Grantland*, for which I'll always feel lucky. I got to write the kind of stuff I always wanted to write, the kind of stuff I'd always worried I'd never get to write. My third real job was at the *Fader*, where I got to hang out every day with a rare group of people who sincerely love pop culture. So thank you to Ben Mathis-Lilley, Lane Brown, Dan Kois, Ben Wasserstein, Sean Fennessey, Juliet Litman, Rafe Bartholomew, Bill Simmons, Mark Lisanti, Naomi Zeichner, Duncan Cooper, Rawiya Kameir, and every other person and every other outlet that's ever let me write.

Thanks to Brian Evenson, Leon Vitali, T. K. Park, Abe Martinez, and all the other experts and strangers who went out of their way to help me on this book when asked. And special thanks to Douglas Smith, who not only wrote the best Rasputin biography around, but also made himself available for insightful, authoritative interviews and provided definitive answers on a long string of nitpicky questions. Thanks to Dmitry and Natalia for bringing me into your (Rasputin's) home. And thanks to Rasputin, for being you.

Thanks to my editors Jamison Stoltz and Garrett McGrath, and to *weepy Rod Tidwell voice* my agent, David Patterson. Mensches, the lot of you. And since David had first gotten in touch with me after reading a Beastie Boys piece I'd written, *big* thanks to the Beastie Boys, too.

Thank U 2 my pals Zak Kahn, Danny Yagoda, Rich Kim, Mike Grinshpun, Matt House, Dan "Jupiter's Gonna Win" Rainwater, Katie Mack, Ray Malo, Jocelyn Guest, Nitasha Tiku, Ira Boudway, BML (again), Caroline Zancan, Lauren Bans, Sarah Goldstein, Ben Yaster, Susan Goldberg, Willa Paskin, David Marchese, Luke McCormick, Linsey "The Coffee Filter Kid" Fields, Jackson Fratesi, Corban Goble, Jason Parham, and Patrick McDermott. Let's be honest, most of you did almost nothing to help me with the book, but you are all deeply great and you deserve gratitude! Thank you to the Food Boys, you are so, so real. And thank you to Paula, Jamie and James McCann and Eddie, Kelly and Rudi Douglas. I couldn't have done it without you (especially you Rudi).

I have a family that's a true and endless source of joy and support for me, and I'm deeply grateful for that fact. I've been trying and failing to sum it up in a pithy manner, but just know I love and respect you all so much, and you make me so proud, and also there's no one in the world I'd rather be stuck in a Volvo with for hours while Rodi pretends a dolphin or a body part is talking. And Ima: for some reason, you always believed in me. It made all the difference. *Toda, toda, toda*!!!

And finally, to Allison—you're the best thing that ever happened to me. I'm going to work every day (of the foreseeable future) to make sure I don't fuck it up. I love you so (sooooiiiiiiiii) much.

NOTES ON SOURCES

I WROTE THIS BOOK using a wide variety of primary and secondary sources.

For the lives and legends of Rasputin, that included Maria Rasputin's *Rasputin: The Man Behind the Myth*; Prince Yusupof's *Rasputin: His Malignant Influence and His Assassination*; Colin Wilson's *Rasputin and the Fall of the Romanovs*; the documentary *Rasputin: The Devil in the Flesh*; and Nadezhda "Teffi" Lokhvitskaya's firsthand accounts of partying with the dude. Above all, I relied on interviews and conversation with the historian Douglas Smith and on his biography *Rasputin: Faith, Power, and the Twilight of the Romanovs*.

For chapters two and three I relied on reporting on the Dr. Luke–Kesha scandal and on the various adventures of Justin Bieber from outlets including *Billboard*, the *Hollywood Reporter*, *Complex*, *New York* magazine, and the *New York Times*.

In chapter four my sources include Brian Evenson's *Raymond Carver's What We Talk About When We Talk About Love: Bookmarked* and Evenson's original notes from his classes with Gordon Lish; D.T. Max's *New York Times Magazine* piece "The Carver Chronicles"; Carol Sklenicka's *Raymond Carver: A Writer's Life*; and the *Paris Review*'s interviews with Gordon Lish.

For chapter five I relied on reporting on the *Blue Is the Warmest Color* scandal from outlets including the *Daily Beast*, the *New Yorker*, and the *Independent*. On Stanley Kubrick I relied on Amy Nicholson's *Tom Cruise: Anatomy of an Actor*; Frederic Raphael's *Eyes Wide Open*; and the documentary *Stanley Kubrick: A Life in Pictures*.

For chapter six I relied on reporting on Alex Guerrero (and his particular relationship with Tom Brady) from ESPN, the *New York Times Magazine*, and, most of all, *Boston* magazine's Chris Sweeney, who's revealed more than anyone about Guerrero's past.

In chapter seven I relied on reporting on the Arellano Félix cartel from *Zeta* and *Proceso*.

For chapter eight I utilized information from the terror-network manual *A Course in the Art of Recruiting* and the ISIS publication *Rumiyah*.

For chapter nine I relied on Shakespeare's *Macbeth* and on reporting on the Nicaragua democratic crisis from the *Guardian*.

In chapter ten I used source material from Busan Presbyterian University professor Ji-Il Tark and contemporaneous reporting on the Choi Soon-sil scandal from *Bloomberg Businessweek*, BuzzFeed, the *Hankyoreh*, and the remarkably helpful and remarkably thorough news blog *Ask a Korean!*

For chapters eleven through fourteen I relied on reporting from a wide variety of outlets that have exhaustively blanketed the mania within the first few years of the Trump administration. That includes the *Washington Post*, *Politico*, and the *New York Times*.

In chapter fifteen, I relied on Masha Gessen's *The Future Is History: How Totalitarianism Reclaimed Russia* and on Andreas Umlaund's academic work on Aleksandr Dugin.

The bulk of the book is based on my firsthand interviews with Scooter Braun, Leon Vitali, Douglas Smith, Brian Evenson, Sam Nunberg, Adela Navarro Bello, Mike S. Vigil, D.T. Max, Alberto Fernandez, Hind Fraihi, Daniel Koehler, Johannes Saal, Alex Guerrero, Abdul Kamouss, Zoilamerica Ortega Murillo, T. K. Park, Dan Pfeiffer, Professor Ji-Il Tark, Rade Serbedzija, and M. C. Bogy. I owe them all for their time.

ADDITIONAL SOURCES

Introduction

Teffi. "My Dinner with Rasputin." *Longreads*. https://longreads
.com/2016/05/03/my-dinner-with-rasputin/.

Chapter One

2Pac. "Thugz Mansion." *Better Dayz*. Death Row Records, 2002.

Wilson, Colin. *Rasputin and the Fall of the Romanovs*. New York:
Citadel Press, 1971.

Yusupov, Prince Felix. *Rasputin: His Malignant Influence and His
Assassination*. Translated by Oswald Rayner. London: Jona-
than Cape, 1934.

Chapter Two

Abramovitch, Seth. "Boy Band Mogul Lou Pearlman's Prison
Interview: My Ponzi Scheme Was Smarter Than Madoff's."
Hollywood Reporter. January 22, 2014. https://www.holly
woodreporter.com/news/backstreet-boys-lou-pearlmans
-prison-672724.

Coscarelli, Joe and Katie Rogers. "Kesha vs. Dr. Luke: Inside Pop
Music's Contentious Legal Battle." *New York Times*. February 23, 2016. https://www.nytimes.com/2016/02/24/arts
/music/kesha-dr-luke.html.

Fagen, Donald. "The Devil and Ike Turner." *Slate*. December 17,
2007. https://slate.com/news-and-politics/2007/12/donald
-fagen-on-the-legacy-of-ike-turner.html.

Graff, Gary. "Johnny Rotten Pays Tribute to Malcolm McLaren."
Billboard. April 9, 2010. https://www.billboard.com/articles

/news/958676/johnny-rotten-pays-tribute-to-malcolm
-mclaren.

"Malcolm McLaren: 'I Don't Mind Being Accused of Being the Fagin, in Many Respects I Was.'" British *GQ.* October 28, 2017. https://www.gq-magazine.co.uk/article/malcolm -mclaren-sex-pistols-interview.

Palmer, Robert. "Commentary: What Ike Had to Do with It: Tales from His Dark Side Still Cloud Ike Turner's Reputation as a Pioneer in American Rhythm and Blues." *Los Angeles Times.* June 20, 1993. http://articles.latimes.com/1993–06 –20/entertainment/ca-5089_1_tina-turner-revue.

"Ronnie Spector: 'Amy Winehouse Saved Me!'" *MOJO.* January 29, 2015. https://www.mojo4music.com/articles/18704/ronnie -spector-amy-winehouse-saved.

Chapter Three

Hoffman, Jan. "Justin Bieber Is Living the Dream." *New York Times.* December 31, 2009. https://www.nytimes.com/2010/01/03 /fashion/03bieber.html.

Chapter Four

Lish, Gordon. "Gordon Lish, the Art of Editing, No. 2." By Christian Lorentzen. *Paris Review* 215 (Winter 2015). https://www .theparisreview.org/interviews/6423/gordon-lish-the-art-of -editing-no-2-gordon-lish.

Sklenicka, Carol. *Raymond Carver: A Writers Life.* New York: Scriber, 2009.

Chapter Five

Brody, Richard. *"Filmworker,* Reviewed: A Documentary About Stanley Kubrick's Right-Hand Man." *New Yorker.* May 9, 2018. https://www.newyorker.com/culture/richard-brody

/filmworker-reviewed-a-documentary-about-stanley
-kubricks-right-hand-man.

Raphael, Frederic. *Eyes Wide Open: A Memoir of Stanley Kubrick.*
New York: Ballantine Books, 1999.

Stern, Marlow. "The Stars of *Blue Is the Warmest* Color on the Riveting Lesbian Love Story." September 1, 2013. https://www
.thedailybeast.com/the-stars-of-blue-is-the-warmest-color-on
-the-riveting-lesbian-love-story.

Chapter Six

Guerrero, Alex. "Alex Guerrero: In My Own Words." *TB12* (blog).
January 2018. https://tb12sports.com/blog/alex-guerrero-in
-my-own-words/.

Itzkoff, Dave. "Piven Leaves Show Amid Concerns for His Health."
New York Times. December 18, 2008. https://www.nytimes
.com/2008/12/19/theater/19pive.html.

Moskovitz, Diana. "Here's How Tom Brady Pushes His Sketchy
Body Guru on People." *Deadspin.* October 9, 2015. https://
deadspin.com/heres-how-tom-brady-pushes-his-sketchy
-body-guru-on-peo-1735747044.

Petchesky, Barry. "Bomani Jones on Tom Brady's Bizarre Training
Schemes: 'This Just Reeks of "Con."'" *Deadspin.* November 1,
2017. https://deadspin.com/bomani-jones-on-tom-bradys
-bizarre-training-schemes-t-1820038413.

Sweeney, Chris. "Tom Brady's TB12 Center Was Investigated by State
Agencies." *Boston* magazine. December 19, 2015. https://www
.bostonmagazine.com/news/2015/12/19/tb12-investigated/.

Wickersham, Seth. "For Kraft, Brady and Belichick, Is This
the Beginning of the End?" *ESPN.* January 5, 2018.
http://www.espn.co.uk/nfl/story/_/page/hotread180105
/beginning-end-new-england-patriots-robert-kraft-tom
-brady-bill-belichick-internal-power-struggle.

Chapter Eight

Creswell, Robyn and Bernard Haykel. "Battle Lines." *New Yorker.* June 8 and 15, 2015. https://www.newyorker.com /magazine/2015/06/08/battle-lines-jihad-creswell-and -haykel.

Heil, George. "The Berlin Attack and the 'Abu Walaa' Islamic State Recruitment Network." *CTCSentinel* 2, no. 10 (February 2017). https://ctc.usma.edu/the-berlin-attack-and-the -abu-walaa-islamic-state-recruitment-network/.

Chapter Ten

"Secret Confidante of Ousted South Korean Leader Park Gets 20 Years in Prison Over Scandal." *Japan Times.* February 13, 2018. https://www.japantimes.co.jp/news/2018/02/13/asia-pacific /politics-diplomacy-asia-pacific/secret-confidante-ousted -south-korean-leader-park-gets-20-years-prison-scandal /#.XDSDGZP7RQI.

Tark, Ji-il, email message to author.

Chapter Eleven

Nuzzi, Olivia. "Troll Daddies Roger Stone and Chuck Johnson Fight Over Bill Clinton's 'Son.'" *Daily Beast.* October 31, 2016. https://www.thedailybeast.com/troll-daddies-roger-stone -and-chuck-johnson-fight-over-bill-clintons-son.

Chapter Twelve

Bertoni, Steven. "Exclusive Interview: How Jared Kushner Won Trump the White House." *Forbes.* December 20, 2016. https://www.forbes.com/sites/stevenbertoni/2016/11/22 /exclusive-interview-how-jared-kushner-won-trump-the -white-house/#1d5d3e293af6.